Key Terms in Discourse Analysis

Key Terms in Discourse Analysis

Paul Baker and Sibonile Ellece

continuum

Continuum International Publishing Group

The Tower Building	80 Maiden Lane
11 York Road	Suite 704
London SE1 7NX	New York, NY 10038

www.continuumbooks.com

British Library Cataloguing-in-Publication Data
A catalogue record for this book is available from the British Library.

ISBN: 978-1-8470-6320-5 (hardcover)
ISBN: 978-1-8470-6321-2 (paperback)

Library of Congress Cataloging-in-Publication Data
Baker, Paul, 1972-
    Key terms in discourse analysis / Paul Baker and Sibonile Ellece.
       p. cm.
    Includes bibliographical references and index.
    ISBN 978-1-84706-320-5 (hardcover)
    ISBN 978-1-84706-321-2 (pbk.)
    1. Discourse analysis. 2. Discourse analysis–Terminology.
    3. Linguistics–Terminology. I. Ellece, Sibonile. II. Title.

    P302.B285 2010
    401'.41–dc22

                                                         2010012771

Typeset by Newgen Imaging Systems Pvt Ltd, Chennai, India

Contents

Notes on Examples

Rather than always inventing examples to illustrate points, we have tried to take them from real life uses of language. To achieve this, we have used corpora – large collections of naturally occurring texts that have been collected and electronically transcribed for the purposes of linguistic analysis. The corpora we have used are

The British National Corpus (BNC), consisting of approximately 100 million words of written (90%) and spoken (10%) British English mainly produced in the early 1990s.

The British English 2006 (BE06) Corpus, consisting of 1 million words of standard British English, collected from 15 written genres and published circa 2006.

Where we have included examples from corpora, we have also included file reference numbers.

The Key Terms

absence

An absence is something that *could* be present in language use or discourse, but is not, possibly for ideological reasons (see van Leeuwen 1996, 1997). For example, Hollway (1995: 60) notes that 'there is no currently available way of conceptualizing women's pleasure and active sexual desire . . . in heterosexual sex which is regarded as consistent with principles of women's liberation'. Absences can be difficult for discourse analysts to identify because the text itself is unlikely to reveal what is absent, so the analyst is required to refer to additional sources. One method of identifying absence in a particular TEXT is to carry out some sort of comparison, for example, by comparing two similar texts against each other or by comparing a single text against a much large set of 'reference texts' via CORPUS LINGUISTICS techniques. Another technique would involve asking multiple analysts to examine the same text in order to gain a range of possible perspectives on what could have been present but is not. See also BACKGROUNDING, ERASURE, EXCLUSION, SILENCE.

access

Access, in relation to CRITICAL DISCOURSE ANALYSIS, is concerned with who has access to certain types of discourse or roles and who gets to control the access of other people – therefore access is strongly related to POWER. Van Dijk (1996: 86) points out that in some discourse situations certain roles afford more access than others – so in education, teachers have more control over educational discourse than students, while in health settings, doctors have more control over the discourse – such as what can be discussed or the setting or timing of an interaction. Access (or lack of it) therefore plays an important role in reinforcing existing power relations. While many westernized societies stress concepts like 'free speech' or 'equal opportunities', at times patterns of access in those societies may not reflect these ideals.

For example, Fairclough (1989: 62–68) discusses a number of ways in which access to discourse is unequally distributed across societies. Literacy plays an important role in determining access – people who have poor literacy (the vast majority who are working class in the United Kingdom) are unlikely to have access to higher education. Fairclough (1989: 65) argues that 'the educational system reproduces . . . the existing social division of labour, and the existing system of class relations'.

In addition, *formality* represents another way that access is constrained – many contexts which involve the exercise of power (such as politics, law, education, medicine or the media) tend to require people to participate in formal situations. Therefore, special knowledge and skills normally need to be acquired in order for people to gain access to those situations. Particular forms of jargon or POLITENESS strategies need to be learnt. As some people do not have access to ways of learning how to participate in these formal situations, they will therefore never be able to be participants in them (see also CAPITAL).

accounts

Scott and Lyman (1968: 46) define accounts as the social process of how people present themselves, particularly when engaged in lapses of conventionality. Such people are likely to use an 'account . . . a statement . . . to explain unanticipated or untoward behavior'. Scott and Lyman categorize excuses and justifications as types of accounts. The examination of accounts is a key aspect of DISCURSIVE PSYCHOLOGY (e.g. Potter and Wetherell 1987), which has shown that people attempt to construct cohesive accounts of their behaviour and attitudes that may actually be contradictory when subjected to qualitative analysis.

adjacency pair

In CONVERSATION ANALYSIS, an adjacency pair consists of two functionally related turns, each made by a different speaker (Schegloff and Sacks 1973). The first turn of the pair requires a relevant response (the second turn). Pairs can take various forms, for example,

invitation – acceptance (or rejection)
request – acceptance (or denial)
greeting – greeting
assessment – agreement (or disagreement)
blame – denial (or admission)
question – answer

The response in the second part of the turn can be categorized as preferred or dispreferred. Generally, the preferred second is the shorter, less complicated response, while the dispreferred second tends to be longer and requires more conversational work. In example 1 below from Atkinson and Drew (1979: 58), the second part of the adjacency pair is a preferred response, while example 2 shows a typical dispreferred second which contains a delay: 'hehh'; a marker: 'well'; an appreciation of the offer: 'that's awfully sweet of you'; a declination: 'I don't think I can make it this morning'; a further delay: 'hh uhm'; and an ACCOUNT: 'I'm running an ad . . . and I have to stay near the phone'. (See also TURN-TAKING.)

Example 1
    A: Why don't you come up and see me some time?
    B: I would like to.

Example 2
    A: Uh, if you'd care to come and visit a little while this morning, I'll give you a cup of coffee.
    B: Hehh, well, that's awfully sweet of you. I don't think I can make it this morning, hh uhm, I'm running an ad in the paper and uh I have to stay near the phone.

adjective

An adjective is a word which describes something, usually being used to give additional information about a noun or pronoun. Many adjectives can be evaluative and are thus important in discursive representation as they reveal author stance: 'The waiter was a portly middle-aged man, deferential but dignified' (BNC, ASN). Leech (1966: 151) notes that adjectives tend to be extremely common in advertising discourse. Some adjectives can be gradable, *happy, happier, happiest*, although others are not, *dead*.

Another distinction can be made between attributive and predicative adjectives, which can have consequences for discourse representation. An attributive adjective directly modifies a noun (*the gay man*), whereas predicative adjectives are often used with copula (*he is gay*). In the former, the adjective appears as one descriptive component of a person's IDENTITY, potentially allowing for other representations, whereas in the latter, the adjectival trait becomes foregrounded, with the referent appearing to be the sum of the adjective and nothing more. Another strategy, where adjectives are transformed into nouns (*he's a gay*), even further represents a person as embodying a single, essential trait.

agency

Agency is an important aspect of the REPRESENTATION of SOCIAL ACTORS. A grammatical agent is a participant in a situation who carries out an action.

Linguistic agency refers to how characters or objects are represented in relation to each other. In example 1, the policeman is the agent, while the woman is the patient.

Example 1
    The policeman attacked the woman.

The term *agent* is sometimes confused with the term SUBJECT – and in some cases, an agent and a subject are the same things, as in example 1. However, agency is determined by a thing's explicit relationship to a verb, while a subject is defined by flow of information, word order and importance in a sentence. So in example 2, the agent is the still the policeman, although the subject is the woman.

Example 2
    The woman was attacked by the policeman.

van Leeuwen (1996: 32–33) points out that sociological agency is not always realized by something taking the grammatical role of 'agent'. Other linguistic techniques, such as using prepositional phrases like *from*, can make the grammatical agent sociologically patient, as in example 3 (ibid.) where the grammatical agent is 'people of Asian descent'.

Example 3
　　People of Asian descent say they received a cold shoulder from neighbours
　　and co-workers.

Agency can also be absent from a sentence, as in example 4, where we do not know who attacked the woman.

Example 4
　　The woman was attacked.

Agency can be attributed to processes (e.g. via nominalizations), abstract nouns or inanimate objects, obscuring the real agent, as in example 5 from Fairclough (1989: 123).

Example 5
　　Unsheeted lorries from Middlebarrow Quarry were still causing problems
　　by shedding stones.

In this example, the agent is an inanimate object: the 'unsheeted lorries from Middlebarrow Quarry' (we are not told who did not put sheets on the lorries, causing them to shed stones). Agency could be made clearer if it were attributed to the people who controlled the lorries, rather than the lorries themselves. Fairclough (1989: 52) argues that there may be ideological aspects to the ways that agency is presented (or misrepresented): 'The power being exercised here is the power to disguise power . . . it is a form of the power to constrain content: to favour certain interpretations and "wordings" of events, while excluding others . . . It is a form of hidden power.' See also
ABSENCE, BACKGROUNDING, EXCLUSION, NOMINALIZATION, SUBJECT, TRANSITIVITY.

aggregation

A type of ASSIMILATION which involves collectively representing people by referring to numbers or amounts. van Leeuwen (1996: 49) notes that 'aggregation is often used to regulate practice and to manufacture consensus opinion even though it presents itself as merely recording facts'. Aggregation can involve actual statistics, 'eight out of ten cats prefer it', but can also use less specific determiners like *some* or *most*, for example 'some men have a check up every few months just to be sure they haven't got any infections without knowing' (from man{sex}man, a Terrance Higgins Trust booklet about safer sex produced in 2002). See also COLLECTIVIZATION.

anaphora

Anaphora involves one term referencing another which has previously been mentioned. This is often carried out by the use of pronouns or determiners as in the example below where the word *them* anaphorically refers to 'gypsies and travellers'.

John Prescott yesterday unveiled proposals to stop Gypsies and travellers from exploiting legal loopholes which have allowed them to buy up green belt land then set up camp. (BE06, A02)

See also CATAPHORA, DEIXIS, SUBSTITUTION.

anti-language

A way of understanding subcultural language use developed by Halliday (1978). An anti-language is the form of language used by anti-societies – societies which are resistant to mainstream society. Such anti-societies might be involved in activities which the mainstream society considers to be illegal or socially tabooed in other ways. Anti-languages are often secret, being communicated through speech rather than being written and they can be subject to rapid change (or OVERWORDING), as new words need to be invented to replace old ones that have become known to mainstream society.

Anti-languages are not normally completely different languages but instead tend to contain new lexical words (mainly nouns, verbs and adjectives, which are central to the activities of the subculture), often retaining the grammatical rules of the language used by mainstream society. For example, an anti-society based around illegal drug use would have words for types of drugs and their effects, dealers, the police, money etc. As well as allowing members of the anti-society to recognize each other, and creating a shared sense of IDENTITY, Halliday (1978: 166) notes that the social values of words and phrases tend to be emphasized more in anti-languages, as compared to mainstream languages, a phenomena which he terms *sociolinguistic coding orientation*. Halliday (1978: 171) also points out that anti-languages enable users to reconstruct their own subjective reality: 'Anti-language arises when the alternative reality is a *counter*-reality, set up *in opposition to* some established norm.' Anti-languages are therefore a good example of *symbolic power* (Bourdieu 1991). See also CAPITAL.

Beier (1995: 65) argues that Cant, a language variety used by sixteenth and seventeenth century rogues, is more appropriately classed as jargon than anti-language, as it has few words attacking social, religious and political systems, while Baker (2002: 15) views Polari (used by gay men in early to mid-twentieth century United Kingdom) as an anti-language, as its lexicon mocked and feminized institutions like the police, helping to demarcate social boundaries and reconstructing an alternative value system according to the attitudes of its members.

anti-semitism

Prejudice or discrimination against Jewish people. Pauley (2002: 1) writes that anti-semitism 'attributes to the Jews an exceptional position among all other civilisations, defames them as an inferior group and denies their being part of the nation[s]' in which they reside. See also Reisigl and Wodak (2001).

archaeology

A form of analysis suggested by Michel Foucault (1972) which focuses on the ways that discourse operates as a system for creating authoritative statements. This form of analysis, while historical, differs from other forms of historical analysis (such as anthropology) in that it does not try to identify 'truths' or what people actually meant or said when they wrote particular texts or acted in certain ways but is instead more concerned with the mechanisms and structures that allowed certain people to have their ideas expressed and taken seriously at various points in time. This form of analysis is therefore concerned with discursive practices and rules.

argumentation

In the field of critical thinking, Bowell and Kemp (2002: 8) define an argument as a 'set of propositions, of which one is a conclusion and the remainder are premises, intended as support for the conclusion'. See also Walton (1990). An argument differs from rhetoric in that arguments tend to appeal to people's critical faculties, whereas rhetoric relies on the persuasive power of certain linguistic techniques to influence a person's beliefs, desires or fears.

Argumentation theory is used in the DISCOURSE-HISTORICAL APPROACH to CRITICAL DISCOURSE ANALYSIS, which focuses on the identification, reconstruction and evaluation of arguments as well as showing how arguments are used by certain groups in order to justify or legitimize the exclusion and discrimination of other groups. Wodak (2001: 73) defines argumentation as a DISCURSIVE STRATEGY, which has the objective of providing a justification for a particular position. See also FALLACY, TOPOI.

assimilation

According to van Leeuwen (1996: 48–50), assimilation is a way of representing social actors as groups. There are two main types of assimilation: AGGREGATION and COLLECTIVIZATION. See also INDIVIDUALIZATION.

attitudes

An attitude is a person's judgement towards something. Attitudes are generally positive or negative, although people can potentially also possess ambivalent attitudes (e.g. be both positive and negative) or profess to have no attitude (e.g. not really care). In traditional social science research, attitudes were often measured by using questionnaires or surveys which asked people to tick a box to indicate where their attitude fell on a scale (with one end representing an extreme negative attitude and the other end being extreme positivity). These scales are often referred to as Likert scales (see Likert 1932). A typical Likert scale would have 5 points (although sometimes point 3 is removed in order to force respondents to make a choice):

1. Strongly agree
2. Agree
3. Neither agree nor disagree
4. Disagree
5. Strongly agree

Since the 1980s, this sort of questionnaire-based attitude research has been criticized, as people may hold complex and contradictory sets of beliefs or opinions around a particular topic, which they may not be fully aware of or be able to adequately articulate. For example, Potter and Wetherell (1987) conducted interviews with people to find out their attitudes towards race relations and showed that within the spoken transcripts the respondents tended to produce incompatible and varying statements, often contradicting themselves, thus making it very difficult to categorize their attitude on a Likert Scale. Rather than asking people to rate their attitudes on a scale then, Potter and Wetherell suggest that we examine what people do with their talk, in order to obtain a clearer account of how they make sense of a topic and position themselves in relation to it. Such an approach therefore rejects the idea that attitudes are stable, consistent internal structures but instead views people as drawing on different discourses. See also the treatment of attitudes by Van Dijk (1998).

audience design

A theory developed by Allan Bell (1984) which argues that speakers change styles in response to their audience. Bell identified a classification system for different types of audiences, depending on three criteria: whether the audience is *known* to be part of a speech context, whether the speaker *ratifies* or acknowledges the listener's presence, and whether the listener is directly *addressed*. According to Bell, an *addressee* would be a listener who is known, ratified and addressed. An *auditor* would be one who is not directly addressed but is known and ratified. *Overhearers* and *eavesdroppers* would not be ratified, but the speaker would be aware of the former and unaware of the latter. See also RECEPTION.

back channels

A term identified by Duncan (1973) to describe feedback that is given by a hearer in order to indicate that they are attending to someone else's speech. They can be (1) non-verbal, for example, consisting of nods, gestures or facial expressions, or (2) verbal, for example, words like *yeah*, *right*, *okay* or vocalizations like *mm* and *uh-huh*. They can also include cases where a hearer completes part of a speaker's turn.

backgrounding

A form of EXCLUSION less radical than SUPPRESSION. van Leeuwen (1996: 39) notes that 'the excluded social actors may not be mentioned in relation to a given activity, but they are mentioned elsewhere in the text, and we can infer with reasonable (but never total) certainty who they are. They are not so much excluded, as de-emphasized, pushed into the background'.

As an example, Sunderland (2004: 34, 40) notes that in a newspaper article about 'dream weddings', the focus is on the *bride* who is described as making a 'breathtaking entrance' down a flight of stairs. There are references to *couples* and *people* but no specific mentions of *bridegrooms*: '[I]f the groom is backgrounded in this "fairytale" text, his important, grounded, "real life" concerns must be elsewhere' (ibid.: 40).

biological sex

Biological sex is usually a binary assignation. A person's sex is based on their reproductive organs (either male or female – although in a small number of cases, a person may be inter-sexed). In addition to reproductive organs, there are other differences: males have one X and one Y chromosome, whereas females have two X chromosomes. Researchers have also found differences in the brains of males and females (Baron-Cohen, 2004). Biological sex has been used in a great deal of variationist linguistic research, for example, how do males use language differently to females? However, many linguists have noted that sex is different to GENDER, which is socially constructed, although the two terms are sometimes used interchangeably, and sex roles often dictate gender roles (so men are expected to speak, dress, think and behave in ways that are different to women, thus producing, reinforcing or exaggerating certain differences). Wittig (1992: 2) takes a more radical position, arguing that biological sex is a social construct propagating IDEOLOGY and that *man* and *woman* are not fixed categories: 'There is no sex. There is but sex that is oppressed and sex that oppresses.'

bourgeois

A term used by Karl Marx (1977) to describe the upper or ruling class in a capitalist society. The bourgeois own the means of production and are defined in contrast to the proletariat (those who work for a wage). Marx attacked the bourgeois for believing that its view of society and culture was universally true (e.g. for their support of the capitalist system which enabled them to maintain power), pointing out instead that these concepts were ideologies. See HEGEMONY.

capital

There are many types of capital, although they all relate to the concepts of advantage and POWER. People who hold capital (or have access to it) will be advantaged over those who do not. The term can be applied to a wide range of spheres: symbolic capital, physical capital, intellectual capital, natural capital etc. Bourdieu (1986) makes a distinction between social capital, economic capital and cultural capital. Economic capital refers to factors of production that are used to create goods or services; this can include land, labour and management. Social capital refers to connections between individuals or social networks as well as group membership. Cultural capital refers to ACCESS to education, knowledge, attitudes and skills (as well as social skills) that will help a person to have a higher status in society, for example, if a person applies for a job, he/she would not only need to have the requisite skills and experience to be eligible for the job but also would need to know how to write an application letter and a c.v. The applicant would also need to know how to conduct him/herself in an interview situation, by dressing appropriately, using formal and polite language, perhaps modifying their accent and being able to follow the interview's 'script'. Capital can often involve a relationship between physical, material objects and more abstract phenomena. For example, owning an expensive work of art is an aspect of cultural capital, although the cultural capital can only be fully realized if the owner is aware that the art has a high cultural value.

capitalism

A system of economics which emphasises private ownership, free markets, choice, competition and entrepreneurism. Proponents of capitalism include the economists Adam Smith, who argued that capitalism promotes economic growth, and John Maynard Keynes, who believed capitalism was important for freedom. Philosopher Ayn Rand also advocated capitalism, on the grounds that it allowed people to act in their rational self-interest. As Klein (2007) notes, in the latter half of twentieth century, under the influence of Milton Friedman and Friedrich Hayek, many countries moved towards a model of 'laissez-faire' capitalism (removing state interference in economic affairs), including America and the United Kingdom. Capitalism has been criticized for helping to create, maintain or exaggerate social and financial inequalities. It is also argued that it results in cycles of boom and recession or depression, while environmentalists have argued that capitalism requires continued economic growth and will eventually deplete the world's resources. At the time of writing, the majority of critical discourse analytical research has taken place in rich, westernized, capitalist countries, and much of this research is underlain by a critique of capitalism, to varying degrees.

cataphora

A cataphoric reference is an expression which refers to a later expression. As with **ANAPHORA**, cataphoric references are often pronouns or determiners. The example below is from a newspaper article – here the cataphoric reference 'he' occurs in the headline, referring to the later reference of 'David Blunkett' in the main body of the story.

He'll be cleared says Blair
   Tony Blair threw a protective shield around David Blunkett yesterday, insisting he would be cleared of using high office to help his ex-lover Kimberly Quinn. (BE06, A02)

categorization

1. In terms of discourse analysis, this can involve assigning something to a particular category; for example, words can be assigned to grammatical or semantic categories, whereas utterances could be assigned to pragmatic categories according to their function (apology, request, disagreement etc.). Categorization schemes can sometimes be difficult to implement if ambiguous cases are found. In addition, categories can proliferate if instances are found that do not fit into the existing set. Such schemes may therefore develop during the process of categorization, although a final scheme ought to be robust enough to cover all instances, including dealing with those which are ambiguous. A categorization scheme also ought to be transparent so that other researchers could arrive at the same decisions.

2. van Leeuwen (1996: 55) describes categorization as a way of representing social actors, and makes the distinction between two types: **FUNCTIONALISATION**

(what people do) and IDENTIFICATION (what they are). He notes that with categorization 'the English language allows us to make a choice between functionalisation and identification and that the use of this choice in discourse is of critical importance for discourse analysts'. Foucault (1979a) demonstrates how the categorization of sexuality changed in the late nineteenth century, for example, from sodomites (who engage in a sex act) to homosexuals (a species).

classroom discourse

The language used by teachers and students to communicate with each other in the classroom. Here, the use of *discourse* refers to the type, genre or context of language used. An analysis of classroom discourse may not only use recordings of actual speech but could also involve reflexive feedback interviews with participants or consultation of teaching texts. Cazden (2001: 3) notes three questions that classroom discourse analysis can try to address: 'How do patterns of language use affect what counts as "knowledge" and what counts as learning? How do these patterns affect the equality or inequality of students' educational opportunities? What communicative competence do these patterns presume and/or foster?' There is no single way of carrying out classroom discourse analysis, although a number of schemes have been developed; for example, Walsh (2006) uses a framework for examining classroom discourse called Self-Evaluation of Teacher Talk (SETT).

clause

A set of words consisting of a SUBJECT and a PREDICATE, and expressing a proposition. Halliday's SYSTEMIC FUNCTIONAL GRAMMAR considers the clause, rather than the sentence, as the basic unit of grammatical analysis. A clause can exist on its own as a sentence, for example, '*The man replied*' (BNC, A0R), but more complex sentences can contain multiple clauses or clauses embedded within clauses. Clauses which cannot exist on their own as a sentence are referred to as dependent clauses. Clauses can be classified further; for example, adverbial clauses function as adverbs: 'I left *when I was about eight*' (BNC, CH8). Relative clauses modify nouns: 'We can return for a moment to talk to the girl *who went to Italy*' (BNC, A04), while complement clauses are arguments of predicates: 'I am sure *that it would be welcomed by them*' (BNC, K98). See also PHRASE.

code switching

The use of multiple languages or language varieties (usually in conversation, although the term can be applied to other registers such as COMPUTER-MEDIATED COMMUNICATION). While borrowing occurs at the level of the lexicon only, code switching occurs at the grammatical or discourse level. Code switching was initially viewed as evidence for substandard language ability, but since the 1980s it has been seen as being related to group membership and a normal product of interaction between bilingual or multilingual people. Code switching is one way that ethnic minorities maintain a sense of IDENTITY; it can also be used to shift FOOTING or to structure talk in interaction (Auer 1984).

Meyerhoff (2006) differentiates between 'code switching' and 'code mixing': The former refers to the 'phenomenon of moving between distinct varieties'; it is 'the alternation between varieties, or codes, across sentences or clause boundaries' (p. 116); the latter 'generally refers to alternations between varieties, or codes, within a clause or phrase' (p. 120).

coherence

Coherence refers to the ways that a text is made semantically meaningful (as opposed to COHESION, which is concerned with grammar). Coherence can be achieved through techniques like IMPLICATURE or BACKGROUNDING actors. De Beaugrande and Dressler (1981: 4) view coherence as one of seven 'standards of textuality', being concerned with 'the ways in which the components of the **TEXTUAL WORLD**, i.e. the configuration of **CONCEPTS** and **RELATIONS** which *underlie* the surface text, are *mutually accessible and relevant*'.

cohesion

Cohesion refers to the way that a text makes sense syntactically. Halliday and Hasan (1976) note that common cohesive devices include forms of reference (e.g. ANAPHORA and CATAPHORA), ELLIPSIS, SUBSTITUTION, LEXICAL COHESION, conjunction and replacement. De Beaugrande and Dressler (1981: 3) view coherence as one of seven 'standards of textuality', claiming that coherence 'concerns the ways in which the components of the **SURFACE TEXT**, i.e. the actual words we hear or see, are *mutually connected within a sequence*. The surface components depend upon each other according to grammatical forms and conventions, such that cohesion rests upon **GRAMMATICAL DEPENDENCIES**'. See also COHERENCE.

collectivization

A type of ASSIMILATION which involves collectively representing people (without using statistics). According to van Leeuwen (1996: 49–50), the word *we* can be used to represent collectivization, or terms like *this nation*, *the community* or even the name of a country (*Australia*) can represent a collective IDENTITY. The following text excerpt, from President Barack Obama's inaugural speech (20 January, 2009), contains a number of examples of collectivization (shown in bold).

> . . . AMERICA has carried on not simply because of the skill or vision of THOSE IN HIGH OFFICE, but because WE THE PEOPLE have remained faithful to the ideals of OUR FORBEARERS, and true to OUR founding documents. So it has been. So it must be with THIS GENERATION OF AMERICANS. That WE are in the midst of crisis is now well understood. OUR NATION is at war . . .

See also AGGREGATION and INDIVIDUALIZATION.

collocation

Collocation refers to the ways that certain words tend to regularly occur next to or close to each other. It can be thought of as the 'company that a word keeps'. Most native speakers of English are probably aware of some collocations (such as *tough* and *luck*), although there are many which are less noticeable (particularly to non-native speakers) and can only be revealed by CORPUS LINGUISTIC methods. Stubbs (1996: 172), in noting the ideological effects of collocations, suggests that their analysis helps to 'show the associations and connotations they have, and therefore the assumptions which they embody'. Some collocations became naturalized and therefore it is difficult to unpack the information and assumptions within them; an example that Stubbs gives is *working mother*, which contains an IMPLICATURE that when mothers stay at home to look after children they are *not* working, suggesting society only considers 'work' to be of value if it is paid work. In addition, Stubbs (1996) argues that collocations may also prime readers to think of groups in certain ways – so with the strong collocational relationship between *illegal* and *immigrant*, we may be primed to think of illegality, even if we encounter the word *immigrant* on its own. See also SEMANTIC PROSODY, SEMANTIC PREFERENCE.

colonization

Initially used in the natural or social sciences referring to a species (plant, animal, human) populating a new area, the term was taken up by Habermas (1984) in an analysis of contemporary CAPITALISM to describe how systems such as the economy, the state and institutions have had an enormous impact on people's lives. Fairclough (1989: 197–198) adapts the term to refer to colonizations in the societal order of discourse, noting the way in which 'discourses of consumerism and bureaucracy have "colonized" other discourse types or expanded at their expense'. In writing about the colonization of advertising, Fairclough (1989) notes 'the dramatic increase in advertising in the last three decades . . . the extent to which people are exposed to advertising on a daily basis . . . the penetration of advertising into non-economic aspects of life . . . into the home through television'. Further examples of the colonization of advertising would involve phenomena such as product placement in films or marketing firms hiring academics to carry out research that will then be cited in the media along with reference to the company which sponsored the research.

colony text

A term coined by Hoey (1986), which is taken from natural science where it describes ant hills and beehives. The components of a colony can be moved around but the colony's meaning remains the same. This applies to certain texts made up of many discrete and similar entries, for example, shopping lists, horoscopes, dictionaries and personal advertisement columns.

community of practice

A term developed by Lave and Wenger (1991) to describe the ways that people who have shared sets of common goals interact with each other, particularly related to contexts where people learn to carry out certain practices in 'apprenticeship' situations. It is 'a set of relations among persons, activity and world, over time and in relation with other tangential and overlapping communities of practice. A community of practice is an intrinsic condition for the existence of knowledge' (ibid.: 29). Eckert and McConnell-Ginet (1998: 491) advocate that a community of practice is where 'observable action and interaction do the work of producing, reproducing, and resisting the organization of power in society and in societal discourses of gender, age, race etc.'. Communities of practice can range from being very formal to informal, short lived and spontaneous (e.g. a group of people who do the washing up together after a meal). The term has some similarities to DISCOURSE COMMUNITY.

computer-mediated communication (CMC)

Forms of interaction such as email, chat rooms, instant messaging, blogging and commenting that occur between people who are using computers, although the term is also sometimes used to refer to other electronic means of communication such as text messaging via mobile telephones. A distinction is made between synchronous and asynchronous types of CMC (the former involves instantaneous 'real-time' interactions such as chatrooms, the latter involves ongoing interactions where there may be long breaks between communicative 'turns' (such as emails needing no immediate response). Discourse analysts have considered how participants in CMC make use of various affordances in order to effectively communicate (e.g. the use of emoticons) and maintain relationships, how aspects of discourse like TURN-TAKING are managed and how language is used to construct online identities, including anonymous identities.

connotation

Connotation is an aspect of sign theory. According to de Saussure (1966), a SIGN consists of a signifier (the representation of something) and what is signified (the mental construct of what is being represented). Words are signifiers, for example, the word *blue* signifies the mental concept of the colour blue. The relationship is arbitrary and not necessarily fixed. Signifiers do not have to be words but can involve other forms of representation, such as images, traffic lights or gestures. Language users agree on the relationship between signifiers and signifieds. Such relationships can be denotative (literal), whereby the word *blue* signifies the mental concept of the colour. However, the relationship can also be connotative, whereby further (often nonliteral) signifiers are ascribed to the signified. For example, *blue* has a range of different connotative meanings which can differ across different cultures. Among other things, it can connote nobility (*blue blood*), sex (*blue movie*), sadness (*feeling blue*), rarity (*once in a blue moon*) or coldness (*turning blue with cold*). Such meanings require additional knowledge of social context in order to be correctly interpreted. Connotations often express positive or negative attitudes.

consumerism

The consumption of a range of goods and services collectively referred to as commodities, and a key aspect of modern CAPITALISM; the concept is therefore central to western CRITICAL DISCOURSE ANALYSIS. Fairclough (1989: 199–201) notes that three sets of conditions relate to the rise of consumerism: (1) economic conditions, such as the ability to produce large varieties of commodities in large quantities coupled with increased wages and leisure time in a population; (2) technological conditions, such as the development of mass media and (3) cultural conditions, such as the rise of individualism and the decline of cultural communities. Advertising discourses are essential to consumerism, and Fairclough's critical discourse analysis has not only examined advertising texts but has also shown how advertising discourses pervade into other contexts (see COLONIZATION). The term is often used critically, for example, *consumer feminism* refers to ways that advertisers claim to 'empower' women by encouraging them to purchase targeted products such as plastic surgery (see also Talbot's [1998] work on *consumer femininity*, which positions women as consumers).

content analysis

A method for studying the content of communication developed by Alfred Lindesmith in the 1930s but becoming popular in the 1960s when it was adapted by Glaser (1965). Content analysis involves the development and use of coding frames, often to make comparisons between different texts, for example, the analyst might focus on comparing the frequencies of certain types of KEYWORDS in different political or media texts. Classification systems need to be reliable in that different human raters ought to be able to make the same categorizations (Weber 1990: 12). In addition, the analysis tends to focus on the 'manifest' meaning of the text (e.g. what has been written or said) rather than attempting to interpret author intentions. Krippendorff (2004) lists six questions which content analysis must address: (1) which data are analysed? (2) how are they defined? (3) what is the population from which they are drawn? (4) what is the context relative to which the data are analysed? (5) what are the boundaries of the analysis and (6) what is the target of the inferences? Content analysis is normally carried out on electronically coded texts, allowing large amounts of data to be quickly and accurately processed (giving it similarities to CORPUS LINGUISTICS).

context

An important aspect of many strands of DISCOURSE ANALYSIS – which helps in the interpretative process of linguistic phenomena as well as providing explanations. The analysis of context forms part of most CRITICAL DISCOURSE ANALYSIS approaches. Van Dijk (2001: 108) makes a distinction between local contexts which are 'properties of the immediate interactional situation in which a communicative event takes place' while global contexts are 'defined by the social, political, cultural and historical structures in which a communicative event takes place'. Wodak (2001: 67) identifies four levels of context that are used in the DISCOURSE-HISTORICAL APPROACH:

1. the immediate, language or text internal CO-TEXT
2. the intertextual and interdiscursive relationship between utterances, texts, genres and discourses
3. the extralinguistic social/sociological variables and institutional frames of a specific "context of situation" (middle-range theories)
4. the broader sociopolitical and historical contexts, which the discursive practices are embedded in and related to (grand theories).

conversation analysis (CA)

A form of linguistic analysis which focuses on transcripts of real-life spoken interactions. It is often referred to as the study of talk in interaction. While analysts study private, informal conversations, they also examine institutional interactions (e.g. doctor–patient, legal interactions, police interviews, talk in the classroom; see Drew and Heritage 1992).

CA was developed in the 1960s by the sociologist Harvey Sacks along with Emanuel Schegloff and Gail Jefferson (e.g. Sacks et al. 1974), who were influenced by ETHNOMETHODOLOGY. CA focuses on structures within speech, particularly TURN-TAKING organization, sequence organization (see ADJACENCY PAIR) and REPAIR. A key aspect of CA is the belief that conversations tend to follow regular structures and that breakdowns in such structures are of interest. CA therefore involves carrying out a close reading of a transcript, focusing on 'small' phenomena like pauses, interruptions and laughter. Most conversation analysts prefer to work with detailed transcripts. Gail Jefferson developed a TRANSCRIPTION scheme which allows analysts to consider the speaker's volume, intonation, speed and emphasis as well as phenomena like breathing or lip-smacks (see Atkinson and Heritage 1984).

Conversation analysts focus on the transcript of the talk and therefore do not usually use other sources of information to aid their analysis. For example, they tend to not make inferences about what people are thinking, and they do not interview the participants to ask them about their inner feelings. In addition, many conversation analysts do not try to explain their conversational data by relating it to a person's IDENTITY or personality or by considering the wider social CONTEXT or any existing theories (which is where CA differs from CRITICAL DISCOURSE ANALYSIS).

conversationalization

A term used by Fairclough (1994: 260), who describes it as 'a restructuring of the boundary between public and private orders of discourse'. Fairclough also notes that it involves the use of language that is normally associated with conversation (such as colloquial vocabulary, use of accent, prosodic and paralinguistic features and particular genres, such as the conversational narrative) being increasingly used in genres and contexts where they were not found before. With conversationalization, language is used to create and maintain a (sometimes synthetic) relationship between a speaker and hearer rather than just being informational, so this can involve emotional, subjective linguistic strategies, such as using appraisal lexis (*very*, *really*), vagueness (*sort of*, *kinda*), repetition (*that's really really great!*), first- and second-person pronouns, contractions, active sentences, informal TERMS OF ADDRESS, slang and swearing, and humour and irony.

Conversationalization has similarities to terms like 'fake intimacy' (Hoggart 1957), public-colloquial style (Leech 1966) and 'SYNTHETIC PERSONALIZATION' (Fairclough 1989). Conversationalization could reflect a movement towards democratization in society, enabling more people to participate in social and political debates, and it could also reflect and create a more relaxed, informal way of interacting. However, it is also argued that in CAPITALIST societies conversationalization is often used as a way of securing customer loyalty by helping to create the appearance of a personal relationship between, say, a service provider and a consumer or a politician and a voter. In addition, conversationalization has been criticized as only giving the *appearance* of an equal or close relationship – generally, those who really do hold POWER can decide when conversationalization is appropriate and when an interaction should be of a more explicitly hierarchical nature. So a doctor may use conversationalization with her patients, but ultimately she has most of the power in the interaction, which she can demonstrate at any point.

conversational maxims

Four maxims or guiding principles developed by Paul Grice (1975) to explain how people conduct conversations. The maxims are not etiquette guidelines (see POLITENESS) but can be best thought of as expectations that people have about how conversations will normally be carried out. The maxims can be flouted for various reasons. Speakers might secretly violate them to mislead, opt out of them or be faced with a clash of maxims (ibid.: 49). Together, the maxims relate to Grice's COOPERATIVE PRINCIPLE. Mey (2001: 76–77) argues that the maxims cannot be universally applied as different cultures may have different principles about how co-operation should be achieved. The maxims are as follows.

The Maxim of Quantity (which governs the appropriate amount of information or speech that someone makes in a conversation): (1) Make your contribution as informative as is required for the current purposes of the exchange, and (2) do not make your contribution any more informative than is required.

The Maxim of Quality (which governs truthfulness): (1) Do not say what you believe to be false, and (2) do not say that for which you lack adequate evidence.

The Maxim of Relevance: Be relevant. Some researchers (e.g. Sperber and Wilson 1986) have argued that this is the most important maxim and actually subsumes the other maxims within it. See RELEVANCE THEORY.

The Maxim of Manner: (1) Avoid obscurity of expression, (2) avoid ambiguity, (3) avoid unnecessary prolixity or wordiness (e.g. be brief) and (4) be orderly (e.g. describe events in the order in which they occur).

When a maxim is intentionally flouted in conversation, other participants make inferences for the reason behind the flouting. For example, the Maxim of Quality might be flouted in order to convey irony or sarcasm, for example, if someone says 'That's great!' after hearing bad news.

cooperative principle

A general principle of conversation postulated by Grice (1975: 45), who describes it as 'Make your conversational contribution such as is required, at the stage at which it occurs, by the accepted purpose or direction of the talk exchange in which you are engaged'. The cooperative principle is supported by four CONVERSATIONAL MAXIMS.

corpus-assisted discourse studies (CADS)

A form of discourse analysis that uses CORPUS LINGUISTICS methods and tends to take a critical approach to analysis. Influential work related to this field could be characterized by Hardt-Mautner (1995) and Stubbs (1996, 2001), although the term CADS was coined by Alan Partington (2004). CADS involves using computer software in order to identify linguistic patterns (such as frequencies and COLLOCATIONS) in large bodies of language data, which can be used as evidence for the existence of a particular discourse or ideological stance. Baker (2006: 13) notes that the corpus approach enables researchers to take into account the 'incremental effect of discourse'. CADS research also places importance on providing explanations for findings, which often means using additional methods of analysis as a form of TRIANGULATION, and taking into account contextual information regarding methods of PRODUCTION and RECEPTION of texts as well as INTERTEXTUALITY. Examples of research that could be subsumed under or related to CADS include Fairclough's (2000a) examination of KEYWORDS in New Labour discourse, Hunston's (2002) research on representation of the deaf, Partington's (2003) work on US press conferences and Baker's (2005) research on the construction of gay men in public discourse.

corpus linguistics

McEnery and Wilson (1996: 1) describe corpus linguistics as the 'study of language based on examples of "real life" language use', noting that it is 'a methodology rather than an aspect of language requiring explanation or description'. Corpus linguists use computer software to examine frequencies and relationships between words in (often large) sets of authentic texts that have been electronically encoded. According to Baker (2006: 10–12), the benefit of such a method is that it can help to reduce researcher bias, enabling existing theories of language use to be tested on a large, representative sample of language data as well as allowing processes such as KEYWORDS or COLLOCATIONS to reveal language patterns that nobody would have hypothesized. Hunston (2002) describes some of the many applications of corpus linguistics including language teaching, stylistics, dictionary creation, forensic linguistics, language variation, studies of IDEOLOGY and translation studies. See also CORPUS-ASSISTED DISCOURSE STUDIES.

co-text

The parts of TEXT (e.g. sentences or utterances) that come before and after a particular piece of text under examination. See CONTEXT.

critical discourse analysis (CDA)

An approach to the analysis of discourse which views language as a social practice and is interested in the ways that ideologies and power relations are expressed through language. Critical discourse analysts are particularly interested in issues of inequality, sometimes keeping in mind the question 'who benefits?' when carrying out analysis.

Unlike many other forms of linguistic analysis, CDA is not only concerned with words on a page but also involves examining social context – for example, asking how and why the words came to be written or spoken and what other texts are being referenced by them (see INTERTEXTUALITY). The approach was first developed by Norman Fairclough (1989), who adopted a three-dimensional framework to analysis. The first stage (DESCRIPTION) involves text analysis, correlating with CRITICAL LINGUISTICS, which itself was developed out of Halliday's SYSTEMIC FUNCTIONAL GRAMMAR. The second stage (INTERPRETA-TION) focuses on the relationship between text and interaction, seeing the text as both a product of the process of production and a resource in the process of interpretation. The final stage (EXPLANATION) examines the relationship between interaction and social context, considering the social effects of the processes of production and interpretation.

Other approaches to critical discourse analysis have been proposed, although all tend towards combining text analysis with consideration of wider social context. Reisigl and Wodak's (2001) DISCOURSE-HISTORICAL APPROACH uses ARGUMENTATION theory, whereas van Leeuwen (1996, 1997) concentrates on social actor representation. Jäger's approach (2001) is based on using theoretical and methodological aspects of Foucauldian critical discourse analysis with dispositive analysis. Van Dijk's SOCIO-COGNITIVE APPROACH to CDA employs a three-part model of memory, while Hart and Luke (2007) focus on the synergy between cognitive linguistics and CDA. O'Halloran (2003) develops a model of the interpretation stage of CDA, taking ideas from connectionism, cognitive linguistics, inferencing and RELEVANCE THEORY, while Partington (2004) and Baker (2006) have suggested an approach to CDA which utilizes corpus linguistics methods to identify large-scale patterns (see CORPUS-ASSISTED DISCOURSE STUDIES). Even within these specific 'flavours' of CDA, there is generally no step-by-step, fixed approach to analysis. The analyst is given considerable freedom in choosing texts, combinations of different analytical techniques and the order in which they are carried out. This can sometimes make analysis challenging to novitiates, and this freedom, combined with the fact that CDA is concerned with highlighting social problems like prejudice and exclusion, can open up practitioners to the accusation of bias (e.g. they could select texts that prove their point while ignoring those which do not). CDA has responded to this criticism in two ways: (1) by acknowledging that the concept of the 'neutral' researcher is a fallacy and advocating REFLEXIVITY, so the researcher reflects on his or her own position and how it develops as the research progresses, and (2) by incorporating TRIANGULATION, such as combining small-scale qualitative analysis with practices from CORPUS LINGUISTICS such as SAMPLING and quantitative techniques, which give evidence for wider trends.

critical linguistics

A socially concerned approach to linguistics, which was first pioneered by Roger Fowler and Gunther Kress in the 1970s, emerging from the book *Language and Control* (Fowler et al. 1979). Critical linguistics used Halliday's SYSTEMIC FUNCTIONAL GRAMMAR to examine how phenomena are represented in texts, for example, via the use of nominalizations or agentless passives, pointing out that grammatical systems are closely related to social and personal needs. However, critical linguists have also adopted other models such as SPEECH ACT THEORY and CONVERSATION ANALYSIS. Critical linguistics was used as the basis for the 'descriptive' level of Fairclough's CRITICAL DISCOURSE ANALYSIS and has also been influential in the development of other critical approaches to discourse analysis such as the DISCOURSE-HISTORICAL APPROACH or the SOCIO-COGNITIVE APPROACH.

cultural relativism

A concept developed by Frank Boas (1887: 589): '[C]ivilisation is not something absolute, but . . . is relative.' The term itself was coined in the 1940s after his death. Originally, an epistemological claim, it was used as a methodological tool and a response to the ETHNOCENTRICISM of western researchers. An example of cultural relativism that Boas (1889) pointed out is to do with the appearance of 'alternating sounds'. English lacks certain sounds that are used in other languages. When English speakers hear someone use such a sound, they misperceive it as another sound (sometimes inconsistently – for example, they may perceive Japanese speakers as alternating between saying *rice* and *lice* when in fact they are always pronouncing the word in the same way).

data-driven approach

A way of carrying out analysis involving the use of actual 'data', as opposed to say, an introspective position. In addition, the data should be naturally occurring rather than consisting of invented texts. In its most extreme form, the researcher tries to avoid imposing existing linguistic theories or categorization schemes (such as grammatical categories) from the outset or setting out to investigate specific hypotheses about language use on the data. Data-driven analysis is sometimes characterized as a bottom-up approach, in contrast to theory-driven analysis which is top-down.

Instead, the researcher approaches the data with an 'open mind' and allows whatever emerges as interesting, salient or frequent to 'drive' the analysis along. The data then direct the analyst to choose certain features or adopt a particular analytical framework. In CORPUS LINGUISTICS, Tognini-Bonelli (2001) makes a related distinction between corpus-driven and corpus-based approaches; the former is similar to data-driven analysis, using minimal theoretical assumptions and relying on frequency and other statistical information to direct the analysis, while the latter uses the corpus as a source of examples to check researcher intuition.

deixis

Expressions in language that point to referents (or put more simply 'refer to things'). Such referents can be concrete (e.g. objects, people) or abstract (e.g. points in time, ideas). Examples of deixis include the words *this*, *that*, *here*, *there*, *now*, *then*, *I*, *you*, *he* and *she*. Such words can only be understood by reference to context (e.g. by considering the words, sentences etc. around the word or by addressing extralinguistic context – for example, in a conversation a person may say 'look at that' and point to something). Because deixis locates referents along specific dimensions, they can be classified into different subtypes, for example, spatial, temporal, discourse, person and social. Huang (2007: 132) classifies 'deixis' into two ways: (1) 'basic categories of deixis' (person, time and space) and (2) 'other categories of deixis' (social deixis and discourse deixis)'. See ANAPHORA, CATAPHORA.

description

A form of analysis which attempts to accurately describe the features of a particular language without making value judgements, such as the extent to which the language is correct, clear or manipulative in some way. This is different to PRESCRIPTIVISM. Description is usually an initial stage of CRITICAL DISCOURSE ANALYSIS which usually comes before INTERPRETATION and EXPLANATION. It would involve identifying a set of formal linguistic features in a text, such as pronoun use, metaphor, modality, nominalizations and agency.

diachronic studies

Diachronic studies refer to the study of language as it changes over time. Such studies have a longitudinal aspect in that they may follow a population, group or individual and examine how their language use changes over a particular period of time. Other diachronic studies may try to collect and then compare samples of language from different time periods. Diachronic analysis is therefore linked to historical linguistics. See SYNCHRONIC STUDIES.

direct speech

Direct speech is a form of speech presentation whereby a speaker's utterance is reported verbatim, unlike REPORTED SPEECH. Direct speech is often represented as a sentence with a reporting clause, and the reported words are enclosed in quotation marks: 'There is a 1952 directive that's never been superseded', she said deliberately (BNC, HR4). See Leech and Short (2007: 64).

discourse

A term with several related and often quite loose meanings. (1) Perhaps in its most general usage, it can refer to any form of 'language in use' (Brown and Yule 1983) or naturally occurring language. (2) It can also refer more specifically to spoken language, hence the term DISCOURSE MARKER, which tends to refer to speech. Stubbs (1983: 9) also makes a distinction between discourse, which is interactive, and text, which is a non-interactive monologue.

(3) Another meaning conceives discourse as 'language above the sentence or above the clause' (Stubbs 1983: 1) and would lend itself to the analysis of text structure and pragmatics. (4) Discourse can also be used to refer to particular contexts of language use, and in this sense it becomes similar to concepts like genre or text type. For example, we can conceptualize political discourse (the sort of language used in political contexts) or media discourse (language use in the media). (5) In addition, some writers have conceived of discourse as related to particular topics, such as an environmental discourse or colonial discourse (which may occur in many different genres). Such labels sometimes suggest a particular attitude towards a topic (e.g. people engaging in environmental discourse would generally be expected to be concerned with protecting the environment rather than wasting resources). (6) Related to this, Foucault (1972: 49) defines discourse more ideologically as 'practices which systematically form the objects of which they speak'. Burr (1995:48) expands on Foucault's definition as

> a set of meanings, metaphors, representations, images, stories, statements and so on that in some way together produce a particular version of events . . . Surrounding any one object, event, person etc., there may be a variety of different discourses, each with a different story to tell about the world, a different way of representing it to the world.

(7) Sunderland (2004) takes Foucault's meaning a stage further by explicitly identifying and naming specific discourses such as 'women beware women' and 'male sexual drive' (see DISCOURSE NAMING, GENDERED DISCOURSE). Discourses are not articulated explicitly but traces of them can be found in language use. The more ideological uses of discourses, which occur towards the end of this list, reflect postmodernist thinking. Potter and Wetherell (1987) have shown that people often appear to voice conflicting opinions around a topic, which they argue is due to them accessing a range of competing discourses in their talk. Discourses are therefore contradictory and shifting, and their identification is necessarily interpretative and open to contestation, particularly as it is difficult to 'step outside' discourse and view it with complete objectivity. Foucault (1972: 146) notes, 'it is not possible for us to describe our own archive, since it is from within these rules that we speak'.

32 discourse analysis

discourse analysis

Just as DISCOURSE has numerous meanings, there are equally plentiful conceptualizations of discourse analysis, which have changed over time. Brown and Yule (1983: ix) refer to it as 'how humans use language to communicate'. Stubbs (1983: 1) refers to it as 'attempts to study the organization of language above the sentence or above the clause; and therefore to study large linguistic units such as conversational exchanges or written texts'. He later notes that it also refers to 'the study of naturally occurring language' (ibid.: 9), pointing out that some writers such as Van Dijk have used the term *text analysis*, which could serve as well as discourse analysis (although text analysis implies a particular European tradition). While some discourse analysts focus on how meaning and structure are signalled in texts, others, especially since the early 1990s, have used discourse analysis more critically to examine issues relating to POWER, inequality and IDEOLOGY. All forms of discourse analysis, however, have tended to stress the importance of examining naturally occurring texts, even if methods of analysis, focus (e.g. the extent to which INTERTEXTUALITY, methods of production and reception or socio-historical context is considered) and goals have differed. Burr (1995: 163) claims that the term is an 'umbrella which covers a wide variety of actual research practices with quite different aims and theoretical backgrounds. All take language as their focus of interest'. Burr (1995: 163) implies that CONVERSATION ANALYSIS involves a form of discourse analysis, while it could also be argued that DISCURSIVE PSYCHOLOGY, INTERACTIONAL SOCIOLINGUISTICS and all of the different strands of CRITICAL DISCOURSE ANALYSIS are also forms of discourse analysis.

Discourse analysis has mainly been a qualitative form of analysis; traditionally, it has involved a 'close reading' of a small amount of text, such as a detailed TRANSCRIPTION of a conversation or a magazine article, although in more recent years, discourse analysts have begun to use quantitative or corpus-assisted methods on much larger sets of data (see CORPUS-ASSISTED DISCOURSE STUDIES). Focusing more on the 'critical' form of discourse analysis, adopted by social psychological research, Burr (1995: 160–161) points out that its central tenets include viewing research as a co-production between the researchers and those who are being researched, with an acknowledgement that objectivity is an impossibility. Instead, discourse analysts need to use REFLEXIVITY, with researchers reflecting on their own position and how that has impacted on the research process and findings.

discourse community

A term used by Nystrand (1982) and then developed by Swales (1990: 24–27), who defines a discourse community according to six characteristics: (1) a broadly agreed upon set of common goals, (2) mechanisms for intercommunication among members, (3) participatory mechanisms to provide information and feedback, (4) owns and uses one or more genres to further its communicative aims, (5) has acquired specific lexis and (6) has a number of members who have a suitable degree of relevant content and discoursal expertise. Members of discourse communities adopt a REGISTER of language, making them different from a SPEECH COMMUNITY, which involves inherited or adopted languages. However, being a member of a discourse community also involves understanding and utilizing concepts and expectations that are set up with a particular community as well as being aware of language. Examples of discourse communities could involve users of an email mailing list about a particular television programme, members of a support group (e.g. Alcoholics Anonymous) or people who subscribe to or publish in the same academic journal. Discourse communities tend to function as mechanisms for enabling communication, rather than as an end to themselves. The term is used by some writers (e.g. Cossard 2006) as being interchangeable with COMMUNITY OF PRACTICE, while others use the terms to mean different things, for example, Hewings (2005: 38) suggests that community of practice is a related but broader notion.

discourse-historical approach

A form of CRITICAL DISCOURSE ANALYSIS which was developed in Vienna by Martin Reisigl and Ruth Wodak (2001). It has been influenced by Halliday's SYSTEMIC FUNCTIONAL GRAMMAR, CRITICAL LINGUISTICS, critical theory, ARGUMENTATION theory, German 'politico-linguistics' and forms of critical discourse analysis carried out by Fairclough (1989, 1995), van Leeuwen (1995, 1996) and Hodge and Kress (1988). In order to reduce the risk of biased politicizing, the discourse-historical approach uses TRIANGULATION, combining different methods and data together and places emphasis on finding out as much about context as possible. Analysis of CONTEXT takes into account the use of language in particular texts, INTERTEXTUAL relationships, INTERDISCURSIVITY, social variables and institutional frames which relate to the context of a situation and sociopolitical and historical context: '[T]he discourse historical approach attempts to integrate much available knowledge about the historical sources and the background of the social and political fields in which discursive "events" are embedded' (Reisigl and Wodak 2001: 35). In a typical discourse-historical analysis, the researcher will first outline the contents or topics of a particular discourse, then investigate the DISCURSIVE STRATEGIES (such as argumentation) used to maintain it and finally examine the ways that particular constructions (such as stereotypes) are linguistically achieved.

discourse markers

Sometimes called discourse particles or pragmatic markers, the term is often used to refer to words or phrases that appear to have no grammatical or semantic function, such as *you know*, *like*, *oh*, *well*, *I mean*, *actually*, *basically*, *OK* as well as connectives like *because*, *so*, *and*, *but* and *or*. Schiffrin (1987: 31) defines them as 'sequentially dependent elements which bracket units of talk'. While most discourse markers were ignored by early grammars as having empty meanings or being 'fillers', they were later acknowledged (particularly by corpus linguists) as playing important roles in the organization of discourse and/or fulfilling pragmatic functions. For example, Aijmer (1996) points to two functional classes of discourse markers, local markers like *I mean* which help to mark micro structures, for example, within a single topic, and global markers like *anyway*, which can be used to signpost transition from one topic to another. Jucker and Smith (1998: 197) make a different distinction between reception markers, which signal speaker reactions to information provided by someone else (*yeah*, *oh*, *ok*, *really*), and presentation markers, which modify information presented by the speaker (*like*, *you know*, *I mean*). Rühlemann (2007: 121) makes a third distinction between present-discourse markers (which would include the above examples) and presented-discourse markers (which are used to manage reported speech: *I goes*, *she was like*). Andersen (1998) has shown that contrary to some arguments discourse markers do adhere to grammatical and functional restrictions and cannot occur anywhere in an utterance.

The concept of discourse markers can be expanded to refer to nonlinguistic phenomena. For example, in speech, a rise in PITCH could be used to mark the start of a new topic. In addition, in writing, discourse can be organized with visual elements like paragraph spaces, subheadings etc.

discourse naming

A form of DISCOURSE ANALYSIS developed by Sunderland (2004) in her work on GENDERED DISCOURSES. It involves a close reading of texts in order to identify linguistic traces suggestive of particular ways of looking at the world or discourses. Sunderland (2004: 28) claims that

> [p]eople do not . . . recognise a discourse . . . in any straightforward way . . . Not only is it not identified or named, and is not self-evident or visible as a discrete chunk of a given text, it can never be "there" in its entirety. What is there are certain linguistic features: "marks on a page", words spoken or even people's memories of previous conversations . . . which – if sufficient and coherent – may suggest that they are "traces" of a particular discourse.

Such linguistic *traces* (see also Talbot 1998) can be identified through traditional techniques of discourse analysis including social actor representation, modality, transitivity and collocation. Part of Sunderland's approach involves identifying how discourses relate to each other. They can be conceived as *competing*, *dominant*, *mutually supporting*, *alternative* etc. Another aspect of naming discourses is more evaluative, with labels like *damaging*, *liberating*, *resistant*, *subversive* and *conservative* being utilized. For example, the sentence 'The law says all men are free in England' (BNC, C85) could be viewed as embodying a number of different discourses. It could reference a discourse of equality but also a somewhat contradictory sexist discourse in that it explicitly refers to men but not women. We would need to investigate the context of this sentence in more detail in order to determine how the author orients to it.

discourse prosody

Discourse prosody, according to Stubbs (2001: 65), is 'a feature which extends over more than one unit in a linear string'. Discourse prosody has a great deal in common with SEMANTIC PROSODY and SEMANTIC PREFERENCE, although where semantic prosody/preference tends to focus on relationships between single words, discourse prosodies look at relationships between a word and the context that it is embedded in. For example, the verb *swan* and its associated forms *swanning*, *swanned* and *swans* collocate with a set of words for places (*shops*, *town*, *pub*) and countries (*France*, *New York*), which suggests a SEMANTIC PREFERENCE. However, by examining the fuller context of *swan* as a verb, we get a sense that users of this word disapprove of people they are writing about:

Example 1
When they were *swanning* around looking pretty, our families were work-ing their fingers to the bone for virtually nothing. (BNC, CEY)

Example 2
Most 'organisers' *swan* in at eight-thirty looking important, only to discover there's a big hitch and they have no time to put it right. (BNC, ADK)

Example 3
'So you've opted out of the war effort', he greeted her nastily, 'to go *swanning* all over the Pacific?' (BNC, FPX)

Example 4
Needless to say, these mega-rich popsters just *swan* around in wellies every other weekend for the benefit of the colour supplements 'Day In The Life' features and leave all the actual farming to peasants who get up at dawn and get paid in potatoes. (BNC, CAD)

Example 5
Morrissey ought to get himself a string section and stop *swanning* about pretending to be Melvyn Bragg. (BNC, CK4)

From these examples, it can be seen that *swan* holds a negative discourse prosody – people who 'swan' are constructed as oblivious to their respons-ibilities or other people (examples 1–4) or appear pretentious and delusional (example 5).

discursive competence

Bhatia (2004: 144) defines discursive competence as 'a general concept to cover various levels of competence we all need in order to expertly operate within well-defined professional as well as general socio-cultural contexts'.

discursive practice

Fairclough (1992: 78) defines discursive practice as involving 'processes of text production, distribution and consumption'. These processes are 'social and require reference to the particular economic, political and institutional settings within which discourse is generated' (ibid.: 71). In Fairclough's three-dimensional model of discourse, discursive practice comes between TEXT and SOCIAL PRACTICE.

discursive psychology

A form of discourse analysis developed by Edwards and Potter (1992), but see also Potter and Wetherell (1987). It has a range of influences, including social studies of science (Gilbert and Mulkay 1984), CONVERSATION ANALYSIS, ETH- NOMETHODOLOGY, rhetorical social psychology (Billig 1987) and writings of philosophers like Wittgenstein. It was set up as a means of critiquing ways that traditional psychology understands, topics like ATTITUDES, ACCOUNTS and memory. When analysing interview data, Potter and Edwards noted that many interview respondents produce inconsistent or variable versions or accounts and that rather than the analyst attempting to discount such inconsistencies or identify the 'correct' one, an alternative was to treat such inconsistencies within the context of their occurrence to show how people handle interactional contingencies, argue points or tailor their talk to specific rhetorical uses. Discursive psychology therefore focuses on close qualitative analyses of spoken interactions (interviews, FOCUS GROUPS or naturally occurring conversations within real-world situations like counselling, helplines or dispute resolution), viewing talk as social action. Edwards (2005: 260) writes,

> Rather than people having memories, script knowledge, attitudes, and so on, that they carry around in their heads and produce on cue (or in RESEARCH INTERVIEWS), people are shown to formulate or work up the nature of events, actions, and their own accountability through ways of talking. These ways of talking are both constructive and action oriented. They are constructive in the sense that they offer a particular version of things when there are indefinitely many potential versions, some of which may be available and alive in the setting.

discursive strategy

In the DISCOURSE-HISTORICAL APPROACH, Reisigl and Wodak (2001: 44) define discursive strategies as accurate and intentional plans of practices 'adopted to achieve a particular social, psychological or linguistic aim'. They are realized via systematic uses of language. The authors go on to identify a range of different strategies, including REFERENTIAL STRATEGIES, PREDICATIONAL STRATEGIES, ARGUMENTATION strategies and TOPOI, PERSPECTIVATION, framing or discourse representation, MITIGATING STRATEGIES and INTENSIFYING STRATEGIES.

eco-critical discourse analysis

A form of critical discourse analysis which is focused on the analysis of texts that relate to the environment. Subsequently, eco-critical discourse analysis addresses any discourse which has consequences for ecosystems (such as economic discourses, gendered discourses or consumerist discourses). The aim of such analyses is to expose underlying ideologies in such texts (see, e.g. Harré et al. 1999, Stibbe 2006). The field was inspired by Halliday (1990) who challenged applied linguists to address twenty-first century concerns, particularly ecological issues. Two goals of eco-critical discourse analysis are to expose damaging ideologies and find discursive representations that contribute to ecologically sustainable societies.

ellipsis

A device used to maintain COHESION in discourse (see Halliday and Hasan 1976). Ellipsis usually refers to an intentional omission of a word or phrase from a text, often because the omitted text has already been referred to earlier and is thus not necessary:

Elinor: Where are you going to hide it?
Tim: Somewhere you can't have it. (BNC, KBW)

In the above example, Tim could have said, 'I am going to hide it somewhere you can't have it', but the first six words were omitted.

emphasized femininity

Connell's theory of HEGEMONIC MASCULINITY conceives of a hierarchy of masculinities, with societies viewing certain ways of being male as superior to others. Could a similar hierarchical conceptualization be applied to femininity? Connell (1987: 183) argues that 'there is no femininity that is hegemonic in the sense that the dominant form of masculinity is hegemonic amongst men'. He therefore prefers the term 'emphasized femininity' as it positions *all* femininity as subordinate. See also PRIVILEGED FEMININITY.

entailment

A logical relationship between two propositions, where if one is true then the other must also be true (see Anderson et al. 1992, Routley and Meyer 1973). For example, the statement 'Mary married John' entails that 'Mary got married'. Unlike presuppositions, however, entailments cannot be shown to remain if negation is applied to the first proposition. So if we say 'Mary didn't marry John', we cannot confidently claim that Mary got married (she may have married someone else or she may have married no one – we don't know). See also IMPLICATURE.

erasure

A form of EXCLUSION or marginalization, particularly in relation to IDENTITY categories (see Namaste 2000: 51–52). Subordinated identities (e.g. women and girls) are sometimes erased in language use. For example, in the following excerpt, the generic *man* is used to refer to all humankind: 'Prehistoric man chose to live here because he knew it was unique, endowed with everything he could ever need to survive and thrive' (BNC, HH8). In addition, identities which threaten to disrupt boundaries between hegemonic and subordinate identities can be erased in order to secure the appearance of stable, discrete and different identity categories, helping to maintain a clear power hierarchy – a case in point is bisexuality (see below).

Erasure can occur in a number of different ways. For example, it can refer to a denial of the existence of a particular identity group (e.g. expressing the belief that bisexuals are simply gay people who haven't come to terms with their sexuality yet), or it can involve the SUPPRESSION or BACKGROUNDING of an identity (e.g. the identity is rarely, if ever, talked or written about – as Baker (2008: 146–150) shows, in the 100 million word British National Corpus the term *bisexual* only occurs 81 times while *gay* (referring to SEXUAL IDENTITY) is over 19 times more frequent). Another way is to subsume the erased identity under another identity (e.g. *bisexual* is often tagged on to the word *gay* as in 'gay and bisexual men') rather than it occurring as a separate identity (or occurring alongside *heterosexual*). This strategy also helps to secure a us–them distinction.

ergativity

An ergative VERB can be either transitive (requiring a subject and an object) or intransitive (not requiring an object). Ergative verbs include those which involve changes of state, such as *break*, *melt*, *transform*, and movement, such as *move*, *turn*, *walk*. When an ergative verb is used in an intransitive way, agency is obscured, but also the party undergoing the process being described is sometimes constructed as responsible for causing the action which affects it. Stubbs (1996: 33) gives the following example: *factories have closed*. The use of the ergative with the reflexive voice particularly seems to blame the subject for an action which is carried out on him/her: 'Neurotic enough to have vanished of her own accord — or even to have *got herself murdered*' (BNC, H8T).

essentialism

The view that particular entities (e.g. certain types of human beings) possess specific characteristics that are fixed and internal. An essentialist argument would be that someone is the way they are because they are 'born that way' and are unlikely to change their essential nature. Many sexual and ethnic categorizations are essentialist. Essentialist thinking is often behind quantit-ative research (e.g. sets of questions aimed at revealing a person's 'inner' personality or the extent to which they are masculine or feminine). Biological or evolutionary explanations for 'difference' can also be referred to as essentialist. Since the 1980s, essentialism has been relatively unpopular in social science research, being challenged by SOCIAL CONSTRUCTIONISM and POST-STRUCTURALISM. It could be argued that essentialism results in STEREOTYPES, whereby negative qualities are assigned to everyone who is labelled as a certain IDENTITY category; differences are exaggerated and those who blur, straddle or cannot be categorized into existing identity boundaries are subject to ERASURE. However, some researchers have argued that it is some-times advantageous for particular ethnic or minority groups to present themselves as having a unified, stable identity (e.g. by downplaying intra-group differences) as this may help them to achieve certain political goals. Gayatri Chakravorty Spivak refers to this as *strategic essentialism* (Landry and MacLean 1996: 214), while Judith Butler (1991: 1) uses the term *strategic provisionality*.

ethics

A set of standards in a research community, regarding the conduct of its members, particularly in relation to human subjects. Ethics are often referred to as guidelines rather than rules, as their implementation can be dependent on the nature of the research being carried out and the needs of particular respondents. Ethics ensure that respondents are treated fairly and respectfully by researchers. A key ethical principle is informed consent – respondents must be in a position to give (usually written) consent to be interviewed or recorded for research purposes (and if they are not able to give consent themselves, then permission ought to be obtained from whoever is responsible for them, for example, a parent, guardian or teacher). Some researchers allow participants the opportunity to read transcripts of their speech and 'take back' anything that they do not feel comfortable with the researcher using. In CRITICAL DISCOURSE ANALYSIS, ethical issues may arise around gaining permissions to use and then quote from copyrighted texts, particularly if the analysis reveals manipulative or prejudiced uses of language.

A distinction in ethics is made between confidentiality and anonymity – in the former, the researcher guarantees that anything that the respondent says or does during the research will not be made public, while anonymity means that the respondent's identity (and the identities of anyone he/she refers to) will be altered or anonymized so that they cannot be traced back to the respondent (generally it is easier to offer anonymity than full confidentiality). Another aspect of ethics involves the researcher–respondent relationship, which is unequal and is potentially open to abuses of POWER. Ethical considerations here include the fact that respondents often give up their time (for no reward); they may be prompted to talk about or remember upsetting incidents, or they may incorrectly come to view the researcher as a friend, confidante or counsellor. In addition, ethical issues may arise if a respondent articulates an attitude (e.g. a racist viewpoint) which the researcher finds problematic or confesses to illegal activity. It could be argued that the researcher has a duty of care to protect the respondent, although at the same time the researcher should not compromise his or her own integrity. (See also Israel and Hay 2006.)

ethnocentricism

A term developed by Sumner (1906) which reflects the belief that either one's own ethnic group or culture is superior to others or is to be used as the benchmark with which to compare other groups. Ethnocentricism is often ingrained in cultures and transmitted via discourse as we grow up. Therefore, anthropologists have recommended that ethnographic fieldwork is carried out as a way of countering ethnocentricism. See also CULTURAL RELATIVISM, ORIENTALISM.

ethnography

A branch of anthropology which involves making detailed descriptions of cultures, subcultures or other social groups (see Fetterman 1998, Wolcott 1999, Brewer 2000). Ethnographers often use multiple methods of data collection, typically including RESEARCH INTERVIEWS and PARTICIPANT OBSERVATION but may also draw on diaries of subjects or other relevant texts (see TRIANGULATION). Ethnography tends to be a more qualitative than quantitative form of research, focusing on providing a detailed account of the complexity and specificity of a social world. Ethnographic fieldwork involves the researcher living among the people being researched, collaborating with them and conducting the research in their language.

ethnomethodology

A term coined by Harold Garfinkel in 1954 (Garfinkel 2002: 4), ethnomethodology is a sub-discipline of sociology which involves studying how people produce and share social orders, or rather how they make sense of their everyday lives. Ethnomethodology is a descriptive rather than interpretative form of analysis and was influential in the development of CONVERSATION ANALYSIS. Rawls (in Garfinkel 2002: 6) states that ethnomethodology does not have a formal set of research methods, while Heritage (1991: 1) notes that it also lacks a systematical theoretical statement. However, Rawls (in Garfinkel 2002: 5) writes that ethnomethodology assumes that 'the meaningful, patterned, and orderly character of everyday life is something that people must work constantly to achieve [and that] one must also assume that they have some methods for doing so'.

exclusion

An aspect of social actor representation where particular social actors do not appear in a text or as part of a discourse. van Leeuwen (1996: 38) notes that some exclusions are 'innocent' in that they are details that readers are assumed to know already. For example, in a sentence like 'The man was arrested', a social actor like 'the police' is omitted, but we would probably be expected to infer this from the context. There may be ideological reasons for omitting this actor, but it could be due to something innocuous like space restrictions in a newspaper.

However, some exclusions (consciously or not) serve ideological purposes, for example, by obscuring or downplaying responsibility for various events. So in a newspaper interview with a doctor involved in cases of parents being wrongly accused of child abuse, the doctor says 'Mistakes were made' (BNC, A30), which does not apportion blame to any individual or group. Two types of exclusion are SUPPRESSION and BACKGROUNDING. See also Riggins (1997).

explanation

Usually the final stage of critical discourse analysis, coming after the stages of DESCRIPTION and INTERPRETATION. Fairclough (1995: 163) writes, 'The object . . . of explanation is to portray a discourse as part of a social process . . . showing how it is determined by social structures and what reproductive effects discourses can cumulatively have on these structures, sustaining them or changing them'.

face

The way that people wish to project themselves to others, from the term 'saving face'. Goffman (1967: 5) defines it as

> the positive social value a person effectively claims for himself by the line others assume he has taken during a particular contact. Face is an image of self delineated in terms of approved social attributes – albeit an image that others may share, as when a person makes a good showing for his profession or religion by making a good showing for himself.

POSITIVE FACE involves our desire for appreciation and approval, whereas NEGATIVE FACE involves our desire to remain autonomous and not be imposed on. A face-threatening act (FTA) involves any situation or event which could alter (usually negatively) the maintenance of our face, while facework is any communicative strategy that is used to manage face during interactions. Facework can be preventive (e.g. helping to avoid face-threatening acts) or restorative (helping to restore face that has been lost). See also POLITENESS.

fallacy

A form of ARGUMENTATION which appears convincing but is logically flawed. Hamblin (1970: 12) says, 'A fallacious argument, as almost every account from Aristotle onwards tells you, is one that *seems to be valid but is not so*'. The identification of fallacies is often used in the DISCOURSE-HISTORICAL APPROACH. Reisigl and Wodak (2001: 71–74) describe a number of fallacies, including *argumentum ad baculum* (using threats as a form of persuasion), *argumentum ad hominem* (attacking someone's character to refute their position), *argumentum ad misericordiam* (unjustifiably appealing for compassion), *argumentum ad populum* or *pathetic fallacy* (appealing to populist feelings or the existing prejudices of a group, or pointing out that because many people believe something then it must be true), *argumentum ad ignorantiam* (arguing that because a standpoint has not being refuted, then it is true), *argumentum ad verecundian* (misplaced reference to authorities who are not qualified), *secundum quid* (making a generalization based on an unrepresentative sample), *post hoc, ergo propter hoc* (mixing a temporally chronological relationship with a causal one), *petition principia* also known as *circular argument* or *begging the question* (using a yet-to-be-proven assumption as the starting point of an argument), *rigged questions* (asking a question containing a PRESUPPOSITION, for example, 'when did you stop beating your wife?'), *ignoratio elenchi* (evading the argument by discussing a different and irrelevant point), *straw man fallacy* (inaccurately representing an opponent's argument in order to make it appear weak), *fallacies in dictione* (changing the interpretation of an ambiguous utterance to weaken an opponent's standpoint).

felicity conditions

In SPEECH ACT THEORY, these are the circumstances that are required for a PERFORMATIVE to be successful; they often involve the rights, obligations, beliefs or abilities of participants (see Austin 1962: 14–24). For example, with statements like 'I now pronounce you husband and wife', 'I name this ship the Mary Rose', 'You have passed your driving test', 'I declare war on country x' or 'I sentence you to 10 years imprisonment', the speaker needs to be qualified to make the statement (these are called preparatory conditions). In addition, the person or people who are the recipients of the performative need to be eligible – a person cannot be pronounced to have passed the driving test if he or she has not just taken a driving test. The speaker must also genuinely intend to make the performative statement (these refer to sincerity conditions) – hypothetically a judge could jokingly sentence someone to imprisonment, although not actually mean it.

feminist critical discourse analysis (FCDA)

A form of CRITICAL DISCOURSE ANALYSIS which is used to critique 'discourses which sustain a patriarchal social order: that is, relations of power that systematically privilege men as a social group and disadvantage, exclude and disempower women as a social group' (Lazar 2005: 5). FCDA is thus concerned with taking the analytical tools developed in critical discourse analysis in order to critique the ways that language use sustains unequal gender relations, for the purposes of emancipation and transformation.

feminist post-structuralist discourse analysis (FPDA)

A form of discourse analysis developed by Judith Baxter (2002, 2003) which is used as a supplement (rather than replacement) to other approaches to language and gender research. FPDA is concerned with the way that identities continually shift, particularly in spoken interactions (such as the workplace or classroom situations). Baxter (2003: 9) argues that 'individuals are rarely consistently positioned as powerful across all discourses at work within a given context – they are often located simultaneously as both powerful and powerless'. Like other forms of POST-STRUCTURALISM, FPDA does not subscribe to a 'grand narrative' (e.g. the belief that all men oppress all women) but instead wishes to show the complexity of POWER relationships, noting that powerless people may experience 'moments' of power. In doing so, FPDA aims to give voices to groups which are not normally heard, showing how a range of different discourses interact with each other. FPDA also advocates using REFLEXIVITY and TRIANGULATION, for example, by conducting different versions of analysis on the same text or getting multiple analysts, including the person or people who produced the text, to separately analyse it.

focus group

A qualitative research method which was initially used as a marketing technique to acquire feedback about new products in the 1940s (Merton and Kendall, 1946) but was adopted and adapted for media research in the 1980s and then social sciences research in the 1990s (see Marshall and Rossman 1999). Focus groups generally involve a small group of people (often with shared characteristics such as age or gender) and a moderator who facilitates a focused discussion around a particular subject. Sometimes the group is 'warmed up' by being given a presentation, problem or text which is used to trigger discussion. The interaction is recorded, transcribed and analysed afterwards. Lindlof and Taylor (2002: 82) argue that focus-group data produce insights that would not be found in one-to-one interactions. Focus groups are generally an inexpensive and quick way to gather data. Data from focus groups can help to highlight respondents' attitudes, priorities, language and frameworks of understanding and can make it possible to identify group norms and cultural values that are co-constructed between multiple participants (Kitzinger 1995: 299). However, their small size means that results are generally not representative of an entire population, although Litosseliti (2003: 22) notes that they are instead 'indicative'. Criticisms of focus groups include the potential for irrelevant data to be produced or for the group to be dominated by one or two strong personalities, resulting in 'groupthink'. In addition, Walvis (2003: 404–405) cautions that the researcher is also a participant and may influence the respondents without realizing.

footing

Used in Goffman (1981: 124–129) to describe switches in the mode and frame of a conversation. A participant's alignment towards the interaction changes noticeably; sometimes, this can be linked to POWER relationships. Goffman gives an example of president Nixon teasing a female journalist by making her do a pirouette to show her 'slacks' and then telling her that she should wear a dress so she doesn't look Chinese. In this instance, Nixon shifts the footing of the interaction from a serious business one to an informal and sexualized one, which disempowers the journalist. Footing can involve CODE SWITCHING or switches in pitch, volume, rhythm stress or tonal quality. It can occur quickly (appearing in linguistic units that are smaller than a sentence), and Goffman suggests that there is continuum between gross and subtle shifts in footing. Footing does not mean definitively changing the mode of interaction to another mode, but it allows for the original mode of interaction to be resumed.

In relation to CRITICAL DISCOURSE ANALYSIS, Resigl and Wodak (2001: 82) argue that '"footing" means the speakers' or writer's discursive establishment of the self as a social entity and the discursive transformation of the self'.

frames

A term used in artificial intelligence, linguistics, discourse analysis, media studies, sociology and psychology. While each field uses it somewhat differently, in discourse analysis it can be thought of as a means of conceptualizing the way that background knowledge is used to make sense of and produce discourse. Lakoff (2004: xv) says frames are 'mental structures that shape the way we see the world'. Minsky (1975) defines frames as forms of knowledge that are stored in memory as data structures and represent stereotyped situations. When a new situation is encountered, a person selects an appropriate frame from memory. Frames are structured as labelled slots which contain fillers. The term has also been used by the sociologist Goffman (1974: 21) who says that frames label 'schemata of interpretation', allowing people to make sense of events. Goffman distinguishes between natural frameworks (which are phenomena such as weather that are beyond human influence) and social frameworks (such as weather forecasts) which explain events and connect them to humans. Brown and Yule (1983: 238–241) note that frames can be used to represent physical objects, for example, a frame representing a house would consist of slots labelled 'kitchen', 'bathroom', 'address' etc. However, they show that frames can also represent activities, giving the example of a 'voting-frame' which would have slots for 'voting-place', the person you give your voting card to etc. Fairclough (1989: 159), in his description of the INTERPRETATION stage of CRITICAL DISCOURSE ANALYSIS, notes that 'frames represent the entities which can be evoked or referred to in the activities represented by schemata'. See SCHEMA, SCRIPTS.

functionalisation

According to van Leeuwen (1996: 54), this is a form of CATEGORIZATION which represents social actors in terms of what they do. This can be achieved in the following ways:

1. Using a noun formed from a verb via a suffix like -er, -ant, -ent, -ian or -ee. For example, *stripper*, *participant*, *recipient*.
2. Using a noun formed from another noun associated with an activity that the social actor engages in, again via suffixes like -ian, -ist, -eer. For example, *electrician*, *artist*, *engineer*.
3. Compounding nouns that denote places or tools linked to an activity the social actor engages in, with more general nouns like *man*, *women* or *person*. For example, *fireman*, *chairwoman*.

See also IDENTIFICATION.

gender

1. A euphemistic way of referring to BIOLOGICAL SEX, for example, 'Each visitor receives a 'passport' bearing the story of an actual victim or survivor who was the same age and gender as the visitor' (BNC, CKW).

2. A set of agreed-upon differences that are used to denote male and female behaviour in particular societies (see Money 1955, Stoller 1968). By the 1980s, most academics used gender to refer to socially constructed traits, whereas sex refers to the biological distinction between males and females. The two concepts are often mapped on to each other, making gender appear naturalized and fixed (see GENDER PERFORMATIVITY), although in fact understandings about what constitutes gender tend to be specific to particular periods in time or cultures. In its most simple form, gender is perceived as a binary masculine/feminine distinction, with equivalent pairings of oppositional traits (e.g. rational = masculine, emotional = feminine). However, it could be argued that there are more complex models. For instance, the view that gender is a linear scale with femininity at one end and masculinity at the other, or actually two linear scales (one with increasing levels of femininity and the other with increasing levels of masculinity), which allows for a person to hold both masculine and feminine traits (or neither) at the same time. In addition, some gender theorists have pluralized the terms (e.g. Connell [1995] writes of masculinities) in order to show that there are multiple ways of being masculine or feminine. See also HEGEMONIC MASCULINITY.

gender differences

The belief that men and women are fundamentally different in various measurable ways. Explanations for such differences can be social (e.g. boys and girls are treated differently by their parents, teachers etc.), biological (references to different types and amounts of chemicals in male and female bodies, differences in brain size, types of chromosomes, primary and secondary sexual characteristics, average weight, height and muscularity etc.), or evolutionary (the view that males evolved to be hunter-gatherers while females cooked and cared for children). Tannen (1990: 42) argues that males and females grow up in different cultures and use different 'genderlects', which is used as an explanation for 'cross-cultural miscommunications'. Linguistically, females are supposed to be more gossipy, involved and cautious about offending others than males who engage in more joke-telling, report talk, problem solving, giving orders and talking about themselves. Larger, meta-analytical studies have found little evidence of gender differences (e.g. Wilkins and Anderson 1991, Dindia and Allen 1992, Canary and Hause 1993), while corpus studies (Rayson, Leech and Hodges 1997, Schmid and Fauth 2003) have found that differences tend to be based on gradients rather than absolutes, and Harrington (2008) cautions that results may be skewed by small numbers of unrepresentative speakers. The gender differences theory has been criticized as a 'non-engaged and apolitical stance' which aims at 'the cementation of patriarchy' (Troemel-Plotz 1991: 489) and a self-fulfilling prophecy (Hyde 2005). Cameron (2007) describes gender differences theories relating to language as a 'myth'. See also WOMEN'S LANGUAGE.

gendered discourse

Gendered discourses are representations and expectations that males and females will act in particular gendered ways (Sunderland 2004: 20–22). Sunderland's approach is influenced by CRITICAL DISCOURSE ANALYSIS, FEMINIST POST-STRUCTURALIST DISCOURSE ANALYSIS and CONVERSATION ANALYSIS, although it differs from other approaches in that Sunderland describes how discourses (including gendered discourses) can be 'spotted' and named via the analysis of linguistic traces in texts. For example, in a newspaper article about the numbers of first-class degrees awarded to males and females, Sunderland identifies four gendered discourses: 'battle of the sexes', 'gender differences', 'poor boys' and 'gender equality now achieved'. The identification of such discourses involves a subjective form of interpretative analysis, based on making sense of the text and its context. Sunderland (2004: 47) notes that discourse identification and naming therefore may say something about the namer as well as the discourse (e.g. she says that a pornographic text could contain a discourse of liberation or a discourse of misogyny depending on the analyst's stance). See DISCOURSE NAMING.

gender performativity

A concept developed by Judith Butler who built on Austin (1962) and Searle's (1969) SPEECH ACT THEORY which stated that language was performative, bringing certain states of affair into being. Butler argues that language is used to construct gender and that gender itself is performative (ultimately a form of copying) rather than something fixed and essential: 'Gender is a kind of imitation for which there is no original; in fact, it is a kind of imitation that produces the very notion of the original as an effect and consequence of the imitation itself' (Butler 1991: 21). As well as being an imitation, gender performance is necessarily repetitious: 'Gender is the repeated stylization of the body, a set of repeated acts within a highly rigid regulatory frame that congeal over time to produce the appearance of substance of a natural sort of being' (Butler 1990: 33). Language is one way (out of many) that people perform gender. By accessing society's gendered discourses about acceptable ways of being male or female, most of us develop gendered linguistic performances, based on features including pitch, speed, lexical choice and topic (explaining to an extent why writers such as Lakoff (1975) claimed that women use hyper-correct language and refer to rare colour terms). Gender performativity theory does not imply that we are completely free to assume 'any' gender at any point (most of the time we are constrained by society's notions of what are acceptable gender performances for our sex – see GENDERED DISCOURSES), but it offers a postmodern explanation for why gender differences exist and appear to be constant and stable in a society (whereas in fact they are constantly in flux and differ between societies).

genericization

According to van Leeuwen (1996: 46–48), genericization is a way of repre-senting social actors as classes rather than as specific individuals (see SPECIFICATION). This can be achieved by the use of plural nouns and the zero article: 'It's not the first time this has happened: he's gone with prostitutes before' (BNC, CBN). It can also be realized via a singular noun combined with a definite article: 'Central to this coercive policing was a concerted effort to isolate the prostitute from working-class culture' (BNC, G0D). Finally, an

genre   53

indefinite article can be used with a singular noun: 'If you were talking to a
prostitute on the beat, you'd get booked for gossiping – for idling your time'
(BNC, B24). Sometimes the present tense can be used for making generic
reference: '. . . prostitutes frequently change their names and appearances'
(BNC, CE2).

van Leeuwen (ibid.: 48) comments on the potential ideological effects of
genericization by noting that groups who are treated in this way are 'symbol-
ically removed from the readers' world of immediate experience, treated as
distant "others" rather than as people "we" have to deal with in our everyday lives'.

genre

A genre refers to a categorization of a particular type of text or social practice.
Such categorizations are normally subjective and can often be broken down
into sub-genres. For example, the genre of fiction could be subdivided into
historical, adventure, mystery, romance, spy, western and so on. Bakhtin
(1986) refers to speech genres – socially specified ways of speaking or writing
that people use, manipulate and combine together (such as university lecture,
shopping list, gossip). Fairclough (1995: 14) defines a genre as 'a socially ratified way of using language in connection with a particular type of social
activity' and later (2003: 26) refers to them as 'different ways of (inter)acting
discoursally'.

Swales (1990) uses the term *pre-genre* to refer to categories which are found
across a range of different social practices – for example, narratives are pre-
genres as they can occur as 'stories' in everyday conversation, in television
reports, in client counselling and so on. In addition, Fairclough (2003: 68–69)
notes that genres can be lifted out of particular networks of social practices
from which they were originally developed. An interview, for example, can
now be found as part of a range of different social practices: job interview,
celebrity interview, political interview. He refers to such cases as *disembedded
genres*. A *situated genre*, however, is one which is specific to a certain network of practice.

hegemonic femininity

Bordo (1993: 316) describes hegemonic femininity as having 'a strong emphasis on appearance with the dominant notion of an ideal feminine body as thin and toned' and is identified as having strong associations with hetero-sexual sex, romance and whiteness. Choi (2000) and Krane (2001) write about sportswomen who are expected to perform hegemonic femininity (e.g. wearing pink) while distancing themselves from behaviour seen as masculine – a difficult feat as in order to be successful athletes they must develop characteristics that are stereotypically associated with masculinity, such as strength, independence and competitiveness. However, Connell (1987), who coined the term HEGEMONIC MASCULINITY, prefers the term EMPHASIZED FEMININITY. See also PRIVILEGED FEMININITY.

hegemonic masculinity

A framework of masculinity proposed by Connell (1995) which views GENDER relations as hierarchical yet complex. Hegemonic masculinity has four central typologies – first is the concept of hegemonic masculinity itself: the 'corres-pondence between cultural ideal and institutional power' (ibid.: 77). Hegemonic masculinity is the often-idealized version of perfect masculinity, embodied by film heroes like James Bond or Rambo, as well as being reflected by real-life powerful men such as presidents of countries or business leaders. While such men are viewed as exemplars of masculinity, they only represent a small minority of actual men (and many may be fictional). However, we are conditioned to view such men as desirable and/or identify with them and their goals. The second typology is SUBORDINATION, 'specific gender relations of dominance and subordination between groups of men' (ibid.: 78). This involves subordination of gay men by heterosexual men, working-class men by middle-class men, counter-cultural men by mainstream men, 'nerds' by 'jocks' and so on. The third typology is complicity: 'Masculinities constructed in ways that realize the patriarchal dividend, without the tensions or risks of being the frontline troops of patriarchy, are complicit in this sense' (ibid.: 79). Complicity involves accepting, or even helping to propagate the gender sys-tem, even though you may not greatly benefit from it. An extreme example would involve a closeted gay politician voting against equal rights for gay people although other cases could involve inaction, such as remaining silent if someone makes a homophobic or sexist remark. The final typology is marginalization – referring to those who are different from hegemonic or subordinated masculinities as they are outside the 'relations internal to the gender order' (ibid.: 80). So Connell notes that black sporting stars in America may be exemplars of hegemonic masculinity, being rich and physically fit, but their power does not trickle down to other black men in America, who are marginalized rather than authorized by hegemonic masculinity. Bisexual men may be another marginalized group, as they threaten the homosexual/heterosexual binary divide. See also HEGEMONIC FEMININITY, HEGEMONY.

hegemony

A term popularized by Gramsci (1971, 1985), who theorized that it involves the exercise of POWER, whereby everybody in a society acquiesces in one way or another to a dominant person or social group. It could be the case that dominated people are not fully aware of their status or have been convinced that it is the natural state of affairs, or they accept their position because they receive some form of benefit from it. Gramsci applied the concept of hegemony to early twentieth century politics in order to explain why a socialist revolution, predicted by Marxism, had not occurred. He suggested that it was because power was maintained, not just through physical and economic coercion but through IDEOLOGY: The values of the bourgeoisie (the powerful class) had become established in wider society as commonsense values, applicable to everybody. Therefore, a culture of consensus had developed, whereby even people who belonged to the lower classes helped to maintain the status quo because they also identified with bourgeois values. Hegemony is thus maintained through the manufacture of consent. The dominant acquire the consent of the dominated to the point where those who are dominated see the world from the point of view of the dominant. They *misrecognize* power and *recognize* it as legitimate. Van Dijk (1997: 19) argues that consensus can be discursively established via 'hegemonic power'.

heteronormativity

A term conceived by Warner (1993) as social practices which are based around the presumption of universal heterosexuality. Heteronormativity normally involves EXCLUSION, SUPPRESSION or BACKGROUNDING of gay or lesbian identities, behaviours or desires but may also involve more active practices such as stereotyping, tabooing, punishing or stigmatizing homosexuality (see HOMOPHOBIA). Rich (1980: 653) conceives of a related term *compulsory heterosexuality*, arguing that '[h]eterosexuality has been forcibly and subliminally imposed on women' so that men can wield power over them.

homophobia

An irrational fear or hatred of same-sex identities, desires and practices. This can be expressed in language via nominations like *faggot* but can also involve negative STEREOTYPES, stigmatization, criminalization, EXCLUSION or denial of ACCESS (e.g. laws which forbid same-sex marriage) or physical attacks. A range of argumentation strategies are often given in order to legitimate homophobia, including reference to religion.

Homophobia often goes hand in hand with SEXISM. For example, many pejorative homophobic terms aimed at gay men focus on GENDER deviance, for example, *sissy*. Gay men are viewed negatively because they (supposedly) act like women. There is therefore an IMPLICATURE that female identities are subordinate to male ones.

hypotaxis

A grammatical construction of functionally similar yet unequal constructs. It is often achieved via SUBORDINATION or premodification in a complex sentence. For example, consider the words *different* and *artistic* in the following: 'Giacometti was an artist with very different artistic aims (BNC, A04). Both function as adjectives; however, *artistic* only modifies *aims*, whereas *different* modifies *artistic aims*. The oppositional construct is PARATAXIS.

ideology

Ideology can generally be thought of as the set of ideas, beliefs and aims that a person or group holds. Fairclough (1992: 87), drawing on Althusser (1971), views ideologies as 'constructions of reality . . . which are built into various dimensions of the forms/meanings of discursive practices, and which contribute to the production, reproduction or transformation of relations of domination'. Language is one way that ideologies are constructed, maintained and challenged. Fairclough (1992: 88–89) notes that it is not possible to 'read off' ideologies from texts because 'meanings are produced through interpretations of texts'.

identification

A way of defining social actors according to what they are as opposed to what they do (**FUNCTIONALISATION**). van Leeuwen (1996: 54–55) notes that this can achieved via three ways:

1. Classification – using existing societal categories such as age (e.g. *youth*, *pensioner*), gender (*man*, *woman*, *sissy*), class (*duchess*, *peasant*), ethnicity (*Caucasian*, *African-American*, *black*, *white*), religion (*atheist*, *Jew*). Such categories change over time and across different societies.
2. Relational identification – referring to someone via their relation to someone else, for example, *mother*, *friend*, *co-worker*. In western societies, relational identification is no longer viewed as important as other forms of identification (some surnames initially acted as form of relational identification though, e.g. *Johnson*). Also Von Sturmer (1981) shows how Australian Aborigines place a high premium on relational identification.
3. Physical identification – referring to people via their physical characteristics, for example, hair colour (*redhead*, *blonde*), size (*giant*), attractiveness (*stunner*, *hunk*).

Some identification words can include more than one category, for example, *crone* refers both to someone's age but also contains elements of physical categorization. See also **CATEGORIZATION**.

identity

Gleason (1983: 918) points out that the term identity is relatively new, emerging into social science literature in the 1950s and made popular by the psychoanalyst Erik Erikson. For Gleason, most definitions tend to fall into one of two opposing conceptions. In one sense, identity can be called 'intrapsychic' in that it comes from within, is fixed and stable and is what people speak of when they talk about 'who we really are'. A second conception holds that identity can be 'acquired' in that it is a conscious or internalized adoption of socially imposed or socially constructed roles. Epstein (1998: 144) points out that Habermas's (1979: 74) discussion of ego identity (as a socialized sense of individuality) makes a useful mediation point between the two definitions.

Woodward (1997: 1–2) says identity 'gives us an idea of who we are and of how we relate to others and to the world in which we live. Identity marks the ways in which we are the same as others who share that position, and the ways in which we are different from those who do not. Often identity is most clearly marked by difference'. She points out that identities are frequently constructed in terms of oppositions: man/woman, black/white, straight/gay and so on. However, while many people may view identity in terms of binaries, it may also be the case that these binaries are not mutually exclusive, or they may exist as gradations or blends. Identity could therefore be said to be composed of a number of (possibly infinite) interacting, internal and external characteristics by which a person can be defined that change over time. At certain points, particular aspects of identity may become foregrounded. For example, Goffman (1963: 14) notes that stigmatized identities need to be constantly managed, while Epstein (1998: 145) argues that deviant identities are likely to subsume other aspects of identity – all behaviour of people with a stigmatized identity will therefore be seen by others as a product of the stigmatized identity. See also NATIONAL IDENTITY, PUBLIC IDENTITY, SEXUAL IDENTITY, SOCIAL IDENTITY.

imagined community

A concept outlined by Anderson (1983) referring to the social construction of a nation or community, based on the fact that very large numbers of people will never meet each other but still feel that they belong to the same community because they have similar interests or attitudes or a part of the same nation. Anderson notes that 'print-capitalism' (the fact that books were printed in national languages to maximize circulation) has made imagined communities possible. See also DISCOURSE COMMUNITY.

impersonalization

According to van Leeuwen (1996: 59–61), impersonalization is a way of representing social actors as something other than human (see PERSONALIZATION). This can involve *abstraction* – assigning a label based on a quality, for example, referring to refugees as 'problems'. It can also involve *objectivation*, where 'social actors are represented by means of reference to a place or thing closely associated with either their person or with the activity they are represented as being engaged in' (ibid.: 59). A number of subtypes of objectivation exist, for example,

1. Spatialization – referring to a group via a place, for example, 'Unlike Europe, *America* is against welfare payments available to everybody without a job, even those who have never worked' (BNC, ABK).
2. Utterance autonomization – referring to a social actor via their utterances, for example, 'Older workers face widespread and increasing discrimination in European Community countries, *a report* said today' (BNC, K2W).
3. Instrumentalization – referring to a social actor via an object that they used to carry out an activity, for example, 'Earlier eight people died when *bombs* rained on the city's crowded streets' (BNC, CH6).

implicature

Information which is implied in a statement but cannot be derived from applying logical inferencing techniques to it. An implicature is therefore what is suggested but not formally expressed. Instead, the reader or hearer must either understand that part of the statement has a conventionalized, special meaning or take context into account in order to decode the implicature (Grice refers to these as conversational implicatures). For example,

John: I've made a strawberry flan.
Fanny: I had strawberries for breakfast dear.

Here we might make the implicature that Fanny does not want to eat John's strawberry flan (as it is unusual to eat the same meal twice in one day, and Fanny seems to be using this as an excuse, rather than saying something like 'How lovely, can I have a big slice'). However, unlike ENTAILMENTS, the implicatures we make do not necessarily have to reflect truths (Fanny might have intended to mean that she loved strawberries). See also PRESUPPOSITION.

indexing

A way of signalling one social meaning over another (often through linguistic means). The term was popularized by Ochs (1992: 338) who writes, 'In every community, members have available to them linguistic resources for communicating such social meanings at the same time as they are providing other levels of information'. Such signals are interpreted by other members of a community. Although indexes are used to signify certain types of IDENTITY distinctions, they are often 'non-inclusive' – most indexes can be used by anyone and can also be used to mark a range of different types of social information. Sunderland (2004: 25) notes, for example, how TAG QUESTIONS can be used to index female identities but are also associated with hesitancy and confirmation checks.

individualization

A way of specifically referring to a social actor as an individual, for example, by using a person's name ('Mrs Smith') or by singling them out in some other way (e.g. through use of an indefinite article 'a 35-year-old woman'). In illustrating how individualization can be used in ideological ways, van Leeuwen (1996: 48) states that middle-class newspaper tends to individualize members of the elite, while working-class newspapers individualize 'ordinary' people. See also GENERICIZATION, ASSIMILATION.

informalization

A term used by Wouters (1977) which referred to increasing permissiveness and leniency in codes of conduct in (western) societies occurring in the 1920s and again in the 1960s/1970s. It was adopted by Fairclough (1995: 19) to refer (partly) to CONVERSATIONALIZATION of public discourse. Linguistically,

Goodman (1996: 42–43) refers to it as involving shortened terms of address, contractions of negatives and auxiliary verbs, the use of active rather than passive sentence constructions, colloquial language and slang. It can also involve the adoption of regional accents (as opposed to say Standard English) or increased amounts of SELF-DISCLOSURE of private feelings in public contexts (e.g. it can be found in talk shows or in the workplace). Goodman argues that informalization of English is the result of a range of interacting factors, including urbanization of society, improved transport links, relaxed social attitudes, new media, erosion of class distinctions, increased participation in society via democracy and the competitive demands of CAPITALISM. Informalization can therefore be potentially empowering and/or disempowering depending on the context of its use and can also place more complex demands on members of society, who need to judge when and the extent to which informalization is appropriate.

intensifying strategies

In the DISCOURSE-HISTORICAL APPROACH, this is a way of strengthening a discourse or argument. At the linguistic level, it can involve using intensity markers or gradable adverbs which emphasize or amplify a proposition (e.g. *very*, *really*, *absolutely*), modal and semi-modal verbs (*should*, *must*, *have to*) or other lexis which carry a strong evaluative load or evoke emotions. At the paralinguistic level, it can involve the use of particular types of stress, speed or volume in order to emphasize particular points, while at the nonverbal level, it can involve the adoption of certain facial expressions or gestures.

interactional sociolinguistics

A term popularized by John Gumperz, who used it as an approach which combined anthropology, linguistics, pragmatics and CONVERSATION ANALYSIS into an interpretive framework for analysing meaning. It was initially often used in cross-cultural comparisons, particularly to analyse intercultural miscommunications, although it has also been employed in cross-gender analysis by researchers like Deborah Tannen. Interactional sociolinguistics argues that sociocultural knowledge does not exist simply in values and judgements that are outside interactions but that such knowledge is contained within interactions themselves and are signified through contextualisation cues.

interdiscursivity

A term used by Foucault (1972) and also adopted in CRITICAL DISCOURSE ANALYSIS by Fairclough (1995: 134–135) to refer to the 'constitution of a text from diverse discourses and genres'. Fairclough's use of the term is inspired by and related to the concept of INTERTEXTUALITY and is sometimes referred to as 'constitutive intertextuality' (Fairclough 1992: 124). Interdiscursivity can involve the way that some genres or structures associated with genres seem to 'seep into' others – for example, Fairclough (1995: 135–166) describes how promotional discourses (associated with marketing or advertising) occur in university prospectuses and newspaper advertisements for university lectureships (an advert for a job also functions as an advert for a university's own achievements). See also COLONIZATION.

Interdiscursivity can also refer to identifying relationships between discourses. For example, a discourse which constructs women as emotional may be a smaller part of the higher order 'gender differences' discourse.

interpretation

A stage of CRITICAL DISCOURSE ANALYSIS, which generally comes between DESCRIPTION and EXPLANATION. To illustrate,

Curbs fail to halt flood of refugees. (BNC, A4H)

For the above example, the descriptive stage of the analysis would identify a water metaphor 'flood' being used to refer to refugees. The interpretative stage of analysis might then focus on asking 'what does this metaphor mean, what is it being used to achieve?' We could say, for example, that the water metaphor has the effect of representing refugees as an out of control, unwanted disaster as well as presenting them as a collective, indistinguishable, dehumanized mass. The interpretation of this metaphor is that the writer intends to represent refugees in a negative way. The explanation stage would then try to focus more on the wider social context, asking why refugees are being represented in this way and what consequences this may have for society and various groups in it.

So interpretation is generally generated through a combination of what is in a text and the analyst's interpretative procedures (also called members' resources). Fairclough (1989: 142) lists six types of interpretative procedures which each result in different yet related types of interpretation: (1) social orders; (2) interactional history; (3) phonology, grammar, vocabulary; (4) semantics, pragmatics; (5) cohesion, pragmatics and (6) schemata. For example, interactional history results in the analyst referring to intertextual context – how do text producers orient to existing discourses which are 'out there' in other texts, and what do they assume that the reader already knows? Interpretations can be problematic in that they depend on the perspective of the researcher. McKee (2003: 66), for example, asks whether there 'must be a correct interpretation of each text'. A reflexive analysis would try to identify the range of possible interpretations instead.

interpretative repertoire

A term used particularly in DISCURSIVE PSYCHOLOGY to refer to

> relatively coherent ways of talking about objects and events in the world. In discourse analytical terms, they are the 'building blocks of conversations', a range of linguistic resources that can be drawn upon and utilised in the course of everyday social interaction. Interpretative repertoires are part and parcel of any community's common sense, providing a basis for shared social understanding. (Edley 2001: 98)

Some writers, for example, Potter and Wetherell (1995), have noted that there are similarities between interpretative repertories and discourses. However, Edley (2001) argues that interpretative repertoires are used to emphasize human agency, noting that people can choose from a pool of available repertoires.

interpretative positivism

Interpretative positivism, identified by Simpson (1993: 105), is a potential problem when carrying out discourse analysis, involving making the assumption that a particular linguistic feature is always used with the same function or same intent. However, Fowler (1991: 90) notes 'there is no constant relationship between linguistic structure and its semiotic significance'. Hardt-Mautner (1995) gives the example of agentless passives. Passive constructions obscure agency; however, this may be intentional (the writer wishes to background who is to 'blame' for a particular act), or it may be due to a variety of other reasons. Perhaps the agency can easily be inferred from the context or the agent is mentioned earlier in the text. The agent may be obscured due to word limitations or simply to make writing style less repetitive.

intertextuality

A term coined by Julia Kristeva in 1966 (see Moi 1990) which refers to the ways that texts refer to or incorporate aspects of other texts within them. This can take many forms, for example, parodies, retellings, sampling, direct reference or quotation and allusions. It is often only possible to make sense of a text by fully understanding how it refers to other texts. For example, Martin Luther King's famous 'I Have a Dream' speech incorporates a great deal of intertextuality. He refers to Abraham Lincoln's Gettysburg Address by using the phrase 'Five score years ago' as well as adopting quotes from the Bible, Shakespeare and the United States Declaration of Independence. The concept has been adopted, particularly within CRITICAL DISCOURSE ANALYSIS (see Fairclough 1989: 55, 1995: 187–213), as an aspect of considering the wider (historical and social) context of a text under analysis. Fairclough (1992: 117) makes a distinction between 'manifest intertextuality', which involves using actual content from one text in another, and constitutive intertextuality', which involves using structures from existing texts (this latter type is sometimes referred to as INTERDISCURSIVITY). See also POSTMODERNISM.

Islamophobia

Prejudice or discrimination against Islam or Muslims. A 1997 report by the Runnymede Trust identified a number of perceptions which relate to Islamophobia: It is seen as monolithic, barbaric, sexist, violent, supportive of terrorism, a political IDEOLOGY, separate and 'other' and that anti-Muslim hostility is thus natural. Halliday (1999: 898) is critical of the term, arguing that the stereotypical enemy 'is not a faith or a culture but a people' and that the term itself produces an unhelpful distortion – 'that there is one Islam: that there is something out there against which the phobia can be directed' (ibid.). He also points out that the term 'inevitably runs the risk of denying the right, or possibility of criticisms of the practices of those with whom one is having the dialogue' (ibid.: 897). See Richardson (2004) for a CRITICAL DISCOURSE ANALYSIS of the (mis)representation of Islam/Muslims in British newspapers.

keyness

In CORPUS LINGUISTICS, keyness is the relative frequency of a particular linguistic item in one text or corpus when compared against another text or corpus via statistical tests of significance (usually chi squared or log likelihood). Many tests of keyness are carried out on single words, deriving a list of KEYWORDS. However, keyness can also be used on LEXICAL BUNDLES or clusters (short fixed sequences of words) or semantic or grammatical groups of words (as long as the texts being used have been annotated according to their semantic/ grammatical categories accordingly). For example, Baker (2006) wanted to identify aspects of argumentation in a series of UK parliamentary debates on the subject of banning fox hunting. He compared the speech of politicians who wanted to keep hunting with those who wanted to ban it, by assigning semantic tags or codes to each word that was spoken. Corpus analysis software was then used to identify which semantic codes were statistically more frequent (or 'key') in the 'ban hunting' speeches when compared to the 'keep hunting' speeches. Politicians who wanted to ban hunting used more words in the semantic category for 'toughness' (*strong*, *toughen*, *weakness*) to argue that their position was tough and their opponent's was weak, whereas those who wanted to keep hunting used more words in the semantic category 'sensible' (*reasonable*, *absurd*, *rational*), arguing that their position was the 'commonsense' one while their opponents were illogical.

keyword

1. A cultural keyword is a word which reveals something important about a particular culture or society. The concept was initially proposed by Benveniste (1954: 336) but has been developed by Williams (1976) who created a dictionary of keywords for English. Wierzbicka (1999) claims that cultures can be understood through the use of particular keywords, for example, German has *Heimat* (homeland) and Russian has *dusha* (soul). Such keywords are usually nouns or adjectives (often abstract concepts like *heritage*, *care* or *community*). Cultural keywords are generally identified via subjective means – for example, the researcher makes a decision to categorize a word as a cultural keyword. Such subjective keywords can sometimes be used in CONTENT ANALYSIS.

2. A keyword in CORPUS LINGUISTICS is any word whose relative frequency in one text or corpus is statistically significant (using chi-square or log-likelihood tests) when compared against another text or corpus (often a reference corpus). The concept was created by Mike Scott and was first implemented in the corpus analysis software Wordsmith Tools. Because keywords are based upon statistical tests, any word can be potentially key if it is frequent enough (although it is up to the researcher to specify the cut off point for statistical significance). Some keywords (such as proper nouns) reveal information about the content of a corpus or text; others (such as closed class items) can tell us about particular stylistic choices, while others can be indicative of cultural keywords (see above). Keywords can also help to act as signposts for discourse, IDEOLOGY or argumentation. For example, Baker (2006) found that members of parliament who wanted to ban fox hunting used the keyword *barbaric* (to argue that hunting was cruel) in debates, whereas those who wanted to keep hunting used the keyword *illiberal* (to argue that people should have freedom to hunt if they wanted to). Grammatical words, if key, can also tell us something about discourse or argumentation strategies. For example, McEnery (2006) showed how the word *and* was key in texts which wanted to ban swearing in the media because the word was used so often to create associations between swearing and other negative phenomena (such as drunkenness and sin). See also KEYNESS.

langue

Saussure (1966) makes a distinction between la langue and parole. Langue
is a language system as a series of signs. It covers the systems of grammar,
spelling, syntax and punctuation. While langue refers to the system of
language, PAROLE refers to the *use* of the system; it is the external manifesta-
tion of langue, characterized by individual, personal usages of language.
Structuralist linguists were interested in investigating langue.

legitimation

Legitimation is a process whereby something becomes legitimate according
to the values of a particular society. Habermas (1985) notes that legitimation
is negotiated in societies – for example, citizens give the state legitimacy
in return for certain benefits (e.g. welfare). Fairclough (2003: 219) defines
legitimation as 'widespread acknowledgement of the legitimacy of explanations and justifications for how things are and how things are done', while
van Leeuwen (2007) identifies four legitimation strategies: *authorization*,
moral evaluation, *rationalization* and *mythopoesis*. Beetham (1991: 39)
implies that legitimation does not occur at the end of a power struggle; it is
not the 'icing on the cake of power' but instead is 'more like the yeast that
permeates the dough and makes the bread what it is'.

lexical bundle

A fixed set of words (usually between three to five words in length) which are
reasonably frequent in natural language use. They are sometimes referred to
as *clusters*, *chunks*, *multi-word sequences*, *lexical phrases*, *formulas*, *routines*,
fixed expressions and *prefabricated patterns*. Unlike idioms like *kick the
bucket*, lexical bundles tend to be difficult to identify (and are thus overlooked
in language grammars and teaching materials) because they often bridge two
structural units, for example, *the lack of the*. CORPUS LINGUISTICS approaches
have been able to identify such bundles and facilitate their categorization into
particular functions. Referential expressions are used to identify something as
being important or to be specific about something, for example, *something
like that*, *a little bit about*, *in the United States*. Stance indicators express
modality or attitude towards a proposition: *I don't know if*, *it is important to*,

I want you to. Discourse organizers introduce, clarify or elaborate on a topic: *I want to talk about, you know what I mean, has to do with the.* See Biber et al. (1999, 2004).

lexical cohesion

A way of achieving COHESION by way of repeating the same word or phrase or using chains of related words that contribute towards the continuity of lexical meaning: 'Each day she had gone with Tom and Peter or just with Tom down into the Underground and played her violin' (BNC, EDN). In the above example, *Tom* is repeated a second time, in order to make it clear who is being referred to. A pronoun like *him* would have been ambiguous. In other cases of lexical cohesion, a related word can occur in place of the original reference: 'Father Death climbs the tree to gather a rosy apple but directly he touches the fruit he is caught' (BNC, HH3). Here, *apple* is later referred to by the superordinate category *fruit*. Another type of lexical cohesion involves repetition of another member of a semantic category: 'To the right, a brick-red dune stood alone among golden yellow ones' (BNC, AT3). Here, *brick-red* and *golden yellow* both belong to the category of colours.

Mediated Discourse Analysis (MDA)

A form of discourse analysis which considers texts in their social and cultural contexts. MDA focuses on the actions that individuals take with texts and the consequences of these actions (see Scollon 1998, 2001, Norris and Jones 2005). While MDA is interested in discourse, unlike CRITICAL DISCOURSE ANALYSIS, it does not take discourse, text or language as its central focus; instead, it is interested in the analysis of social action. In order to achieve this, it considers six central concepts: mediated action, site of engagement, mediational means, practice and mediational means, NEXUS OF PRACTICE and COMMUNITY OF PRACTICE. Analysis is achieved through TRIANGULATION of different types of data (e.g. using participant observation, focus groups, surveys, analysis of media content), participants' definition of significance and issue-based analysis. MDA tends to be well suited to the analysis of the intersection of everyday social practices with broad issue-based public discourses in societies. For example, Scollon (2001) gives an example: When purchasing a cup of coffee, he is surprised when the waiter asks his name and then later calls his name when the coffee is ready to collect. This reflects an 'erosion of the distinction between institutional and non-institutional actions' (ibid.: 180).

members' resources

See INTERPRETATION.

metaphor

A way of representing something in terms of something else. The identification and analysis of metaphors are often used in the DESCRIPTION stage of CRITICAL DISCOURSE ANALYSIS as a way of revealing ideologies or discourses surrounding a subject.

> The Arts Council and Sports Council have enthusiastically welcomed the move, but all Roy Hattersley can do is trot out allegations of electioneering and say he'll 'consider' keeping it. (BNC, K52)

In the above example, Roy Hattersley is represented as 'trotting out' allegations. This is a metaphorical usage, suggesting that the way Hattersley makes allegations is well rehearsed (as if he is riding a horse at a showjumping contest) and thus contrived. The metaphor 'trot out' is therefore used to dispute Hattersley's claims. See also SIMILE.

mitigating strategies

Reisigl and Wodak (2001: 45) identify mitigating strategies in discursive presentation as ways of modifying the epistemic status of a proposition by mitigating the illocutionary force of an utterance. Some examples involve use of impersonal constructs, 'it seems quite clear that . . .'; forms indicating degrees of reservation, 'I'm not an expert but . . .'; using a question instead of an assertion, 'Shouldn't we go further?'; framing assertions with plural pronouns, 'We proposed this yesterday . . .' and use of vague expressions, 'There may be some points you didn't mention before' (ibid.: 84). See also INTENSIFYING STRATEGIES.

modality

Ways of expressing possibility (epistemic modality) or necessity (deontic modality), as the two examples below, respectively, show:

'You must be out of your mind,' Nick said. (BNC, EFJ)

You must promise me that this will be our little secret. (BNC, JXS)

Modality can be expressed via a set of verbs known as modal verbs, including *should*, *would*, *will*, *could*, *can*, *may*, *must* and *shall*. In addition, 'semi-modals' such as *have to*, *need to* and *want to* are increasingly used to express modality (Leech 2002). Modal adverbs include *perhaps*, *probably*, *necessarily* and *inevitably*.

Aspects of modality are sometimes focused on in CRITICAL DISCOURSE ANALYSIS, particularly because modal verbs often highlight POWER inequalities or IDEOLOGY – deontic modality can be used to express authority, whereas epistemic modality can construct different representations of the world.

moral panic

A term popularized by Cohen in 1972. Moral panics arise when a particular group, usually led by what Cohen calls 'moral entrepreneurs', attempts to exert collective moral control over another group or person. They begin with the identification of a 'problem' which is perceived as a threat to a community or section of a community's values or interests (sometimes reflecting political or religious beliefs), for example, pornography on television. Cohen labels those who are the subject of a moral panic as 'folk devils'. There follows a build up of public concern, often with the media helping to propagate the panic. As a result, a number of solutions are proposed, until the panic recedes or results in social change (see also Thompson, 1998: 98). Goode and Ben-Yehuda (1994) say that a moral panic consists of the following features: concern, hostility, consensus, disproportionality and volatility.

narrative

Narrative has been defined as stories about human cognition, actions (and their consequences), events, and descriptions of circumstances in which those events occur. They are normally structured with a beginning, middle and end. Altman (2008: 26) defines a 'narrative text as a series of individual following-units, joined by modulations and arranged in a particular manner'. 'Each narrative text', according to him, 'thus displays a specific "following-pattern" ' (ibid.). Examples of narratives include myths and legends which are found in all human societies and are sometimes used to explain phenomena in nature. Lyotard (1979) in his critique of ideological and institutional forms of knowledge argued that narratives are not used merely to explain but also to construct dominant forms of knowledge and beliefs. For example, religions such as Christianity, Islam, and Buddhism have institutionalized narrative knowledge and use it as the basis for their moral codes. Lyotard theorized that a form of narrative known as a grand narrative provides a connection between sets of events and social systems such as CAPITALISM and class STRUGGLE. However, POSTMODERNISM does not see grand narratives as holding universal truths, but instead it views them as oppressive, contestable, fragmented and fluid.

national identity

National identity is a concept that is built around the idea of the nation state. According to Barker and Galasinski (2001: 123), a nation state refers to the political and administrative apparatus that has a claim of 'sovereignty over a space or territory'. Wodak et al. (2009: 3) point out that the concept of IDENTITY in general and national identity in particular is 'context dependent and dynamic'. Thus there are different constructs of national identity, and these depend on the society or nation concerned. Every nation state discursively constructs its own identity, although such identities are 'malleable, fragile, and frequently ambivalent and diffuse' (Wodak et al. 2009: 4). For example, one way of constructing national identity could be geographical, being delineated by boundaries separating different countries. Alternatively, it could be ethnic; for example, a certain ethnic group may be discursively constructed as the legitimate 'nation' of a particular geographical 'country'. Wodak et al. (2009) identify a number of assumptions which inform their conceptualization of national identities. First, nations are 'IMAGINED COMMUNITIES which nationalized political subjects perceive as discrete entities' (ibid.: 3, see also Barker and Galasinski 2001). Secondly, national identities are special forms of social identities which are produced, reproduced and transformed through discourse. Thirdly, national identity involves a complex of 'similar . . . perceptual schemata . . . emotional dispositions and attitudes, and of similar behavioural conventions which bearers of this "national identity" share collectively and which they have internalized through socialisation' (Wodak et al. 2009: 4). According to Barker and Galasinski (2001: 124), 'The symbolic and discursive dimension of national identity narrates and creates the idea of origin, continuity and tradition'. Members of a certain 'national identity' also share certain attitudes and emotional dispositions towards those they consider to be outsiders. Therefore, national identity is constructed as unified, being created through symbols, images and rituals that represent the shared meanings of nationhood (ibid.).

nationalist discourse

Nationalist discourse enables the construction of NATIONAL IDENTITY. It is the discursive means whereby national identity is produced, reproduced, cemented and transformed. Nationalist discourse is therefore a means of representing shared experience through NARRATIVES, symbols and rituals which are regarded as the core of a national identity. Discourse analysts have examined how nationalist discourses can sometimes be based around STEREOTYPES which distinguish between 'us' and 'them', and such discourses can be employed in order to justify discrimination or exclusion of out-groups.

naturalization

A term used to describe how certain practices and/or discourses have become dominant, even universal, usually because such practices or discourses originate from dominant classes or groups. For example, the discourse and practices surrounding women being nurturers is viewed as commonsensical in many societies, having been naturalized. Fairclough (1989: 75) notes that naturalized practices or discourses can be used to sustain unequal POWER relations: 'Naturalization is the royal road to common sense . . . in the naturalization of discourse types and the creation of common sense, discourse types actually appear to lose their ideological character. A naturalized type tends to be perceived not as that of a particular grouping . . . but as . . . neutral in struggles for power, which is tantamount to it being placed outside ideology' (ibid.: 92).

negative face

A concept used in POLITENESS theory to refer to a person's desire to act out of their own volition and not to be imposed upon by others (Brown and Levinson 1987). In other words, negative face is our desire for freedom to do what we want, how we want to and when we want to. Linguistic examples of people taking negative face into consideration would be 'Please, you go first' or 'Welcome to my humble abode'. See also POSITIVE FACE.

neoliberalism

A term used to describe a dominant economic system which emerged after the Second World War and is particularly associated with the United States. In this case, liberalism refers more to economic rather than human rights and freedoms. Neoliberals thus advocate economic measures that they believe will ensure that the world remains economically stable or prosperous. They advocate transferring some control of the economy from public to private sectors along with moderate tax and interest rates, privatization of state-owned enterprises, deregulation and property rights. The term neoliberalism is often used critically, and the system has been viewed by opponents as a systematic dismantling of democratic institutions and the rise of a form of governance where the state no longer protects the interest of the people but is instead controlled by the interests of large multinational corporations. Neoliberalism policies have also been viewed as responsible for widening economic inequalities between individuals. Critical discourse analysts such as Fairclough (2000b) have focused on the political discourse of neoliberalism. For a description of the term's history, see Harvey (2005). See also CAPITALISM.

nexus of practice

A nexus of practice refers to a group of people who come together to engage in a number of related social actions. According to Scollon (2001), the concept signifies a genre of activity (like having a beer or coffee) and the SOCIAL ACTORS involved in that particular activity. See also COMMUNITY OF PRACTICE.

nominalization

Nominalization refers to the conversion of processes into nominals (or verbs into nouns), for example,

1. Move (verb) → movement (noun)
2. Difficult (adjective) → difficulty (noun)

This has the effect of backgrounding the process itself and can sometimes omit the participants who are the agents in the processes:

Surely Tony Blair getting tough on *immigration* now is too little, too late. (BE06, B05)

In the above example, *immigration* is a nominalized form of the verb *immigrate*. The nominalized form does not necessarily have to specify who is carrying out the process (the example does not reveal who is immigrating). Fairclough (1992: 179) notes that medical and scientific texts favour nominalization, possibly to appear 'objective'. In other cases, nominalization may be used in order to obscure blame or serve to dehumanize certain groups.

non-discursive

The term non-discursive refers to social processes that are said to not involve the use of discourse. Eagleton (1991: 219) makes a distinction between practices and discourses, noting that there is a difference between giving a sermon and taking a pebble from your left ear. The latter is more likely to be a non-discursive practice. Discursive practices are shaped by the non-discursive dimensions of social practice and vice versa and are therefore said to be in a dialectical relationship (Fairclough 1992). However, other discourse theorists see all social practices as discursive (Laclau and Moufe 1985), which means that discursive practices are fully constitutive of the social world.

non-sexist language

Sexist language can be defined as language which discriminates on the basis of GENDER or BIOLOGICAL SEX (see SEXISM). For example, generic uses of the pronoun *he* and other male generic terms like *early man* and *fireman* could be said to background female members of the English speaking community. It could also be argued that there is inequality in the TERM OF ADDRESS system. Adult males are called *Mr* whereas adult females use *Miss* or *Mrs*, forcing them to reveal their marital status.

Non-sexist language involves a deliberate attempt to avoid using gender discriminatory words. For example, terms such as *Ms*, *chair* or *director of ceremonies* have been suggested as replacements for their more sexist counterparts such as *Miss/Mrs*, *chairman* and *master of ceremonies*. Some people have opposed non-sexist language as a form of POLITICAL CORRECTNESS.

Baker (2010) found increases in the frequency of non-sexist language usage across four general corpora of written British English from 1931 through 1961, 1991 and 2006, noting that the most successful strategies seemed to involve getting people to stop using a particular word, rather than persuading them to change over to a new invented one, especially if it was difficult to use in spoken contexts (such as *him/her*). Terms based on existing words like *chair* proved to be more popular than more inventive strategies like the *-person* suffix and *Ms*. Instead, he found that use of *Mr* had strongly declined over time, suggesting a different sort of resolution to the unequal term of address system.

nonverbal communication

The use of non-oral language to communicate. Examples include 'body language' (hand gestures, posture, touch) and sign language. Nonverbal communication also can be achieved through facial expressions, eye contact (or lack of it) or via styling choices such as clothing or hairstyles. Aspects of speech such as tone, speed, volume, stress, rhythm and so on can be viewed as nonverbal, while in writing, nonverbal elements could include phenomena such as the colour of the ink or the handwriting style used. SILENCE could also be viewed as a form of nonverbal communication.

norm

In general, a norm refers to the average or typical performance of a group of people. This could involve results from a test or refer to phenomena like the average weight of a population. However, in social research norms refer to conventionalized ways of acting or behaving (see NATURALIZATION). Social norms are usually unwritten expectations about the appropriate ways that people should behave. They are handed down from generation to generation through socialization, often via NONVERBAL COMMUNICATION or through discourses.

normalization of discourse

Normalization of discourse refers to ways that certain discourses, practices and identities are constructed as normal (see also NATURALIZATION). This can sometimes result in existing discourses being challenged. For example, Tasker (2004, 2005) conducted a study of lesbian and gay parenting texts and found that there are often similarities drawn between heterosexual and gay parenting. They argue that such similarities indicate a tendency to construct gay parenting along the lines of heterosexual parenting in order to 'normalize' gay parenting. The discourse used to construct gay parenting this way can therefore be said to be a normalization of gay parenting discourse.

noun

A noun is any word that can be used to name something. Nouns can be concrete (*dog*) or abstract (*idea*), singular (*goose*), plural (*geese*), uncountable (*sheep*) or proper (*Tom*). Nouns can also modify other nouns (*coffee morning*). Nouns are an open grammatical class, meaning that they have many members and that new nouns can be created. Nouns function as heads of noun phrases which in turn perform the functions of SUBJECT, OBJECT and complement in a sentence. Nouns can be created from verbs, adjectives or adverbs, sometimes via a process called NOMINALIZATION (e.g. *accept* → *acceptance*).

object

In grammatical terms, 'object' refers to the entity that is represented as being acted upon. It contrasts with other grammatical categories such as subject, verb and adverbial. For example, in the clause 'Kelly hit the ball', there are three grammatical categories, namely, SUBJECT, VERB and OBJECT. *Kelly* is the subject, *hit* is the verb and *the ball* is the object.

objectification

1. The means of constructing an abstract concept as if it is something concrete or real (similar to reification).
2. The construction of human subjects as inanimate objects. This often occurs linguistically, for example, involving avoidance of attribution of agency to a human (or group or people), suggestions that the human is owned by someone else or that it is acceptable to hurt the human or not show concern for their feelings (see Nussbaum 1995). The following is an example of objectification from a magazine article: 'Two years later, at 18, she found herself pregnant by Smith' (BNC, CD5). Here the woman (the singer Neneh Cherry) is depicted as having no agency in her pregnancy.

objectivity

Objectivity in science refers to an impartial, rational analysis of a natural phenomenon that is not influenced by the characteristics of the analyst studying the phenomenon. In that sense, objectivity means that the object of study has been measured and evaluated in such a way that the same results can be reproduced by another analyst.

The objective approach has been criticized from a post-structuralist perspective as being difficult to apply to the social sciences, as it assumes that an analyst can impartially select phenomena to study and that the methods and process of analysis are not affected by the analyst's personal prejudices and IDENTITY. For example, Harré and Secord (1972), Brown (1973) and Armistead (1974) have argued that the social psychology research of the 1960s and 1970s implicitly voiced the values of dominant groups. Secondly, the objective stance presupposes that a text can be separated from the social and historical conditions in which it is produced and consumed, while thirdly it could be argued that objectivity (or the desire for it) is a 'stance' in itself, albeit unacknowledged. Critical and post-structuralist analysts have therefore viewed objectivity as problematic, instead suggesting that researcher REFLEXIVITY and transparency of their own (changing) positions should become part of the research process. Objectivity is associated with POSITIVISM. See also SUBJECTIVITY.

observer's bias

The observer's bias refers to the ways that a research outcome can be influenced by the researcher (see OBJECTIVITY). For example, if the researcher sets out to investigate whether men dominate women in mixed-sex interactions, and hypothesizes that they do, he or she may conduct the research in such a way that the outcome of the study supports rather than rejects the hypothesis.

observer's paradox

This term, coined by William Labov (1973), refers to the difficulties experienced by researchers when they try to obtain naturally occurring linguistic data. This is because the researcher needs to systematically observe and record language as it is used in a natural context. However, the presence of the observer or recording equipment may cause those who are being observed to alter their behaviour. The following is a (simplified) example of transcribed spoken data, taken from the British National Corpus (file KP0).

> Speaker A: It's fucking brilliant . . . Shit they didn't record that did they?
> Speaker B: It doesn't matter.
> Speaker A: Well I said a rude word . . .
> Speaker B: Well no it doesn't matter. Anonymity guaranteed. . . . They won't use the bit where we say fuck fuck fuck.
> Speaker A: Fuck.

Researcher presence can thus result in language use that is not representative of the 'everyday language' of the researched community, and yet it is only through such systematic observation that the researcher can obtain the required data, hence the paradox.

A potential solution could be to secretly record the subjects, although this would be viewed as a breach of researcher ETHICS and not recommended. A more ethically sensitive solution to overcome the observer's paradox would be to use family members and friends to record speech (in the absence of the researcher) in the hope that those being researched will feel more at ease and therefore produce 'natural' speech. The researcher could also try to carry out analysis on a group that he/she already 'belongs' to, as there would already be pre-established ways of interacting. Another solution could be to ask informants to recount tales of personal experience, which would be likely to produce an emotional response, resulting in more naturalistic speech. The researcher may also decide to disregard the first ten minutes or so of the recording, in order to allow the subjects to acclimatize to being recorded. Finally, the researcher could acknowledge the paradox when carrying out the analysis. Depending on our research focus, the above example does not give completely useless data – it could still be of interest to see how the participants oriented to being recorded, how they conduct TURN-TAKING and which words they used under these circumstances (why did they say *fuck* and not some other word?).

oppositional discourses

Discourses always exist in networks and are related in mutually supportive or contradictory ways (see INTERDISCURSIVITY). Oppositional discourses draw upon each other in order to contradict each other. For example, in the context of some African countries, a 'women as victims of poverty' discourse seems to exist in an oppositional relationship with a 'women as agents of development' discourse, suggesting that women are constructed simultaneously as being vulnerable and prone to poverty and disease as well as being the backbone of rural economies. Oppositional discourses can be indicators of a dominant discourse being challenged by marginal or emerging discourses (see also ORDER OF DISCOURSE).

oppositional practices

These are sets of SOCIAL PRACTICES that have conflicting consequences. For example, democracy as a social practice is the opposite of dictatorship. Democracy as a social practice implies equality, respect for human rights, consultation and freedom of expression. On the other hand, dictatorship implies inequality, violation of human rights and lack of freedom. Additionally, an oppositional practice can refer to any practice which is in opposition to a socially sanctioned practice – for example, rebelling against authority or cross-dressing.

oppression

Oppression refers to the way that POWER is exercised over a person or group of people in an unjust and/or cruel manner. Oppression can affect victims at a physical or emotional level and can be based on aspects of IDENTITY, such as ethnicity, religion, gender or sexuality. It can involve ERASURE, exclusion, negative STEREOTYPING or denying ACCESS. A goal of CRITICAL DISCOURSE ANALYSIS is to identify ways that language and discourse is used in order to maintain or resist oppressive practices. Other approaches, such as FPDA (FEMINIST POST-STRUCTURALIST DISCOURSE ANALYSIS), are concerned with directly giving voices to oppressed groups. See also HEGEMONY.

oral discourse

In traditional (older) forms of discourse analysis, the term TEXT was used inter-changeably with DISCOURSE so that written texts were referred to as written discourse as opposed to spoken texts which were referred to as oral discourse (Levinson 1983). Today there is a distinction made between text and discourse where texts are seen as the material realizations of discourses. In other words, discourses are articulated through texts.

order of discourse

A term coined by Foucault (1971, 1984). Fairclough (1992: 43, 1993: 138) defines order of discourse as the 'totality of discursive practices in an institu-tion and the relationships between them'. He later describes an order of discourse as 'a particular combination of genres, discourses and styles which constitutes the discoursal aspect of a network of social practices . . . In general terms [they are] . . . the social structuring of linguistic variation or difference – there are always many different possibilities in language, but choice amongst them is socially structured' (Fairclough 2003: 220).

Orientalism/orientalist discourse

1. Earlier Orientalism gained recognition in the nineteenth century when scholars from the West (mainly France and England) wrote about and attempted to interpret aspects of Asian and Arab cultures against a backdrop of colonialism. Nineteenth century western constructions of 'The Orient' often depicted an exotic, irrational, passive and backward alien culture in opposition to a normalized, rational, active and civilized westerner. At other times, oriental men were constructed as hyper-sexual and thus threatening to white women.

2. Contemporary Orientalism is a critical **POST-COLONIAL THEORY** that tries to deconstruct stereotypical depictions of Asian and Arab cultures and of the former colonized subjects in general. Perhaps the most well-known Oriental critique is that which is provided by Edward Said (1979) whose rejection of the earlier Orientalism is also a rejection of the biological generalization, cultural and religious prejudices that earlier Orientalism entailed.

orthography

Orthography refers to a system of writing which includes conventions of punctuation, capitalization, hyphenation and word breaks as well as the symbols (graphemes) and diacritics used in a particular language. Phonemic orthography is a writing system in which each sound (phoneme) has a distinct letter used to represent it and which it does not share with another sound (such as the International Phonetic Alphabet). Morphophonemic orthography considers both sound and word structure. For example, in English, the voiced /z/ sound at the end of *birds* and *shoes* is spelt with the same orthographic character as the voiceless /s/ counterpart in *rats* and *lips*.

Defective orthography refers to a system where there is no correspondence between the sound (phoneme) and the character used to represent the sound. In English the vowel sound /iː/ is represented by different characters in the words am**oe**ba, succ**ee**d, repl**e**te, b**ea**t, bel**ie**ve, rec**ei**ve and mach**i**ne. Finally, a complex orthography, such as writing systems used to represent Chinese, combines a number of symbols and punctuation rules.

In CONVERSATION ANALYSIS, orthographic TRANSCRIPTION generally refers to conventions that are used in order to represent spoken recordings (such as conversations) in written form. Such conventions often reassign punctuation marks or formatting styles to indicate different aspects of speech. For example, [square brackets] to mark sections of overlapping conversation, a number in round brackets (1.0) to indicate the length of a pause, CAPITAL LETTERS to show raised volume or colons to show a draw:::n-out sound.

overarching discourse

A discourse which subsumes several other discourses under it. For example, 'woman as domestic' discourse can be regarded as an overarching discourse under which are more specific discourses such as 'woman as cook', 'woman as nurturer', 'woman as cleaner' (see DISCOURSE NAMING). The 'woman as domestic' discourse itself can also be subsumed under higher order discourses such as 'gender differences' or 'patriarchal society'. See Sunderland (2004: 69).

over-determination

According to van Leeuwen (1996: 61), over-determination is a process of social actor representation whereby a person or group is described as 'participating, at the same time, in more than one social practice'. A subtype of over-determination is *inversion*, whereby social actors engage in two practices which are oppositional in some way (van Leeuwen (ibid.) points to the cartoon characters in the television series The Flintstones, who live in prehistoric times but also engage in many activities that are common to the twentieth century). Another form of over-determination is *symbolization*, whereby a fictional social actor or group stands in for a nonfictional social actor. A third subtype is *connotation*, whereby a 'unique . . . nomination or physical identification . . . stands for a classification or functionalisation' (ibid.: 63). For example, a term like *trailer trash* (a pejorative term for people who live in trailer parks) connotes a wide range of behaviours and attitudes which are popularly associated with such people (e.g. that they are uneducated, bigoted, have poor taste, are substance abusers etc.). Finally, *distillation* 'is a form of over-determination that connects social actors to several social practices by abstracting the same feature from the social actors involved in these several practices' (ibid.: 64).

The example that van Leeuween (ibid.: 64–5) gives involves a list of different types of therapists, which includes groups like school teachers and lawyers. van Leeuween argues that this taxonomy has abstracted peripheral qualities of these jobs (teachers and lawyers are not really therapists but their roles may involve some therapy-like work) and elevated them to generalizations.

overwording

The extensive use of synonymous or near-synonymous words to reference a particular domain or social practice (also referred to as overlexicalization). Overwording may indicate a preoccupation with a particular issue or domain and is often found where there is ideological struggle. For example, the drug *marijuana* has been referred to as *cannabis*, *weed*, *ganja*, *pot*, *mary-jane*, *hemp*, *dope*, *grass*, *hash* and *hashish*, while people who are described as *freedom fighters* can also be called *terrorists*, *rebels*, *insurgents* or *assassins*, depending on the ideological perspective of the namer.

parataxis

Parataxis refers to placing linguistic items side by side so that they have (or appear to have) equal status (without using coordinating or subordinating conjunctions). The most famous example of parataxis is Caesar's 'I came, I saw, I conquered'. If multiple adjectives are used to modify a noun (or noun phrase), then, unlike HYPOTAXIS, it is possible to put commas after each one to show that they all modify the noun; for example, consider 'Glasser still stands in awe of this formidable, feckless man' (BNC, A05). Here *formidable* and *feckless* both modify the word *man*. The word *formidable* does not modify *feckless man*.

parole

This term is associated with the Swiss Linguist Ferdinand de Saussure (1966) and refers to actual instances of language use. It contrasts with LANGUE, which refers to the abstract system of language such as its grammatical system. Parole is about utterances (language as used by individual speakers in a specific context) rather than the abstract system.

parsing

Parsing, or *syntactic analysis*, refers to the analysis of a sentence in terms of its constituent parts. This can be done manually by diagramming or putting brackets around sentences to show the different parts of the sentence such as the Noun Phrase (subject), the Verb Phrase (predicator) and Noun Phrase (object) in an subject verb object (SVO) structure.

participant observation

Participant observation is a qualitative research strategy that has its origins in traditional ETHNOGRAPHY. It involves the researcher immersing herself in the researched community's environment and joining in with their daily activities and routines, often over a long period of time. It helps the researcher to understand the research phenomenon from the participants' perspective, what is sometimes referred to as an 'insider perspective'. A disadvantage of participant observation is that it can be very time consuming. The participatory nature of the research means that it can also be difficult to collect a complete record of data, as the researcher may need to rely on their memory of events.

participants

1. Human participants are people who take part in a social activity. In discourse analysis research that could involve acting as a subject – for example, interview participants are the people who are reviewed by a researcher.
2. In grammatical theory, participants are components of a clause. In English clauses, for instance, there are three components: the participants, the process and the circumstances.

[Sasha] [arrived] [yesterday afternoon]

In the example above, 'Sasha' is the participant in the clause, 'arrived' is the process and 'yesterday afternoon' describes the circumstances in which the process takes place.

The participants in a clause are used to represent participants in real life, but this does not necessarily mean that language users always represent every participant in an explicit or equal way. Some participants may be represented as active while others could be passive or excluded (see PASSIVE AGENT DELETION).

passive agent deletion

Passive agent deletion refers to the conversion of an active pattern to passive voice which results in the agent of the process being omitted or backgrounded. For example, the sentence 'But the police have killed 46 people in the past five years, including 12 last year' (BNC, ABD) is an active sentence with 'the police' as the agent. The sentence could be rewritten as a passive sentence, 'Forty six people have been killed in the past five years, including 12 last year', so that the agent is deleted (see also AGENCY, PASSIVIZATION). In such cases, this can make the perpetrators of an action appear to be discursively absolved from responsibility.

passivated social actors

Social actors can be represented as 'doing' things (as actors/agents) or as having things done to them or for them (as goals or beneficiaries of other social actors' actions). The latter type of social actors are said to be passivated while the former are activated. Activated social actors make things happen and can therefore influence their environment. On the other hand, passivization of social actors can be interpreted as a linguistic trace of disempowering discourse in that it constructs such actors as inactive and therefore not having any meaningful influence on their environment (see also AGENCY, PASSIVIZATION, PASSIVE AGENT DELETION). For example, in the British National Corpus, the group 'the elderly' is often composed of passivated social actors, being the goal of verbs like *visit, befriend, help, support* and *protect*.

passivization

Passivization is a term used in grammar to refer to the transformation of an active sentence into a passive one. An active sentence is one with an subject verb object (SVO) basic pattern, such as 'John hit Mary'. Here 'John,' the SUBJECT, performs the act of hitting on 'Mary', the object. When the same sentence is transformed into a passive, 'Mary was hit (by John)', its structure changes to subject verb adverbial, where the adverbial ('by John' in this case) is optional. From a discourse analytical perspective, this can have the effect of backgrounding certain actors or their role in an activity. See also AGENCY, PASSIVE AGENT DELETION, PASSIVATED SOCIAL ACTORS.

patriarchy

Patriarchy is a social system that is based on the belief and associated practices that men are authority figures in most, if not all, social structures. This places male figures in positions of POWER in structures such as families and communities as well as giving them ACCESS and priority to governance. Patriarchy is enshrined in practices such as inheritance, whereby older male children inherit CAPITAL from their parents, or in marriage practices, whereby a woman is 'given away' by her father and then adopts her husband's surname. Feminists have challenged and deconstructed patriarchy, showing it to be maintained by patriarchal discourses, for example, those which construct men as being natural or good leaders.

pauses

Pauses are silences or gaps in a conversation which occur as a result of the current speaker stopping. Conversation and discourse analysts often take care to mark pauses in spoken transcriptions as they can be revealing of interesting phenomena. For example, pauses can be associated with dispreferred seconds in ADJACENCY PAIRS.

performative

Performatives are (often formulaic) SPEECH ACTS which, when uttered, perform a social act and bring about a new reality (see Austin 1962). Such utterances have no TRUTH CONDITIONS and usually contain a performative VERB. These are called explicit performatives. The performative verb indicates the illocutionary force of the utterance. For example,

> I *declare* the resolution carried. (BNC, HM6)
> I *promise* I will be there in a minute. (BNC, KR1)
> I *vote* that this is a good point. (BNC, J99)

Performative verbs can often be identified by seeing if the word *hereby* can be inserted before them. The meanings of the above sentences do not depend on their truth condition and are not falsifiable. We do not know, for example, if the person voting on the good point above actually believes that the point is a good one or whether it can be independently verified that the point is good. The meaning, or pragmatic force of the performative, depends on certain conditions, known as FELICITY CONDITIONS, being appropriate for them to be uttered and to be meaningful. For example, if someone says 'I resign', for the performative to be felicitous, they have to have a particular job or role that they are allowed to resign from, and they must utter the performative to someone who is able to accept their resignation. If these conditions are not present, the uttering of the sentence would be infelicitous and would have no force.

performativity

The idea of performativity is related to Austin's SPEECH ACT THEORY in which PERFORMATIVE speech acts do not just reflect an existing reality but create that reality. For example, a performative SPEECH ACT such as 'I declare this meeting officially opened' creates a new reality in that before the words were uttered the meeting was not yet happening. However, after they are uttered then a meeting is actually taking place. Butler applied the concept of performativity more broadly to refer to how we constitute our sense of self through a systematic and repeated performance of certain types of acts. See GENDER PERFORMATIVITY.

personalization

A form of social actor representation whereby social actors are represented as human beings (as opposed to IMPERSONALIZATION). Examples of personalization include FUNCTIONALISATION, IDENTIFICATION and OVER-DETERMINATION. See also SYNTHETIC PERSONALIZATION.

personification

Personification is a metaphorical representation, common to literary texts, whereby nonhuman objects are ascribed human attributes or qualities. For example, 'Out of the fifty odd men left, only about thirty would be required to unload the Russian ship, big as she was' (BNC, B3J). In this case, the ship is referenced with the female pronoun *she*, despite the fact that in English inanimate objects are not gendered.

Personification can express abstract nouns in human terms, for example, 'One thing of which capitalism has always been proud, is that it can in a literal sense "deliver the goods" ' (BNC, CDW).

perspectivation

Reisigl and Wodak (2001: 81) refer to perspectivation as the way that 'speakers express their involvement in discourse and position their point of

view in the discursive flux: for example, in the reporting, description, narra-
tion and quotation of discriminatory events or utterances, and not least, in
the discursive practice of discrimination itself'. See DISCURSIVE STRATEGY.

persuasion (persuasive strategies)

Persuasion is an integral part of ARGUMENTATION (see also the DISCOURSE-
HISTORICAL APPROACH), and it involves a speaker or speakers adopting strategies
to convince the listener of the validity of what he/she is saying. Persuasion
thus involves attempts to influence people to change their perceptions,
attitudes towards people, ideas or the world in general.

Persuasive strategies include the use of WARRANTS or TOPOI, which are rules that
connect the argument to the conclusion or claims. One persuasive strategy
involves the speaker or writer appealing to authorities, experts or celebrities
who support his or her point of view. For example, a 1950s advert for the
cigarette brand Camel stated, 'According to a recent Nationwide survey:
More doctors smoke Camels than any other cigarette'.

phatic communication

Phatic communication (or phatic communion) is a term coined by Bronislaw
Malinowski (1923), referring to verbal interaction (sometimes called 'small
talk') that is aimed at acknowledging the existence of other people as well as
establishing and maintaining rapport among participants in a conversation.
For example, in England people might engage in talk about the weather. This
is not because English weather is particularly interesting or extreme, but
because it is an uncontroversial way of establishing common ground before
other topics can be approached. Phatic communication can often occur in
COMPUTER-MEDIATED COMMUNICATION, such as text messaging or social network-
ing sites, where its function is not to impart essential information but to
demonstrate that people care for and are thinking of another person. Some
linguists use the term to refer to cases where people refer to the channel of
communication itself, particular in online contexts.

phrase

A grammatical structure which functions as a single unit in a sentence. It can contain one or more words. Phrases can be classified according to a central word called a head word. Common types of phrases are noun phrases (*John, the black cat, some trees, excitement*), prepositional phrases (*into the woods, to the shops*), adjectival phrases (*sick as a parrot*), adverbial phrases (*really slowly*) and verb phrases (*hit the ball, couldn't have known that*). Phrases can contain other phrases embedded within them; for example, *hit the ball* is a verb phrase which contains a noun phrase. See PARSING.

pitch

Pitch is a perceptual characteristic of speech and refers to the frequency of the vibration of vocal cords in the production of speech sounds. It corresponds to the musical notions of high notes and low notes. The higher the vibration of the vocal cords, the higher the pitch. Pitch gives syllables produced in speech relative prominence. For example, in the English syllable system, if a number of syllables of a word are said with low pitch and one is said with a high pitch, the syllable that has higher pitch will be more prominent (it will be a stressed syllable) (see Kreidler 1989). Pitch can thus be used to signal discourse structure; for example, a change in pitch could mark a new topic, show emphasis or indicate that the speaker requires the listener to pay attention (see Brown and Yule 1983: 164).

politeness

Politeness theory is concerned with how people establish and maintain social cohesion, for example, by using various verbal and nonverbal strategies or avoiding talk that may potentially cause conflict and social disharmony (Brown and Levinson 1987). Politeness, as used in language, is inextricably linked to what linguistics philosophers refer to as FACE (see NEGATIVE FACE, POSITIVE FACE). Leech (1983) conceives of a Politeness Principle, similar to Grice's (1975) COOPERATIVE PRINCIPLE. This Principle has maxims of tact, generosity, approbation, modesty, agreement and sympathy.

Politeness is also closely linked to POWER and power relations. So in an interaction we would often expect less powerful people to use more polite forms of language, although people at extreme ends of a social scale may not attend to a society's politeness norms. Politeness criteria can vary between cultures or regions. For example, in Sengwato, a dialect of Setswana, a language spoken in Botswana, the use of the second person pronoun *wena* (you) in the singular form is considered impolite if used by a young person to address an older person. The polite form is the plural *lona* (you). However, in the Southern parts of the country, where other dialects of the language are spoken, it is acceptable to address an older person using the singular form.

political correctness (PC)

PC is an umbrella term, used in American campuses in the 1980s to designate forms of behaviour, linguistic and otherwise, that had the intention of eliminating discrimination against traditionally marginalized social groups, such as women (see NON-SEXIST LANGUAGE), the disabled, ethnic and religious minorities. This could include, for example, coining new terms such as *African-American* or *wheelchair user* or avoiding language use that was considered to be excluding, pejorative or referenced STEREOTYPES Another example of PC involves 'affirmative action' policies designed to counter earlier incidents of discrimination, such as having quotas in workplaces, schools or governments to ensure that previously excluded groups are given the opportunity to participate.

However, such practices inspired a backlash, and the concept of PC was resignified in order to refer to practices that were viewed (especially by the right-wing media) as ridiculous, interfering with people's freedom of expression, patronizing or moralizing. As a result, Cameron (1995: 123) noted that 'PC now has such negative connotations for so many people that the mere invocation of the phrase can move those so labelled to elaborate disclaimers or reduce them to silence'.

PC (or 'sensitive language use') was debated in media and academic circles in the 1990s, with Dunant (1994: xi–xii) arguing against 'positive discrimination' and assuming that all minority groups wish to be treated in the same way. Pinker (1994) claimed that PC could result in a 'euphemism treadmill,' whereby new terms continually need to be replaced as older ones acquire negative meanings, resulting in confusion, whereas Ehrenreich (1992: 335) points out that changing language does not necessarily alter underlying attitudes.

Cameron, however, writes that '[t]he verbal hygiene movement for so-called politically correct language does not threaten our freedom to speak as we choose . . . It threatens only our freedom to imagine that our linguistic choices are inconsequential, or to suppose that any one group of people has an inalienable right to prescribe them' (Cameron, 1994: 33).

populism

Albertazzi and McDonnell (2008: 3) define populism as 'an ideology which pits a virtuous and homogeneous people against a set of elites and dangerous "others" who are together depicted as depriving (or attempting to deprive) the sovereign people of their rights, values, prosperity, identity and voice'. Populism is not restricted to a particular political position, and thus there can be liberal or conservative populism. Canovan (1981: 5), however, notes that people who expound populist ideologies rarely label themselves as populist and reject the term if it is used on them.

positive discourse analysis

A form of CRITICAL DISCOURSE ANALYSIS (CDA) described by Martin and Rose (2003) and Martin (2004) which foregrounds the fact that CDA need not always be concerned with exposing hidden *negative* agendas or discourses which maintain unequal POWER relationships or mislead readers in some way (although it should be acknowledged that some texts, intentionally or not, do this). Positive discourse analysis suggests that positive readings of texts are possible and that not all discourses are damaging or negative. It therefore focuses on what texts 'do well' and 'get right'.

positive face

Positive face is a concept in POLITENESS theory which holds that every individual has the need to feel appreciated, acknowledged, understood and accepted (Brown and Levinson 1987). For example, when we have done well we expect and want our friends to acknowledge our achievement by complimenting us. Positive face is related to issues of self-esteem, reputation and social standing. Positive face can sometimes be maintained by banter or playful insults, the implication being that two speakers are so close that they can appear to be rude to each other and no offence will be taken. See also NEGATIVE FACE.

positivism

Positivism is a philosophical movement, first theorized by Auguste Comte and later by Émile Durkheim, that holds that true knowledge is that which is based on the physical and sensory world. Logical positivism combines empiricism with rationalism and holds that observation is critical for our understanding of the world. Scientific positivism views all knowledge as scientific, by which it means that science is transcultural and rests on results that are not influenced by the beliefs and IDENTITY of the analyst (see also OBJECTIVITY). Many social scientists have rejected a completely positivist stance, arguing that taking a positivist approach to study human behaviour is problematic because it ignores the role of the researcher in the research and does not take into account the specific historical and social contexts under which research is conducted. It has also been argued that positivism results in reductionism through which one entity is reduced to another entity such as when people are reduced to numbers and tables. In addition, such approaches could lead to the establishment of NORMS, which could be used to stereotype or marginalize certain social actors. See also INTERPRETATIVE POSITIVISM.

post-colonial theory

Post-colonial theory is a philosophical and critical approach to the legacy of colonialism. Post-colonialists examine the relationship between colonisers (normally from the West) and the colonized, often focusing on unequal POWER relationships between the two groups and how they have been legitimized and maintained. For example, post-colonialists may study how the indigenous knowledge of the colonized was used to benefit the colonisers or how the literature of the colonisers justified the subordination of the colonized by representing the latter as inferior and irrational, unable to govern themselves and therefore needing leadership.

Post-colonialism also deals with the reactions of the colonized and how they have reclaimed and reconstructed their own identifies, albeit fragmented, using colonial structures such as schools and universities. It deals with how the colonies use the coloniser's languages, such as French, Portuguese and English, to write their own histories and to creatively resist the images that come from colonial literature and different art forms. Frequently cited post-colonialist writers include Edward Said, Frantz Fanon and Gayatri Chakravorty Spivak. See also ORIENTALISM.

post-feminism

Post-feminism is a term which first became popular in the early 1980s to describe the range of different (sometimes conflicting) discourses and theories that came after the SECOND-WAVE FEMINISM of the 1960s and 1970s. While second-wave feminism was concerned with issues of legal equality such as property rights and the right to vote, some feminists noted that it also tended to construct women as a homogeneous and victimized group that had little or no agency. In post-feminism, women are seen as coming from diverse ethnic, cultural, racial and economic backgrounds. Post-feminism also acknowledges female agency, rather than viewing women as passive recipients of patriarchal structures and practices. Some post-feminists have examined why some women agree with the goals of feminism but do not consider themselves to be feminists; others have examined backlash against feminism or looked at social practices like pole-dancing or the production and consumption of pornography from a post-feminist perspective. A key strand of post-feminist research is the examination of how gender inequality continues to exist in more subtle, complex or negotiated forms – see, for example, Levy's (2005) study of 'raunch' culture or Mill's (1998) examination of Dateline adverts. Perhaps one of the controversial positions of post-feminism is the idea that feminism is no longer (as) relevant as many of the issues it fought for have been achieved and that other issues, such as economic inequality, are of importance. Lazar (2005: 17) conceptualizes a global neoliberal discourse of post-feminism as 'once certain indicators (such as rights to educational access, labour force participation, property ownership, and abortion and fertility) are achieved by women, feminism is considered to have outlived its purpose and ceases to be of relevance'. Some contemporary feminists have thus abandoned the term post-feminism, feeling that it does not accurately reflect their position and instead use the term *third-wave feminism* to describe their perspective.

postmodernism

Postmodernism arose as an intellectual movement associated with a number of philosophers such as Jean-François Lyotard, Jacques Derrida, Jean Baudrillard and Michel Foucault, among others. It has also been seen as an aesthetic, political or literary phenomenon (so, for example, we can talk of a postmodern novel). According to postmodernist philosophers, truth or reality is a product of human social groups rather than something that is essentially 'out there' waiting to be discovered. A central tenet of postmodernism is 'the death of the author', a rejection of the belief that there is only one true meaning of a particular TEXT (such as a poem, novel, film or painting), which is the one that the author intended the audience to understand. Instead, postmodernists hold that there are multiple readings of a particular text, depending on who encounters it. Another belief of postmodernists is the rejection of 'grand narratives' – or large-scale theories that are intended to explain everything. Postmodernists are sceptical of the values of modernity, such as the value of humanity having an essence different from that of animals or of good triumphing over evil. Quentin Tarantino, for example, has been cited as a postmodern film maker, in that his films sometimes combine different genres and discourses together as well as 'dissolving the divide between high and low art' (Hayward 2000: 279). As well as being anti-essentialist, postmodernism is opposed to ways of ordering experience in binary opposites, such as male versus female, rational versus emotional, knowledge versus ignorance, dominance versus submissiveness and so on. Indeed, one goal of postmodernism has been to deconstruct such binary opposites. Postmodernist thinking thus foregrounds notions of complexity, contradiction, ambiguity and interconnectedness in every aspect of life. Some postmodernists have been criticized for foregrounding style over substance, having a nihilistic or amoral worldview or using unnecessarily complex terminology to express relatively simple concepts. See also POST-STRUCTURALISM.

post-structuralism

Post-structuralism is a movement, related to POSTMODERNISM, which is concerned with 'critiquing the ways in which competing forms of knowledge and the power interests these serve, aspire to fix meaning once and for all'

(Baxter 2003: 23; see also Laclau and Mouffe 1985). According to post-structuralism, meaning or reality is discursively constructed. In linguistics, post-structuralism signifies a shift from constructing meanings in terms of binary opposites. Structuralists, such as Saussure, have argued that linguistic signs are composed of two parts – a *signifier* (such as written word or a collection of sounds) and a *signified* (the concept or meaning that is referenced by the signifier). Saussure argued that the relationship between the two was arbitrary yet fixed. However, in the view of post-structuralists, 'social meanings are continuously negotiated and contested through language and discourse' (Baxter 2003: 23–24). Derrida (1978), for example, claims that in addition to the *signifieds* acquiring meaning though their *difference* with others, they also have the identity of *deferral,* which means that the meaning of any representation can only be fixed temporarily because it depends on the discursive context in which the *signifieds* are located. In other words, meanings are not eternally fixed but are discursively constructed and can thus shift over time. Post-structuralists have problematized the notion of a stable self, arguing that individuals hold multiple, changing and interacting IDENTITY traits (social class, age, gender, sexuality, ethnicity) and that any form of knowledge making (such as text analysis) requires the analyst to take into account how such identity traits impact on the process of analysis. In addition, post-structuralists reject the idea that a text has a single 'true' reading or meaning, instead advocating that each reader constructs his or her own reading (or set of readings), which all have validity.

post-structuralist discourse analysis

Post-structuralist discourse analysis (or PDA) is an approach to discourse analysis that focuses on 'what is happening right now, on the ground, in this very conversation' (Baxter 2002: 828, quoting from Wetherell 1998: 395). Baxter claims that PDA is concerned with 'the continuously fluctuating ways in which speakers, within any discursive context, are variously positioned as powerful or powerless by *competing* social and institutional discourses' (ibid.). For PDA, the object of discourse analysis is not so much to find closure to meanings but rather to highlight the 'diverse viewpoints, contradictory voices and fragmented messages' (ibid.) that are represented in spoken data. As a result, no discourse can be said to be completely dominant as language in interaction shows a continuous flux, with individual speakers being powerful at one point and powerless at another (see also Baxter 2008).

power

Power is our ability to control our environment, our own lives and those of others. The German sociologist Max Weber (1925: 28) gave a much-quoted definition of power (Macht), which according to Kronman (1983: 38) translates to 'the probability that one actor within a social relationship will be in a position to carry out his [sic] own will despite resistance, regardless of the basis on which this probability rests'. Foucault (1979b) contrasts *sovereign power* with *disciplinary power* or what Fairclough (1989: 33) similarly formulates as *coercion* or *consent*. The former is exercised by the state or sovereign, who had the power to punish, coerce or kill people. Disciplinary power, on the other hand, is a way of ensuring that people exercise self-control or submit to the will of 'experts'. For Foucault, disciplinary power is a much more efficient method of control than sovereign power, and this has become the main form of power that most people in western societies tend to encounter in their day-to-day lives. Talbot (1998: 193) points out, 'Real social power does not reside in big muscles   Power resides elsewhere: in being at the head of a corporation, a general leading an army, a senator or an MP'.

Critical discourse analysts have tended to focus on how disciplinary power is created, maintained and challenged. For example, Fairclough (1995: 1), following Foucault, defines power not only as asymmetries that exist between individuals participating in the same discursive event but also in terms of how people have different capacities to control how texts and thus discourses are produced, distributed and consumed. Van Dijk (1996: 85) notes that 'social power and dominance are often *organised and institutionalised*, so as to allow more effective control and to enable routine forms of power reproduction'. This means that power is successful precisely because it is reenacted in routine activities which are not questioned but instead seen as normal (see HEGEMONY).

Power is linked to discourse because discourses are ways of representing and constructing reality so that power relations are constructed, maintained and contested via discourses. It is because of the link to discourse that power relations are never static. The inverse of power is RESISTANCE (see also STRUGGLE, SUBVERSION). As discourses compete for ascendancy, formerly dominant discourses may be challenged, and even replaced, by formerly marginal discourses resulting in a shift in power relations as well as social change.

Power is not necessarily a bad thing – for example, a student and teacher are obviously in an asymmetrical power relationship, although here the relationship is usually (hopefully) beneficial rather than detrimental to the student. Indeed, some critical discourse analysts have focused on cases of abuses of power, for example, where power has harmful consequences, while POSITIVE DISCOURSE ANALYSIS focuses on cases where the power utilized by text holders is used for good. A post-structuralist view of power is that it is connected to human agency and that no one individual is placed as powerful across all discourses. Thus, one can be powerful in one context and powerless in another (see also Baxter 2003).

pragmatics

Pragmatics is a branch of linguistics that is concerned with the communicative functions of language (Levinson 1983, Thomas 1995, Yule 1996), particularly examining language and interaction in context. Pragmatics can be thought as subsuming or overlapping with other fields and theories such as SPEECH ACT THEORY, POLITENESS theory, CONVERSATION ANALYSIS and INTERACTIONAL SOCIOLINGUISTICS.

Pragmatics is concerned with meaning – how people make sense of language. While we need knowledge about a particular language before we can use it, such as grammatical rules, what individual words mean and how to pronounce them, pragmatics focuses more on how we achieve meaning in particular contexts, by taking into account things like how, where and when something is said, who says it, what the relationship is between the speaker and hearer, and how we make sense of ambiguous uses of language.

For example, the question 'Can you pass the salt?' appears to ask if someone is capable of passing the salt. However, if it is said with a rising tone, during a meal, to another person who is closer to the salt than you are, then its communicative goal is probably a request for the salt, rather than a question about ability. The meaning of the utterance is more than what is actually said.

predicate

In traditional grammar a sentence consists of two parts, a SUBJECT and a predicate. The predicate must contain a VERB (and can optionally contain other parts of speech such as nouns, adjectives or adverbs), and it modifies the subject.

predicational strategies

Predicational strategies or strategic predications are evaluations, usually realized as predicates, adjectives, appositions, adverbials, relative clauses, metaphors or collocations, that are used to ascribe particular attributes or qualities to social actors, often in discriminatory discourse (Reisigl and Wodak 2001). These are used as elements in ARGUMENTATION in order to justify discrimination against a certain social group. An example of a predicational strategy that Reisigl and Wodak (2001: 55) cite is from an Austrian newspaper, which writes, 'Foreigners are socio-parasites, who exploit the welfare system'. Such a strategy is used to justify why foreigners in that country should be removed from the social welfare system or returned to their countries of origin. See REFERENTIAL STRATEGIES.

preferred reading

RECEPTION theory holds that texts are encoded with certain meanings when they are produced, which are subsequently decoded in the process of text interpretation. Decoding involves both the comprehension and evaluation of a text. Hall (1973) suggests that the preferred reading is when consumers of a text accept the encoded meanings that were intended by the text producer. This is sometimes referred to as the dominant or hegemonic reading, and the readers who align with the dominant readings could be referred as dominant, hegemonic, preferred or passive readers. They contrast with RESISTANT READERS, who reject the dominant meanings encoded in a text, formulating alternative readings.

prejudiced discourse

Prejudiced discourse is discourse that shows evidence of discrimination against a particular social group. Common examples of prejudiced discourse involve discrimination based on ethnicity, race, sex, sexual orientation. While such a discourse may show evidence of discrimination against one group, it can also show favour for another, usually more dominant social group. See Van Dijk (1984).

prescriptivism

Prescriptivism is associated with traditional approaches to the study of language where some linguists tended to be concerned about preserving the 'purity' of language. This approach conceives of a distinction between correct and incorrect uses of language. The strongest prescriptivists would encourage use of correct language, for example, by pointing out perceived mistakes and asking people to correct themselves. An example of prescriptivism would be 'never end a sentence with a preposition'. Prescriptivism is therefore highly rule governed. Prescriptivists could be criticized for imposing their own view of language on others, being over-concerned with rules, not acknowledging that language is always changing and 'owned' by everyone who uses it, even those who may use nonstandard forms associated with less powerful ways of speaking.

Advocates of POLITICAL CORRECTNESS could be viewed as prescriptivist in that they also attempt to regulate how language is used, according to a particular value system. Another example of prescriptivism would be the Campaign for Plain English, which advocates that councils and other bodies avoid unnecessary jargon and complex language use, which they view as excluding and confusing to ordinary people.

Prescriptivism could be contrasted with descriptive linguistics (see DESCRIPTION), which attempts to describe how people actually use language, without making judgements about correctness. A postmodern perspective would argue that a truly descriptive approach is impossible, as that too involves making a judgement (to try to appear neutral).

presupposition

A presupposition is a proposition which, although not formally stated, is understood and taken for granted in order for an utterance or a statement to make sense. For example, the statement 'John's presentation was well received' presupposes that 'John gave a presentation'. Presuppositions differ from ENTAILMENTS in that if the statement is negated, 'John's presentation was not well received', then the presupposition still holds true (John still gave a presentation). Entailments, however, cannot be shown to hold true when statements are negated.

Presuppositions are important in discourse analysis because they can point to speakers' or writers' commonsense assumptions, beliefs and attitudes that are taken as given. Analysis of presuppositions allows the discourse analyst to identify implicit meanings in texts. Presuppositions are also features of INTERTEXTUALITY in that they 'constitute something taken for granted by the text producer which can be interpreted in terms of intertextual relations with previous texts of the text producer' (Fairclough 1992: 121). However, Chapman and Routledge (2009: 179) warn that '[t]here is not a consensus among scholars in the field about what constitutes a standard notion of presupposition in linguistics and the philosophy of language'.

privileged femininity

1. Privileged femininity can be conceived as a pro-female discourse in that it operates as a form of positive discrimination. It could involve practices which acknowledge the existence of male advantage in various contexts, such as education and the workplace, and attempts to improve access and opportunities for females (Kitetu and Sunderland 2000).
2. A different understanding of privileged femininity would refer to women or girls who are relatively advantaged in society, possibly due to other aspects of their IDENTITY that are more powerful or through being linked to a powerful man. An example would be a woman who is married to a wealthy man and does not need to do paid work. While often being linked to social class, privileged femininity can also be connected to ethnicity. For example, in pre-democratic South Africa white femininities could be considered privileged as white women's experience was not characterized by the hardships that defined black women's experience (see also McRobbie 2009: 87). See also HEGEMONIC FEMININITY.

processes

In his SYSTEMIC FUNCTIONAL GRAMMAR, Halliday (1994: 106) writes,

> Our most powerful impression of experience is that it consists of
> "goings-on" – happening, doing, sensing, meaning, and being and
> becoming. All these goings-on are sorted out in the grammar of the
> clause. Thus as well as being a mode of action, of giving and demanding
> goods-&-services and information, the clause is also a mode of reflection,
> of imposing order on the endless variation and flow of events. The
> grammatical system by which this is achieved is TRANSITIVITY. The trans-
> itivity system construes the world of experience into a manageable set
> of PROCESS TYPES.

A transitivity process consists of three elements – the process itself (represented by verbs), the participants (represented by nominals) and the
circumstances (represented by adverbials or prepositional phrases). See
PROCESS TYPES, TRANSITIVITY.

process types

Processes are aspects of TRANSITIVITY. Processes represented in the clause are
processes of doing, being, meaning, becoming and so on. Halliday (1994)
identifies six process types (three main and three secondary). The main types
are (1) material processes (processes of doing), (2) mental processes
(processes of sensing) and (3) relational processes (processes of being). The
three secondary processes appear at the boundaries between the main
process types. So (4) behavioural processes appear between material and
mental processes, (5) verbal processes border the mental and relational and
(6) existential processes border the relational and material. Behavioural
and existential processes only have one participant, while the other processes
may have one or two. A process that has one participant can take an
intransitive verb, whereas processes with two participants make use of
transitive verbs.

For example, material processes are represented as active sentences and can take both transitive and intransitive verbs, for example,

Joseph is kicking a ball (transitive – two participants: Joseph and a ball).
Joseph is running (intransitive – one participant: Joseph)

Mental processes are always attributed to 'human or human-like' participants who do the sensing. The SUBJECT and the theme often coincide, which results in the use of personal pronouns and a tendency to be realized as passive clauses:

I am worried by your silence.

Relational processes are represented as attributive or existential patterns and can be realized in three types of clauses:

1. Intensive: I am tired
2. Circumstantial: I am in my forties
3. Possessive: I have two children. (Halliday 1985: 119)

The choice of representational clause (whether it is transitive or intransitive for material processes) for a real-life process may be ideologically or culturally significant. In addition, a consistent choice of mental processes in representation may indicate a writer/speaker's *perceptions* rather than an objective account of events.

production

Production refers to processes that are involved in the creation of a TEXT. As with analysis of RECEPTION, analysis of text production can be one stage of CRITICAL DISCOURSE ANALYSIS (Fairclough 1989: 24–26). Analysts may ask questions such as under what circumstances was a text produced, who produced it, for what purposes and what constraints were placed on the production of the text (e.g. was censorship involved).

Text production takes place within a specific discursive practice, which is one aspect of social practice. For example, the production of a newspaper text takes place with the discursive practices of news production within the main social practice of the media as an industry. Text production involves processes based on internalized social structures and conventions. Therefore, the production of each text is constrained by the social conventions within which it is produced.

promotional culture

Promotional culture refers to a social phenomenon whose function is to communicate a message which not only provides information but also promotes a particular aspect of social life (see Wernick 1991). Such a phenomenon is linked to the marketization or commodification of discourse. Fairclough (1992) has shown, for example, how university prospectuses which traditionally provided information about courses, have begun to also contain promotional messages, functioning as a form of advertising for the university itself. A degree may be seen as a 'product', students are customers and lecturers are service providers.

proposition

A proposition is the semantic content of a sentence, which is the bearer of truth or falsity. Propositions are sometimes regarded as abstract (or decontextualized) meanings of words, in contrast to their PRAGMATIC meaning.

prosody

Prosody refers to the suprasegmental features of connected speech, such as stress, rhythm, PITCH, volume and intonation. These features can reveal something about the speaker or his/her intentions. For example, volume may indicate emotional state, while a rising intonation at the end of an utterance may be used to distinguish a question from a statement. In writing, prosodic features are sometimes represented orthographically with punctuation marks. For example, an exclamation mark could be used to indicate certain prosodic features such as volume or emphasis.

public identity

Hekman (2004) distinguishes between what she calls individual identity and public identity. She believes that every individual has a unique IDENTITY or core self that is constituted by a variety of experiences and influences from childhood, and it is this identity that allows each individual to function as a mature adult. However, individual identities can be subsumed under what Heckman calls public identities. Public identities are overarching identity categories that are constituted by public discourses. For example, being white, black, working-class, Christian or an immigrant is a public identity. While our individual identity makes us different from everyone else, Heckman says, our public identities identify us as members of a social group, sharing certain attributes with other members of our identity category.

public sphere

A term associated with Habermas (1984), which refers to the relationship between social systems and everyday life. Fairclough (2003: 68) sees the public sphere as 'the sphere in which people act as citizens'. In the public sphere, citizens can debate issues that affect their lives and influence the directions of policies that impact on their way of life. The more powerful members of a society often have more ACCESS to the public sphere, taking part in public debates that influence the direction in which society develops.

qualitative methods

This term refers to a number of research methods which involve non-numerical data collection or explanation. Such methods include ETHNOGRAPHY, PARTICIPANT OBSERVATION, unstructured interview, case study, FOCUS GROUP and CONVERSATION ANALYSIS. Such methods often involve the close analysis of a small amount of data rather than summarizing large amounts of data via QUANTITATIVE METHODS. Qualitative approaches have been criticised for being subjective as the researcher's identities can influence the research process; for example, the researcher may choose to analyse a piece of data which confirms his or her own expectations. See also Bernard and Ryan (2010).

quantitative methods

Quantitative methods rely on mathematical models and statistical tests to systematically and objectively study natural phenomena. It is widely used in the natural sciences, such as physics, chemistry and mathematics, as well as being used in CORPUS LINGUISTICS and CONTENT ANALYSIS. In the social sciences, the use of quantitative research is criticized as being associated with POSITIVISM. See also Blaikie (2003).

queer theory

Queer was a pejorative term aimed at gay people, but it was subject to RECLAIMING in the later part of the twentieth century as a defiant, politicized IDENTITY label. While queer is still often associated with homosexuality, proponents of queer theory argue that the term is potentially anything which mainstream society considers to not be 'normal', particularly in terms of sexual identity or desire. For example, an S/M practitioner, a prostitute or a woman who has a relationship with a much younger man could be seen as queer. In addition, the concept could be extended to cover gender identity, ethnic identity and so on – so a couple who are of different ethnicities could also be viewed from a queer perspective. Rather than seeking 'liberation' or 'assimilation' of minority identity groups into the mainstream, queer theory instead seeks to deconstruct and challenge the concept of fixed and stable identities (particularly binary pairs like gay/straight), arguing that such identities are social constructs and 'performed'. One aspect of queer analysis would be to show that identity categories are specific to particular societies and points in time by examining historical records or looking at other cultures to show that such identities were either not conceptualized or that the discourses about them were very different. Hall (2003: 101) writes, '. . . desires do not necessarily *remain* true. That is not to say that we are "all" really bisexual. The point of queer theories generally is that we are not all "really" any one thing'. Queer theory thus takes POST-STRUCTURALISM as its basis, although it also has links to feminist theory and GENDER PERFORMATIVITY.

racism

Racism refers to the belief that human abilities and traits can be differentiated on the basis of ethnicity and that, as a result, some 'races' are better or worse than others (either generally or with respect to particular characteristics). According to Memmi (1992: 103), racism involves making absolute generalizations that are evaluations of real or fictitious differences which are detrimental to the accused (see also Reisigl and Wodak 2001: 5–10). A racist person judges their victim negatively in order to justify and legitimate his or her own privileged status and the victim's marginalized status. Racism is also understood more broadly as an overarching label for all kinds of discriminatory and aggressive tendencies towards those who are perceived as 'different'. A related term is heterophobia – an irrational fear or dislike of any different group (e.g. Jews, black people, Arabs, women, young people or people with disabilities). Racism is ideological, that is, it is encoded in different sociocultural, religious beliefs and pseudoscientific theories, which are articulated through discourse and result in the stereotyping of certain groups of people. Institutional racism results in certain groups been denied POWER, ACCESS or CAPITAL. Racism can also result in violence and, in some cases, genocide. The DISCOURSE-HISTORICAL APPROACH to CRITICAL DISCOURSE ANALYSIS has often been used to examine ARGUMENTATION strategies, FALLACIES and TOPOI surrounding RACIST DISCOURSE.

racist discourse

Racist discourse refers to different ways by which people are constructed as biologically different and therefore deserving to be treated in particular dehumanizing ways (see ORIENTALISM/ORIENTAL DISCOURSE). RACISM is often based on STEREOTYPES which are used to characterize an ethnic group as possessing particular qualities or essential differences when compared to another group; for example, one ethnic group may be viewed as less generous or intelligent than another group. Racist discourse is also realized in racializing REFERENTIAL STRATEGIES or nominations such as 'nigger' or 'bushmen'. However, racist discourse can construct some groups of people positively through the use of positive stereotypes.

reception

Reception theory is an approach to textual analysis which focuses on audiences and how they interpret texts (such as a magazine, book, film, piece of music etc.). Stuart Hall (1973) developed a theory of encoding and decoding which stipulates that audiences can have three possible reactions to a text. First, there is a dominant or PREFERRED READING which coincides with how the creator of the text wished it to be understood. Secondly, there is an oppositional reading (see RESISTANT READER), whereby the audience interprets the text in a different way to the way it was intended to be understood. Finally, there is a negotiated meaning which involves a kind of compromise position between the first two meanings.

A study of reception may also consider other forms of analysis, looking at what sorts of people actually consumed the text, for what reasons and in what contexts. This could involve quantitative research (e.g. considering viewing figures or comparing different demographic groups) and/or carrying out RESEARCH INTERVIEWS or FOCUS GROUPS with people who have encountered the text. Consideration of reception can also be a consideration of CRITICAL DISCOURSE ANALYSIS.

reclaiming

The appropriation and resignification of a pejorative term by the group that it was aimed at, as a political strategy. Labels such as *slut*, *dyke*, *bitch*, *nigger* and *queer* have been 'reclaimed' as positive concepts. A reclaimed term can often be ambiguous, however, as it may retain elements of its original negative meaning. Thus, context is important in interpreting meaning as well as the IDENTITY of the user, audience and who the term is aimed at. Some speakers, particularly those who do not belong to the group in question, may feel that it is not appropriate for them to use a reclaimed term, for fear that it could be misinterpreted.

recontextualization

Recontextualization refers to ways in which text or parts of text are taken from their original setting or context and then used in different contexts.

Bernstein (1990: 184) points out that semantic shifts take place 'according to recontextualizing principles which selectively appropriate, relocate, refocus and relate to other discourses to constitute its own order and orderings'. Linell (1998) suggests that this can be achieved in three ways: (1) intratextual, where a part of a text is referred to within the same text, either earlier or later; (2) intertextual, where part or all of another text is referred to in another text and (3) interdiscursive, where types of discourses are recontextualized.

referential strategies

Also referred to as 'nominational strategies', this is a term used in the DISCOURSE-HISTORICAL APPROACH to refer to ways of constructing social actors, particular in relation to self and other representation and the construction of in- and out-groups. This often involves the use of nouns as labels for people or groups as well as the adoption of METAPHORS, metonymies and synecdoches (a part standing for a whole). For example, a businessman might be referred to as a *suit*. Referential strategies are used to articulate discriminatory discourses, be they positive or negative. In their analysis of RACIST DISCOURSE, Reisigl and Wodak (2001) identified a number of referential strategies which employ the use of personal reference to represent or construct certain groups of people disparagingly. Certain nouns have discriminatory connotations on their own; that is, they do not need further qualification to convey discriminatory meanings. For example, the use of a term such as *paleface* is derogatory to the people who are labelled as such. However, referential strategies may involve the use of more or less neutral terms which ascribe more positive value to those being labelled.

Many referential strategies are borrowed or adapted from van Leeuwen's (1996, 1997) categories of social actor representation, for example, AGGREGA-TION, IMPERSONALIZATION, EXCLUSION, SUPPRESSION, BACKGROUNDING, SPECIFICATION, GENERICIZATION. The following is an example of a referential strategy from spoken English: 'That could have been painful that could you *bitch*' (BNC, KCE). See PREDICATIONAL STRATEGIES.

reflexivity

Reflexivity (sometimes called *self-reflexivity*) refers to a process of reflecting on the research process as it is being carried out, and it is usually an integral part of discourse analysis. For example, the researcher may try to consider how aspects of his/her IDENTITY and the society he/she has been brought up in could impact on the way that the research proceeds, such as choice of topic, research questions and methods of data collection and analysis. Reflexivity is thus the methodological principal of using one's self-awareness in order to deal with possible inherent researcher bias.

register

A register is a specialized code or variety of language associated with a specific social practice and designed to serve a specific social goal. It consists of distinctive linguistic patterns (vocabulary, grammar, phonology etc.) which have become conventionalized and are relatively durable. Other terms such as GENRE or dialect have sometimes been used in similar ways to register. Halliday and Hasan (1985: 41) differentiate dialects from registers by saying that the former concept is 'a variety of language according to the user', while the latter is 'a variety according to use', and it reflects 'the different types of social activity that people commonly engage in'. So as register tends to be based on the *use rather than the user of language*, variation according to geographical location and demographic categories are not included under register.

Examples of registers include medical interviews, lab reports, weather reports and newspaper editorials. However, registers should be seen as a spectrum of varieties of language rather than clear distinctive varieties. There is no clear boundary between one register and another. Biber et al. (1998) used corpus approaches to identify distinctions between a range of different written and spoken registers, noting that each register could be classified as appearing on a five linear scales or 'dimensions': (1) involved versus informational production, (2) narrative versus non-narrative discourse, (3) elaborated versus situation-dependent reference, (4) overt expression of argumentation and (5) impersonal versus non-impersonal style. For example, telephone conversations occur at the 'involved' end of dimension 1 (speakers use this register to express involvement with the hearer, rather than give a great deal of information). On the other hand, official documents are informational rather than involved. However, for dimension 2, both telephone conversations and official documents are 'non-narrative' rather than narrative (e.g. they do not tend to involve lengthy descriptions of past tense events).

relativism

Relativism refers to a philosophy which holds that truth is not absolute. Relativism thus holds that our understanding of the world is dependent on our own circumstances, experiences and IDENTITY. For example, we often make sense of other cultures through comparing them against our own culture.

But in the developing countries of Asia, Africa and Latin America, parents live in mortal fear of these diseases – and for very good reason. (BNC, A7G)

In the above example (from a British charity leaflet), the term 'developing countries' implies that less wealthy countries are still in the process of developing, as opposed to richer countries which are implied to be 'developed' (and thus do not need to develop any further). In fact, all countries are 'developing', just some have developed in different ways or at different speeds relative to others. As a related concept, *linguistic relativity* states that the limits of the native speaker's language are the limits of their world. Relativism contrasts with such notions as POSITIVISM, monism and universalism.

relevance theory

Relevance theory is a cognitive theory of pragmatics associated with Sperber and Wilson (1986), developed out of Grice's theory of cooperativeness in conversation. While Grice held that there were four CONVERSATIONAL MAXIMS (quality, quantity, manner and relevance), which were used by speakers and listeners in order to encode and decode meaning and IMPLICATURE in interactions, Sperber and Wilson put relevance at the core of their theory. They postulate that when people are engaged in conversational interaction, they produce utterances that are presumed to have relevance to the interaction. The listener is able to infer meaning because he or she assumes that the speaker's contribution is relevant enough to warrant processing for meaning even though a speaker may appear to flout the maxim of relevance (e.g. their contribution may appear not to be relevant).

Example
   Sue: Did you go to Tom's recital?
   Donald: Tracy's here.

On the surface, Donald's response to Sue's yes/no question appears to be irrelevant as he gives information about another person. In order for Sue to process Donald's utterance as meaningful, she must assume that Donald is being relevant to the exchange in that particular context. For example, she needs to take into consideration that Tracy is Tom's ex-partner and that Tracy does not like to hear Tom being talked about. For Sue to interpret Donald's response, she needs to know that Donald is aware of the relationship breakup and also that Donald knows that she (Sue) knows about it too. Don's utterance is therefore a warning to Sue, perhaps to change the subject. Relevance is thus a subjective concept, as it depends on the status of the hearer and his/her knowledge at the time of perceiving an utterance.

repair

Repair is a term used in CONVERSATION ANALYSIS to refer to patterns of naturally occurring conversation where a speaker needs to repeat or reformulate part of his/her utterance in order to 'correct' what he/she had previously said. This can often occur when one or more participants has difficulty with speaking, hearing or understanding. Repair can involve self-repair, or another speaker can attempt to clarify or correct the first speaker's utterance. Repair can also be marked by features such as REPETITION, PAUSES or hesitation markers such as *er* or *erm*.

> I think probably that was probably London but in the north I lived on the north east coast in a very small town and some of I mean my memories are quite different in a way. (BNC, D90)

In the above example, from a conversation, the speaker engages in self-repair after the word *probably*, 'that was probably', in order to correct his grammar.

repetition

Repetition refers to the rearticulation of linguistic phenomena. In naturally occurring talk, repetition is frequent, as is illustrated in the following stretch of speech:

> Yes, could be could be anybody, yes, yes. (BNC, JK1)

Here the repetition of 'could be' is possibly an example of disfluency phenomena. The speaker may be trying to maintain the floor, and repeating part of the utterance helps him to achieve this while he is formulating what to say next. In addition, the speaker may use repetition for emphasis, which seems likely with his use of 'yes'.

In literary texts repetition is used, especially in poetry as a special device to achieve an aesthetic or other poetic goal. The repetition of equivalent grammatical structures is called parallelism, which can be used for the purposes of foregrounding. The repeated structures become perceptually more prominent, and as a result they are stylistically significant (Short 1996).

Halliday and Hasan (1976: 280) regard 'repetition' as being inseparable from 'reiteration': 'When we talk about REITERATION . . . we are including not only the repetition of the same lexical item but also the occurrence of a related item, which may be anything from a synonym or near synonym of the original to a general word dominating the entire class'.

reported speech

Reported speech (also called indirect speech) refers to an aspect of speech representation (also known as speech presentation) by which words are attributed (to a speaker/writer by another speaker/writer) but are not reported verbatim, as they are in DIRECT SPEECH (Short 1996). Reported speech is characterized by the use of a reporting clause without quotation marks, for example, 'She said I was a handsome devil, too' (BNC, A74).

representation

Representation can generally be defined as the creation of a mental image through art, language and other domains where meaning can be created such as theatre. It involves the signifying practices and symbolic systems through which we produce meaning (see Hall 1997).

Discourse analysis often examines how particular phenomena (people, concepts, events etc.) are represented through language use. For example, prejudiced language is characterized by positive self-representation and negative 'other' representation (Reisigl and Wodak 2001), which can be achieved through stereotyping. Sometimes, the term *construction* (associated with STRUCTURALISM and POST-STRUCTURALISM) can be used with similar effect to representation.

repressive discourse

Repression is an attempt to remove from the consciousness any ideas, thoughts, memories or desires that are considered to be painful, unacceptable or otherwise unpleasant. Repressive discourses are therefore those discourses whose effect is to prevent ideas, thoughts, memories and practices that are considered to be unacceptable. For example, during the twentieth century, there were numerous repressive discourses around homosexuality, which constructed homosexuals as deviant, mentally ill, child molesters, women trapped in men's bodies and so on. The word *homosexual* itself was part of the repressive discourse, as it was generally associated with medical and legal practices, which constructed people who experienced same-sex desire as perverted or criminal. Laws which criminalized homosexuals were both a result of such repressive discourses and helped to strengthen them. Repressive discourses tend to be regulatory (see also REPRESSIVE HYPOTHESIS).

repressive hypothesis

The repressive hypothesis posits that Western societies, from the nineteenth century, have sought to suppress human sexuality and sexual urges. Foucault

(1979a) notes that although the repressive hypothesis implies large-scale censorship, in fact, it was a proliferation of discourses around the subject which suppressed human sexuality. Earlier texts on sexuality from India, China, Mesopotamia and other parts of the world indicate that human sexuality used to be discussed without shame, until around the seventeenth century.

reproduction

Reproduction is used in contrast with *transformation* in discourse analysis. Transformative discourses are those that lead to social change while reproductive discourses help to maintain the status quo. Reproduction means that established conventions are recreated and maintained, and this often happens as a result of dominant discourses achieving hegemonic status over a long period of time. Such discourses will reproduce the established conventions and maintain the status quo. However, Fairclough (1989: 39) notes that when people draw on existing orders of discourse they may use creative combinations, which can result in reproduction either being 'essentially conservative, sustaining continuity, or basically transformatory, effecting changes'.

research

Research refers to the systematic investigation of natural and social phenomena using established methods of measurement and analysis. A distinction is often made between scientific research and historical research, where scientific research involves the formulation of a hypothesis, testing (through experimentation) the hypothesis, drawing a conclusion, and making a generalization. If the findings are consistent with the hypothesis, then the experiment supports the hypothesis, and if not, then the experiment does not support the hypothesis. Historical research makes use of historical archives as sources of information which will be used as evidence. Another distinction can be made between QUALITATIVE METHODS and QUANTITATIVE METHODS of research. The former typically using detailed, non-numerical close analysis of particular case studies, while the latter measures and compares larger scale phenomena in terms of quantities (mathematical and statistical values). As a form of social research, discourse analysis often needs to take into account issues of ETHICS and may also adopt practices of REFLEXIVITY and TRIANGULATION to avoid bias.

---

research agenda

A research agenda is a program that is designed to conduct research on a particular scientific or social issue. The research agenda includes the objectives that a researcher hopes to achieve through the research and the research questions that the researcher hopes to answer. Discourse analysts can hold a range of research agendas, depending on their IDENTITY, personal interest or relationship to what is being researched as well as the kind of discourse analysis that they are undertaking. A feminist researcher engaging in CRITICAL DISCOURSE ANALYSIS, for example, may embark on a research project because he/she wants, through the research, to influence public policy to be more gender inclusive. However, a researcher who wants to examine how DISCOURSE MARKERS are used in conversation may not hope to change society, other than to advance our knowledge in a specific academic field. See also Wodak and Chilton (2005).

research interview

A tool used in qualitative research which involves the researcher asking participants questions relating to the topic being researched. The interview covers both fact and meaning levels of the interviewee's experience and is useful for obtaining an in-depth account of the research participant's life experience as well as meanings as constructed by the research participant (Kvale 1996). It also helps to clarify responses to a questionnaire. There are many types of interviews, which are often categorized according to how much freedom the researcher is given to divert from a standard procedure. For example, a *conversational* or *unstructured interview* does not follow a set pattern, and there are no preset answers for the interviewee to choose from. Such interviews follow the pattern of natural conversation and questions can be adapted to the interviewee's own needs and priorities. While such interviews often provide interesting and detailed data, they may lack focus and can be time consuming to administer. A *general guided interview* is designed to obtain information from specific topics or areas, and all interviewees are asked to talk about the same areas, although the questions may not be strictly the same. It has more focus than the unstructured interview. Similar to this is a *semi-structured interview*, where again the interviewer has a framework of themes to explore but may adapt questions as needed. *Structured interviews*, however, have a more fixed and limited set of questions. For example, a *standard open-ended interview* is designed to get quick responses from interviewees, and the same questions are asked to all the interviewees. Finally, the most structured type of interview is a *closed fixed response* interview, which consists of questions with a set of possible responses and all interviewees are asked the same questions. This interview type is both quick and easy to administer although may not provide particular rich data to analyse.

research questions

Research questions are a series of questions which identify and focus on the research phenomenon that the researcher intends to study. Research questions thus translate the objectives of the research into a set of achievable goals. Some research projects contain an overarching research question which is difficult to directly address, so it is then broken down into smaller 'operable' questions, which are linked together. A well-thought-out research question is thus answerable, not too broad, and logically leads to a hypothesis which is a prediction of the findings of the research process. Mason (2002: 20) defines research questions as 'vehicles that you will rely upon to move you from your broad research interest to your specific research focus and project'.

resistance

Resistance is a reaction by social subjects to the imposition of POWER. In every society, dominant discourses acquire hegemonic status, becoming common-sensical. However, as Foucault (1979a: 95) notes, '[W]here there is power, there is resistance'. When dominant discourses ascribe certain subject positions to social subjects, those subject positions can be taken up, affirmed or rejected. A rejection of those SUBJECT POSITIONS proffered by powerful discourses constitutes resistance. Resistance, then, emphasizes human agency and conceives power as a never-ending struggle.

resistant reader

In RECEPTION theory, a resistant reader is one who reads 'against the grain', contesting the intended meanings and subject positions that a text proffers. Unlike passive readers, resistant readers interpret texts with new, unintended meanings. For example, in the 1950s, Hollywood produced many films aimed at female audiences starring actresses like Bette Davis and Joan Crawford. These films were sometimes called 'women's films' or 'weepies' due to their (melo)dramatic content and focus on personal and romantic relationships. However, they became popular with some gay men, who engaged in a resistant reading to view them as a source of camp humour.

rewording

Rewording is a form of elaboration, when a proposition or concept is restated using a different form of words: 'Oh it's great, I love it' (BNC, JT5). It could also be called paraphrasing or relexicalization. Lexicalization is the creation of vocabulary to talk about a particular domain of life, such as business, medicine, disability, education and so on. Through vocabulary, we lexicalize our experience and construct our social life. However, domains of life can be relexicalized, and this can often be a strategy which reflects the construction of discourses. Fairclough (2003: 127) points out that in a text written by two members of the British Labour Party, the term 'transnational companies' is reworded as 'transnational capital' and 'international capital', which suggests the authors are making a relation of equivalence between the concrete concept of 'companies' and the abstract concept of 'capital', as part of a Marxist discourse.

Rewording can also be used to challenge discourses. For example, in Botswana traditional words which were used to talk about disability have been challenged by new words. Terms like *segole* (cripple), *sefofu* (that which is blind) and *semumu* (that which is dumb) have been replaced by expressions such as *monalebogole* (one who has disability), *motlhokapono* (one who has no sight) and *motlhokapuo* (one who has no speech), respectively, reflecting and constructing a more sensitive attitude towards people with disabilities. The latter set of words use human reference compared to the older words, which referred to such people using nonhuman terms. Rewording strategies may not always be successful at changing discourses, particularly if the mainstream discourse is very strong. For example, Pinker (1994) conceives of a 'euphemism treadmill', whereby new terms continually needed to be coined, in place of older ones which quickly require negative meanings, despite being initially devised with good intentions (see OVERWORDING, POLITICAL CORRECNTESS, RECLAIMING).

rheme

A distinction can be made between a THEME, which constitutes a topic, and the rheme, which is what is said about the topic (sometimes called the focus). Although the distinction dates back to the nineteenth century, it was used by Halliday in his SYSTEMIC FUNCTION LINGUISTICS.

sampling

Sampling refers to selection of data in terms of the scope and depth of coverage. When one is carrying out research into language use, it is often infeasible to be able to collect every single example of language from a particular population or dataset. Instead, sampling involves taking a smaller amount of data which is hoped to be representative in some way of the larger population. One method of obtaining the research sample is through random or *probability sampling*, where participants or data are picked at random. This contrasts with *systematic sampling* where the sample is obtained by selecting elements at regular intervals. Another method is *stratified sampling* by which data are selected on the basis of preset criteria in order to reflect the make-up of the population more closely. For example, if a country has 80% of its population under the age of 18, then we might want to sample 400 people from this age group and only 100 people aged above 18.

Sapir–Whorf Hypothesis

The term is named after two linguists, Benjamin Lee Whorf (1897–1941) and Edward Sapir (1884–1939). It holds that the language that people speak determines how they view the world. This view has also been referred to as linguistic determinism or linguistic relativity (see RELATIVISM). Whorf used examples from many Native American Languages as evidence to prove that different cultural concepts inherent in the structures of different languages order the ways that people experience the world. For example, the Hopi language has two different words for water depending on whether the water is in a container or whether it is a natural body, like in a lake. Most western cultures do not make this distinction and only have one word.

scare quotes

Scare quotes are quotation marks that are used to separate the voice of the author from other voices in a text. They therefore can be markers of INTERTEXTUALITY. There may be a variety of reasons why the author wishes to do this, rather than simply attributing a quote to someone else; indeed, the author may not be directly quoting anyone. Scare quotes could be used to question some aspect of a word or phrase, signifying that the author does not agree with it or is aware that others may not agree with it. Or they may be applied in order to show a new usage of an existing term or the introduction of a new term (see Fairclough 1992: 119–120).

schema

A schema (plural schemata or schemas) is information that is stored as packages in our long-term memories which we then use to interpret and understand social phenomena. Around any topic or event, we have a schema or mental model comprising of a set of assumptions and expectations about what that thing is like. For example, we know how to conduct ourselves when we go to a funeral because we have, in our memories, knowledge of what a funeral is, what it involves and how people usually behave in a funeral. See also FRAMES, SCRIPTS. See also Schank and Abelson (1977).

scripts

Scripts are schemata (see SCHEMA) that are ordered sequentially. Schema theory distinguishes between these sequentially ordered schemata and non-sequentially ordered schemata (FRAMES) (Minsky 1975). Scripts thus contain assumptions which involve the order in which things should happen. For example, in a church, a Sunday service starts with a prayer followed by announcements and then other rituals. The key event, the sermon, then follows and so on (depending on which church each individual is familiar with). Frame assumptions, however, include what a church service is about, who is responsible for what activity, who gives the sermon (pastor, priest) and who confesses and to whom.

second-wave feminism

In the West, the 'second wave' of the Feminist movement, sometimes referred to as the Women's Liberation movement, began in the 1960s and continued into the 1970s. It is contrasted with first-wave feminism, which involved the struggle to give voting and property rights to women in the nineteenth and early twentieth century, and third-wave feminism, which is defined as the period from about 1990 to the present day (see also POST-FEMINISM). Second-wave feminism was concerned with a range of issues including

SEXISM and sexist power structures, the notion of the woman as the 'other' in patriarchal society, media representation of women and legal battles around abortion, rape, divorce, sexuality, education and the workplace. It was during second-wave feminism that research on WOMEN'S LANGUAGE became popular.

self-disclosure

Self-disclosure is the act of revealing personal information about oneself to others such as work colleagues or friends. This can be a conscious or unconscious act. Self-disclosure is viewed by some as threatening, especially when one encounters a stranger. However, it is believed to be an important aspect of cultivating intimate relationships between friends or partners. In professional settings, such as counselling and doctor–patient interactions, it is the client and patient, respectively, who self-disclose while the counsellor or doctor listens. Self-disclosure, particularly in counselling, is regarded as a core part of therapy, where just talking helps the client to deal with his or her pain. Self-disclosure could be seen as an aspect of INFORMALIZATION of discourse, and it can also signal asymmetrical power relations as it is only the vulnerable party that discloses personal information about himself/herself (see Fairclough (1992) in his discussion of doctor–patient interaction).

semantic field

A semantic field refers to a set of words belonging to the same conceptual area. They are not synonymous, but they are related to each other (Lyons 1977). For example, *acupuncture*, *physiotherapy*, *dialysis* and *chemotherapy* are terms that belong to the semantic field of medicine.

semantic preference

Stubbs (2001: 65) describes semantic preference as 'the relation, not between individual words, but between a lemma or word form and a set of semantically related words'. Semantic preference can therefore be thought of as an extension of COLLOCATION. For example, collocates of the word *cup* in the British

National Corpus include *tea*, *coffee* and *coca-cola*, suggesting that *cup* holds a semantic preference for drinks. However, an additional set of collocates for *cup* – *FA*, *UEFA*, *world*, *semi-final*, *qualifier*, *gold*, *finalists* – are words which refer to sports matches (normally football), where a trophy is awarded to the winner. These two semantic preferences indicate the polysemious nature of *cup* – as a drinking receptacle and as a sporting trophy. Semantic preferences, unlike SEMANTIC PROSODIES or DISCOURSE PROSODIES, do not normally reveal attitudes, and Stubbs (2001: 66) suggests that semantic preferences tend to involve sets of words that are finite, while discourse prosodies can be more open ended.

semantic prosody

Semantic prosody was popularized by Louw's (1993) paper on irony and is linked to the concept of COLLOCATION. Louw noted that irony tends to rely on a collocative clash; in other words, a writer will deviate from using expected collocates for ironic effect. For example, Louw (1993: 164) quotes this sentence from the novel *Small World* by David Lodge:

> The modern conference resembles the pilgrimage of medieval Christendon in that it allows the participants to indulge themselves in all the pleasures and diversions of travel while apparently *bent* on self-improvement.

Louw points out that the word *bent* normally tends to occur in negative situations, collocating with words like *destroying*, *harrying* and *mayhem*. He suggests then that, in using *bent* with the positive term *self-improvement*, the author is being ironic, implying that the participants of a conference are not really concerned with self-improvement. While semantic prosody seems to involve collocates, a related term is Stubbs' DISCOURSE PROSODY, which involves longer stretches of discourse which have similar meanings collocating with particular words. In addition, while semantic prosody suggests an attitude, SEMANTIC PREFERENCE does not.

semantic relations

Semantic relations are relations that exist between two (or more) meanings or concepts (Lyons 1977). A wide range of different types of semantic relations exist. For example, polysemy refers to the ability of a word, phrase or sign to have multiple meanings although the meanings have the same etymology. So the word *bed* is polysemious because it can refer to something we sleep on or the bottom of a river. A similar concept is homonymy, although here the different meanings also have different etymologies. Synonymy means that different words may have equivalent meanings. For example, the words *glad* and *pleased* could be said to be synonyms. Antonymy refers to meaning relations that are oppositional, for example, *black/white*. Hyponymy is a meaning relation that expresses hierarchical order of concepts and class membership of concepts. For example, the concept of *human* subsumes the concepts *man*, *boy*, *woman*, *girl* as subordinate concepts.

semantic role

A semantic role defines the relationship between a participant in a CLAUSE and the main verb of the clause. For example, the semantic role of agent means that the participant (agent) is the doer of the action expressed by the main verb of the clause.

Example
   Carol kissed Mary.

'Carol' is the agent or doer of the action expressed by the main verb 'hit'. 'Mary', however, has the semantic role of goal. That means that Mary is the recipient of the action expressed by the main verb 'kiss'. See also Kreidler (1998: 66).

sentence types

Sentences can be classified into a number of different types, depending on their syntactic structure and the communicative functions that they perform (see Verspoor and Sauter 2000). English, for example, includes declarative, interrogative, imperative and exclamatory sentence types. A declarative sentence type is structured as a statement (The sky is blue).

An interrogative sentence type is structured as a question and is used in order to get information from someone (Do you love football?) An imperative type is often structured with a main verb in the base form and is used to issue orders or directives (Get out of my house.) Finally, an exclamatory sentence type usually takes the form of a sudden, forceful expression (My God!)

Sentences can also be defined in terms of the number of CLAUSES they have and the relationships between the clauses. A simple sentence contains only one clause. A compound sentence has two or more clauses of equal grammatical status (see PARATAXIS). A complex sentence contains more than one clause, but the clauses are not grammatically equal (see HYPOTAXIS, SUBORDINATION), with one being the main or independent clause, while the others are subordinate. A main clause can stand alone as a complete sentence, while a subordinate clause only forms a sentence fragment.

Examples

I broke my knee [one clause, simple sentence].

I fell and broke my knee [two clauses, of equal status, compound sentence].

When I fell, I broke my knee [two clauses separated by a comma, the second is a main clause and the first is a subordinate clause, complex sentence].

sex

1. Sex refers to the biological make-up of living things which determines their reproductive functions. A distinction is made between male sex and female sex, although there are rare instances where one can be born having both male and female characteristics (sometimes referred to as being intersexed). Sometimes the term GENDER is used as a 'polite' equivalent of sex. See also BIOLOGICAL SEX.
2. Sex is also used in everyday language to refer to a wide variety of sexual acts or behaviour (for either reproduction or pleasure).

sexism

Sexism refers to discrimination against people on the basis of their SEX. It tends to reflect the belief that one sex is inferior in some way to the other.

In language, this can include a range of practices such as using gendered terms which denigrate a particular sex (like *bitch*), labelling certain jobs in order to normalize them to one sex (*fireman, policeman, charwoman*) as well as specifically marking cases believed to be exceptional (*lady doctor, male prostitute*). Sexism can be embedded in language systems – for example, in English, adult males are normally referred to as *Mr*, whereas adult females are referred to as *Miss* if they are unmarried and *Mrs* if they are married. The language system forces women to reveal their marital status, whereas men do not (an alternative term *Ms* was proposed as an equivalent to *Mr* but is still relatively rare). Sexism may also involve exclusion (such as a generic term like *industrial man*) or the use of generalizing or stereotyping remarks about males or females:

> Laura took several sips. Her face was screwed up with grief. 'Is John looking after Margaret and Rose?' John was Laura's husband, Margaret and Rose their two-year-old twins. 'He offered. But he's so useless with them, typical man! I thought it best I leave them with a neighbour'. (BNC, AN7)

Forms of sexual objectification, through inappropriate use of terms like *honey, sweetheart* and so on (e.g. in a workplace context), could be viewed as sexism. Sexism can also be enshrined in law (such as laws which have not allowed women to vote or hold certain jobs) and can involve acts of violence (e.g. women are more likely to be killed or violently attacked by their male partners than vice versa). See also NON-SEXIST LANGUAGE. See also Mills (2008).

sexist discourse

Sexist discourse refers to ways of representing people stereotypically, which leads to their marginalization or social exclusion on the basis of their sex. A discourse that represents women as 'domestic' is sexist because it constructs them in roles that exclude them from participating in public enterprises, such as formal employment, business and politics.

sexual harassment

Sexual harassment can be perpetrated by or directed at males or females, and it is often related to abuse of power or expressions of dominance. It consists of verbal or nonverbal messages relating to a person's sexuality or gender that are physically or emotionally threatening and/or intimidating (see Mumby and Clair 1997). On an individual level, it can involve a suggestive remark which might be framed as a joke, but it could also include attempts to coerce someone into a sexual relationship, perhaps in return for a reward, or it could involve an actual sexual assault.

Sexual harassment can also be seen as a more pervasive practice in which the threatening messages are directed not so much at individual persons but at a particular social group such as women. Mumby and Clair (1997) assert that sexual harassment is a social reality at both the micro-level and macro-levels of society, with the micro-level supporting the macro-level and the macro-legitimating acts of sexual harassment against some members of the society.

sexual identity

The term sexual identity is used to define a number of IDENTITY traits. At one level, sexual identity is used to define a person's biological characteristics. At another level, it is used to define sexual orientation (sometimes called sexual preference); that is, it defines the extent to which a person is attracted to people of the same sex or people of the opposite sex (or both or neither). Sexual identity may also refer to aspects of sexual desire that are not configured around the BIOLOGICAL SEX of the desired partner. For example, an S/M practitioner may base her sexual identity around desire to engage in S/M, and whether her partners are male or female may be secondary. Sexual identity can thus involve reference to sexual desire and/or sexual behaviour.

shared knowledge

This refers to knowledge about the world which two or more people possess and which enable them to understand and live in harmony with each other. People who belong to the same culture, community of practice, family and so on have large amounts of shared knowledge about how things are done, along with mutual beliefs and ideologies, which enables them to work together and to minimize conflict or misunderstandings.

sign

Sign theory was founded by Saussure (see, for example, Saussure 1966). Signs are entities that represent other entities. They are used to make meaning out of our experience of the world. For example, a comma is a sign that signifies a pause in a sentence, and an exclamation mark signifies different emotions such as surprise and anger. The words of any language are signs. They get their meanings (or signification) through convention. For example, in English, the word *cat* signifies a feline animal that is kept as a pet. Signs are made up of two parts, the signifier (the form of representation such as words on a page, a sound or a picture) and the signified (the mental concept that the signifier represents).

A distinction can be made between natural signs and conventional signs. Natural signs represent something that occurs in nature. For example, a fever could be a sign of malaria or another ailment. Conventional signs are those that get meaning by agreement. For example, the word *table* signifies a piece of household furniture. The relationship between the signifier and signified here is said to be arbitrary. There is nothing 'natural' that connects the sound 'table' to the physical entity it signifies. If there was, all languages would use the same word for table. Signs can have both a denotative meaning and one or more connotative meanings (depending on particular contexts). The denotative meaning of a word is normally a non-evaluative description (such as a dictionary definition), whereas a connotative meaning is often more subjective, evaluative and non-literal. For example, the denotative meaning of *owl* would be a nocturnal bird of prey. The connotative meaning of *owl*, however, could involve the notion of wisdom. (See CONNOTATION.) POST-STRUCTURALIST theorists like Derrida (1978) have claimed that the relationship between signifiers and signifieds is not fixed forever but is instead discursively constructed and can change over time.

silence

Silence is a lack of articulation or voice. A discourse analyst would be interested in understanding the context in which silence occurs as well as examining wider societal and cultural norms. For example, by looking at the immediate context of a particular interaction, we would ascertain whether a person's silence was due to them not hearing someone's utterance or due to sulking, impoliteness, agreement or something else. A CONVERSATION ANALYSIS approach would consider how other participants orient to a person's silence.

However, other discourse analysts might consider the context of silence in other ways. For example, silence can be a result of 'silencing' which is in turn a result of certain practices that discourage speaking or where linguistic assertiveness is stigmatized. For example, in some cultures such as the Setswana culture in Botswana, women are not expected to speak in a kgotla (a public meeting place) and young people are not allowed to 'talk back' when they are chastised by adults. These cultural norms lead to silencing and disempowerment of particular groups.

Yet, in other contexts, silence can indicate POWER. For example, a person or organization who refuses to acknowledge or engage with an interlocutor may be demonstrating that they do not consider them important or relevant enough to warrant a response. See also Thiesmeyer (2003).

similes

A simile is a form of comparison in which one entity is expressed in terms of another through the use of an explicit similarity marker such as 'like' or 'as'.

You're saying space is like a wobbly jelly?. (BNC, FNW)

Similes are similar to metaphors, although with similes the two entities are marked as being distinct from each other, whereas with metaphors this is not the case. Both similes and METAPHORS are of interest to discourse analysts in that they involve ways of representing things which can indicate traces of particular discourses.

social action

Social action theory was developed by Max Weber who wrote, 'Action is social in so far as . . . it takes account of the behaviour of others and is therefore oriented in its course' (Weber 1947: 88). An example of social action would be language. We can classify social actions into purposeful rationality (where a goal and the means used to achieve it are rationally decided), value-oriented rationality (where the goal may not be rational but the means used to achieve it is rational), affective action (which are actions that occur due to our emotions, such as crying at a funeral) and traditional actions (actions which are guided by age-old customs).

social actors

Social actors are participants in clauses, who may be represented as subjects (agents) or objects (goals) in the clause. Fairclough (2003: 145–150) distinguishes between those elements of the clause which may be subjects or objects but not social actors. For example, John is eating an apple.

'John' is a social actor represented as the agent of the material action of eating. Apple is the goal of that material action. However, 'apple' is not a social actor as it cannot act on its own volition. In other words, it is inanimate and nonhuman, so it cannot be a social actor. Social actors are normally animate and/or human, but can include groups or abstract entities like 'council' or 'community'. And sometimes, however, inanimate objects or abstract concepts can be represented as if they have agency.

> The rules demanded that a hundred games had to be played within 24 hours; there was no time for sleep and only 20-minute breaks were allowed for snacks. (BNC, A89)

In this example, the rules are represented as 'demanding' various requirements, which has the effect of giving the rules agency, rather than acknowledging the humans who invented the rules (see also IMPERSONALIZATION).

Analysis of the representation of social actors includes concerns with whether they are included or excluded in the representational clause. Social actors can be excluded, a phenomenon called SUPPRESSION, or mentioned but having to be inferred in one or more places (BACKGROUNDING the social actor). See also van Leeuwen (1996).

social change

Social change refers to variation in the structure of society that results from social STRUGGLE. In every society, different discourses 'combine under particular social conditions to produce a new complex discourse' (Fairclough 1992: 4). Social change occurs because the struggle against dominant or hegemonic discourses has been successful. This may result in changes in the ways that particular people are treated or represented, changes to laws, social structures or changes to attitudes or norms.

social class

This term refers to the way in which society is structured by placing different people in different groups according to their economic, cultural and some-times ethnic characteristics. Class, from a Marxist perspective, is a system that classifies people according to whether they own property. Those who have no property have to work for those who own property, a condition which Marx believes is harmful to the society. A conservative view would hold that social class divisions are essential to society and inevitable. In some contexts, social class can be difficult to define and may depend on different types of CAPITAL related to behaviours, attitudes, background and education rather than material aspects like economic status or ownership of property. For example, an unemployed PhD graduate may have a much smaller amount of money to live on than a builder but is likely to be considered to be of a 'higher' social class. Variationist sociolinguists like Labov (1966) have used the concept of social class in order to differentiate aspects of language use such as accent or lexical choice. Generally, working-class people have been found to use local accents or dialects, whereas middle-class people tend to use standard forms of language.

social cohesion

Social cohesion refers to a range of social phenomena that bring together people and cement their relationship to form one unit. Social cohesion is usually relevant when there is some sort of diversity in society (ethnic, religious, sexual, economic etc.) that can potentially cause discord.

social constructionism

This refers to the ways we understand the world which are historically and culturally determined (Burr 1995). Social constructionist theorists are critical of ESSENTIALISM by arguing that there is nothing natural about our perception of reality. For example, our view of how men and women, girls and boys, adults and children should behave has nothing to do with their 'nature' but everything to do with social, cultural, economic and historical circumstances. We understand our world not because of the nature or essence of that world but because we interpret the world through the discourses that are available to us. Social interaction, especially linguistic interaction, is seen as having the greatest influence on how our versions of reality are shaped.

social identity

Social identity refers to the socially constructed attributes that are ascribed to individuals by themselves or others. Examples of social identities include labels which reference familial relations (*mother*), occupations (*nurse*), hierarchical roles (*boss*), religion (*Muslim*), sexuality (*gay*), region (*northerner*) and age (*pensioner*). People thus possess multiple social identities, which change throughout their lives and are understood differently by different people. Social identities are constructed via discourses which proffer SUBJECT POSITIONS which people may take up or reject. Hogg and Abrams (1999: 7) note that 'Social identity theory is a product of postwar European social psychology, and so its development cannot properly be understood without knowing something about the development of European social psychology'. See IDENTITY.

socially constitutive

Socially constitutive refers to the state of being able to influence or shape how society is structured. Fairclough (1993, 1995) theorises that texts, language use and discourses are socially constitutive – they contribute towards the constitution of various aspects of society or culture by creating systems of knowledge, social subjects and the relationships between them. However, this is a two-way process. So language is not only socially constitutive but it is also socially determined. Societies help to shape languages, for example, by determining which concepts are named. So the *Mr/Miss/Mrs* term of address system in English both reflects and constructs societal views about gender. Therefore, society and discourse or society and language are mutually constitutive.

social practice

A social practice is a body of structured, usually institutionalized, activities mediated through language. For example, politics, the media and the law are social practices that have language as an integral part of those practices. Language itself is a social practice because it is an intrinsic part of a society. Fairclough (2001: 122) notes that a social practice has the following elements: productive activity, means of production, involves social relations, social identities, cultural values, consciousness and semiosis. These do not occur as discrete and autonomous entities but are all 'dialectically' related; the different elements of a social practice shape each other. Social practice is one dimension of Fairclough's three-dimensional conception of discourse (the other two being TEXT and DISCURSIVE PRACTICE).

social relations

Social relations are relationships that occur between different social actors, such as doctor–patient, counsellor–client, student–teacher and mother–child. Social relations are constructed, contested and restructured through discourse.

socio-cognitive approach

An approach to carrying out CRITICAL DISCOURSE ANALYSIS developed by Teun Van Dijk (1998, 2001) which makes explicit the link between discourse, cognition and society. In practice, it involves the analysis of topics (or macrostructures), local meanings (relating to phenomena such as word choice), context models and mental models (involving knowledge, attitudes and ideologies) and the relationship between discourse and society. Van Dijk (2001: 118) describes his approach as a 'permanent bottom-up and top-down linkage of discourse and interaction with social structures'.

sociolinguistics

Wardhaugh (2005: 1) describes sociolinguistics as 'the relationship between language and society, although Labov (1972b: 183) notes that the term is 'oddly redundant' because language and linguistics are *always social*. Bloome and Green (2002: 396) stress the dialectical nature of sociolinguistics by noting that '[a] sociolinguistic perspective requires exploring how language is used to establish a social context while simultaneously exploring how the social context influences language use and the communication of meaning'.

Sociolinguists are therefore often interested in identifying how the IDENTITY of a person or social group relates to the way that they use language. For example, they may look at linguistic differences (and similarities) between (and within) certain types or groups of people or attempt to determine the ways that social variables, such as age, sex, social class or level of education (either alone or in combination with other variables), impact on language use. Some sociolinguists focus on why certain languages (or aspects of language) become popular while others fall into disuse. This could be done by either carrying out a detailed, small-scale study of a small group or community, looking at social networks and focusing on the role of 'language innovators' or by focusing a much larger population, relating aspects of language uptake (or decline) to various social contexts. Other sociolinguists consider particular contexts, such as doctor–patient interactions, while others still examine attitudes or beliefs about language, looking at why some forms of language are viewed as 'better' or 'worse' than others and what impacts such views have on different types of people and language use itself. See also Meyerhoff (2006).

somatization

van Leeuwen (1996: 60) defines somatization as being a type of objectivation. It uses a metonymic reference to label a person or group with reference to some place or thing that is closely associated with them or an activity they engage in. Resigl and Wodak (2001: 48) use the term in reference to RACIST DIS-COURSE, listing somatonyms such as *whites, paleface, slit-eyes* and *bush negros.*

spatialization

See IMPERSONALIZATION.

speaking

An acronym devised by Dell Hymes (1974) which refers to a model which shows the components that need to be taken into account before someone can use language in a particular social context. These include

Setting (time and place) and scene (cultural aspects)
Participants (the speaker, the audience and relationship between the two)
Ends (purposes, goals and outcomes)
Act sequence (form and order)
Key (tone, manner or spirit)
Instrumentalities (forms and styles of speech)
Norms (social rules)
Genre (the kind of speech act or event)

specification

A way of representing social actors as specific cases (as opposed to GENERICIZATION).

van Leeuwen (1996: 47) notes that in middle-class newspapers, government agents and experts are referred to specifically and ordinary people are referred to generically (while the reverse is the case for working-class newspapers).

speech act

Speech acts are utterances which perform various social functions such as requesting, greeting, advising, complaining, warning and so on (see also SPEECH ACT THEORY). Austin (1962: 101) classified three types of speech act:

1. Locutionary act – the actual utterance and its ostensible meaning
2. Illocutionary act – the real meaning that the speaker intended
3. Perlocutionary act – the actual effect of the speech act, whether it was intended by the speaker or not

Searle (1975) classified illocutionary speech acts into the following taxonomy:

Assertives – acts that commit the speaker to the truth of a proposition
Directives – acts that cause the hearer to do something
Commissives – acts that commit the speaker to do something in the future
Expressives – acts that express the speaker's feelings towards something
Declarations – acts that change reality (such as baptizing, pronouncing someone guilty etc.)

speech act theory

Austin (1962) theorized that when people talk they are performing actions with their words. They are doing things such as warning, promising, marrying, proposing, inviting and so on. When a priest says 'I pronounce you husband and wife' to a couple before him/her, then he/she is performing the act of marrying the couple. As long as certain FELICITY CONDITIONS are met, the performative act creates a new reality. Searle (1969, 1975) defined a classification system of speech acts as well as introducing the notion of indirect speech acts by showing that a single utterance could contain more than one type of speech act, a primary one which is indirect and not literally performed and a secondary one which is direct and is performed in the literal utterance of the sentence. For example,

Hugh: I wish I was at Toys R Us.
Paul: OK, I'll take you.

Here, the primary act of the speaker (a child) is to persuade Paul (an adult) to take him to Toys R Us and buy him a toy. The secondary act is simply the literal statement of wishing to be at Toys R Us.

SPEECH ACT THEORY helped to inspire Butler's theory of GENDER PERFORMATIVITY.

speech community

The term speech community has been traced back to Bloomfield (1926: 153–154): 'Within certain communities successive utterances are alike or partly alike . . . Any such community is a speech community'. It was also used by early sociolinguists like Gumperz (1968), Hymes (1972) and Labov (1973). Speech communities have been associated with forms of language that are learnt from a community that one grows up in (and are passed on via inheritance or adoption). This is in opposition to a DISCOURSE COMMUNITY, which involves shared language use based around a particular formal or informal social group (such as an email list, a dance club or a law firm).

Speech communities thus involve shared community membership and shared linguistic communication. However, there is disagreement over the extent to which these two factors play a role in defining speech communities. Most societies contain multiple speech communities, and it could be argued that people can belong to more than one speech community. See also COMMUNITY OF PRACTICE.

stereotypes

Kunda (1999: 315) views stereotypes as 'mental representations of social categories'. Stereotypes reduce a person or group to a small number of vivid, easily grasped traits, which are often exaggerated, frequently negative, and enable the solidification of differences between in and out groups. Some members of a social group may possess certain traits (and those same traits may also occur in other social groups), but with stereotyping, these traits become an essential, naturalized feature of a particular group. For example, some gay men talk in a 'camp' voice, but many gay men do not (and some heterosexual men have a camp voice). However, the camp voice has become a stereotype associated with being gay, perhaps because camp-voiced gay men are much more 'different' and thus visible than gay men who do not have a camp voice. Comedians who want to index homosexuality will put on a 'camp voice'. The trait therefore becomes associated with all gay men and is disassociated from heterosexual men.

So stereotyping deploys a strategy of splitting by excluding or expelling everything which does not fit. Dyer (1977: 29) writes that '. . . boundaries . . . must be clearly delineated and so stereotypes, one of the mechanisms of boundary maintenance, are characteristically fixed, clear-cut, unalterable'. Hall's (1997: 223–279) discussion of the stereotyping of racial IDENTITY in the 18th and 19th centuries notes how black people were represented in terms of a few supposedly essential characteristics, a strategy designed to fix difference and thus secure it forever. 'Laziness, simple fidelity, mindless "cooning", trickery, childishness belonged to blacks as a race, as a species. There was nothing else to the kneeling slave but his servitude; nothing to Uncle Tom except his Christian forbearing; nothing to Mammy but her fidelity to the white household – and . . . her "sho" nuff good cooking' (ibid.: 245). Stereotyping tends to occur when there are inequalities of POWER and can lead to social exclusion.

structuralism

Structuralism is an intellectual movement in which all phenomena are viewed as having inherent underlying structures or systems. In linguistics, structuralism is associated with the Swiss linguist Ferdinand de Saussure who viewed language as having an underlying structure. Structuralists tended to focus on the structure of language at a particular moment in time (synchronically), rather than looking at how and why languages change (diachronically). They also viewed SIGNS as deriving meaning through differences to other signs, especially in relation to binary opposites. For example, we understand what is meant by the term *woman* by comparing it to what it is not – *man*. Similarly white is not black, good is not bad and so on. Structuralism has been criticized, especially by discourse analysts (see Baxter 2003, 2008) who argue that seeing the meaning of concepts as consisting of binary opposites tends to set up one of the concepts as the norm and the other as deviant or derivative. Structuralism has also been criticized for being asocial as it tends not focus on the way language is actually used by its speakers.

struggle

Struggle refers to a tension that results from one social group resisting the power and control of another social group or institution. Theories of discourse argue that different discourses and SOCIAL PRACTICES occur in competing and contradictory relationships. The tension between oppositional discourses and practices is a result of a struggle for HEGEMONY. Marginal discourses struggle against mainstream, powerful and hegemonic discourses. The struggle is successful when previously marginalized discourses and practices successfully penetrate and change the dominant discourses, resulting in social change. Fairclough (1989: 34) relates social struggle to the concepts of power relations and class relations.

style

Style refers to the manner of doing things. From a linguistic perspective, there are three views of style: the dualist view, the monist view and the pluralist view (Short 1996; Leech and Short 2007). The dualist view sees form and meaning as separate and defines style as a dress of thought. The monist view sees style (form) and meaning as inseparable and that a choice of form is simultaneously a choice of meaning. The pluralist view claims that 'language performs a number of different functions, and any piece of language is likely to be the result of choices made on different functional levels' (Leech and Short 2007: 24).

Carter and Nash (1990: 15), however, point out that style 'cannot be explained by reference to only one level of language such as grammar and vocabulary'. Fairclough (2009: 164) also defines styles as being related to 'identities or ways of being', pointing out that 'being a "manager" in the currently fashionable way in business or in universities is partly a matter of developing the right semiotic style' (Fairclough 2009: 164).

stylistics

Stylistics is the linguistic study of STYLE. It focuses on examining varieties and properties of language, looking at the principles behind elements such as register, accent, dialogue, grammar, accent, sentence length and so on. Short (1996: 5) notes that stylistics is 'concerned with relating linguistic facts (linguistic description) to meaning (interpretation) in as *explicit* a way as possible' and is thus 'the logical extension of practical criticism' (ibid.: 6).

subject

A subject is one of two main phrasal constituents of a CLAUSE (the other one being the PREDICATE). The subject relates to other elements in a sentence (such as the OBJECT) via a VERB.

Subjects can consist of bare noun phrases (*Men* are working here), determiners with noun phrases (*The girl* went home), gerunds (*Walking* is painful), full clauses (*That she didn't like me* was known to everyone), an infinitive construction (*To lose one's child* is a difficult thing) or the word *it* (*It*'s raining; *it* was known that she didn't like me). Subjects are identified via flow of information, word order and their importance in a sentence. Sometimes subjects can be confused with actors or agents (see AGENCY). Consider the following sentence extract:

Bobby Robson was surrounded by players and coaches. (BNC, A4P)

This sentence is in the passive voice so *Bobby Robson* is the subject, but the actor is *players and coaches*. If the extract was reworded as an active sentence, 'players and coaches surrounded Bobby Robson', then both the subject and actor would be *players and coaches*.

subject position

Davies and Harré (1990: 48) define positioning as 'the discursive process whereby selves are located in conversations as observably and subjectively coherent participants in jointly produced storylines. There can be interactive positioning in which what one person says positions another, and there can be reflexive positioning in which one positions oneself'. Therefore, in discourse, social actors or individuals are ascribed certain roles and identities which are referred to as subject positions. For example, if a man refers to a woman as 'honey', then he is positioning her in a certain way. He could be suggesting that she is desirable or be implying that he has or would like to have a more intimate relationship with her. He may also be positioning her as inferior to him. The woman could respond in a way which confirms the subject position, or she could challenge it, for example, 'I'm not your honey'. Individuals occupy multiple subject positions at various points (e.g. parent, boss, teacher, social activist) depending on the SOCIAL PRACTICE they are involved in and its related discourses (Hutcheon 1989, Jørgensen and Phillips 2002, Baxter 2003).

subjectivity

From a western humanist perspective, subjectivity is a term that is used to describe the relationship between the individual and his/her environment which sees the individual as a unique and autonomous entity (Hutcheon 1989, Jørgensen and Phillips 2002). This view has been criticised by postmodernists who see subjectivities as being constructed through discourse (see SUBJECT POSITION).

subordination

1. In English traditional grammar, subordination refers to a transformational process of joining two clauses to form a complex sentence. One of the clauses is a main or independent CLAUSE and the other is a dependent, embedded or subordinate clause. For example,

I enjoyed doing this because it took people by surprise. (BNC, A06)

In the example above, the sentence is made up of two clauses: 'I enjoyed doing this' is a main clause, while 'because it took people by surprise' is a subordinate clause. The subordinate clause cannot stand on its own as a sentence.

2. Subordination also refers to the construction of certain members of a society as not having equal social status as others. Connell's theory of HEGEMONIC MASCULINITY (1995) views groups in society as subordinating each other, for example, heterosexual men subordinate women and gay men.

substitution

A technique of COHESION whereby a word or phrase which has already been encountered in a text is substituted by another word:

Helen: Can you get me the flan tin down there . . .
Clare: Do you want the bigger one?
Helen: No that one will do. (BNC, KCD)

In the above example, the word *one* substitutes the term *flan tin*. See also ANAPHORA. See also Halliday and Hasan (1976).

subversion/subversive discourses

This term describes acts of dismantling established conventions and traditional taken-for-granted assumptions about how the world works. Subversion is often related to power relations. For example, the RECLAIMING of previously abusive terms such as *nigger* and *queer* is a subversive strategy. Dominant or hegemonic discourses, especially those which involve subordination of certain groups, are likely to produce subversive discourses. As Foucault (1979a) notes, wherever there is power, there is also resistance. For example, the discourses that created the homosexual as a 'deviant' sexual category also provided a lexicon for articulating resistance: '[H]omosexuality began to speak in its own behalf, to demand that its legitimacy or "naturality" be acknowledged often using the same categories by which it was medically disqualified' (Foucault 1979a: 101).

suppression

A form of social actor EXCLUSION, which according to van Leeuwen (1996: 39) is the lack of reference to a social actor anywhere in a particular text. A typical way that this is realized is via passive agent deletion, for example, 'Complaints were made to us about certain members of our staff (who, incidentally, no longer work for us) going into unoccupied floors to make love' (BNC, A6V). In this example, we do not know who made the complaints. See also AGENCY, BACKGROUNDING.

synchronic studies

Synchronic studies refer to the study of language 'frozen' in time. A synchronic study of language may focus on a single population, or it may compare language use across different types of speakers (such as American English vs. Indian English or young vs. old people). This approach has been associated with a structuralist perspective. See also DIACHRONIC STUDIES.

synthetic personalization

A term coined by Fairclough (1989) to describe a way of tailoring interactions that are directed towards a public mass audience so that every member of the audience feels that they are being personally addressed. Fairclough (1989: 62) gives examples from 'air travel (*have a nice day!*) [and] restaurants (*Welcome to Wimpy!*)'. Synthetic personalization uses techniques of CONVERSATIONALIZATION in order to give the appearance of substance to a relationship.

systemic functional grammar (SFG)/linguistics

SFG is a model of grammar that was developed by Michael Halliday (1961, 1978), who was influenced by John Firth. It is an approach to linguistic description which aims to provide a comprehensive account of how language is used in context for communication. Halliday began developing the theory in the 1960s. The 'systemic' part views language as a network of systems, whereas the 'functional' part is concerned with the actual uses that language is put to in real-life contexts (as opposed to viewing language as an abstract system). SFG analyses language in terms of semantics, phonology and lexico-grammar (the relationship between structures and words). Halliday also views language as having three meta-functions: ideational, interpersonal and textual.

SFG was influential in the development of CRITICAL LINGUISTICS (Fowler et al. 1979) and later CRITICAL DISCOURSE ANALYSIS (Fairclough 1989). Halliday's model was used to show how grammatical systems and phenomena can be used in order to achieve particular social functions.

tabloidization

This refers to the phenomenon arising in the media where news is presented in a more personalized, emotive, simplistic and 'populist' format, contrasting with formats which attempt to be more fact oriented and devoid of emotion. Tabloidization is characterized by the use of personalized and often simplified narratives. For example, a news article about a murder may include pictures of the victim and his/her family as well as revealing graphic details about the murder. The victim may be evaluated in positive ways, which emphasize the tragedy and waste of life. The killer, if caught, may be described as a *monster* or with adjectives like *evil*, and the coverage may try to explain the murder in a simple way such as it being linked to taking drugs or watching horror films. The story may evoke a range of emotional states: empathy, sympathy, fear and outrage. Tabloidization has sometimes been called 'dumbing down', another aspect of it being a move away from political and international news and a move towards stories which focus on the lives of individuals from the entertainment industry, celebrities or other people who are not associated with politics. However, tabloidization can be associated with particular political agendas, for example, nationalism. A similar term *tabloidese* is referred to as 'downgrading of hard news and upgrading of sex, scandal and infotainment' (Watson and Hill 2000: 307). Conboy (2006: 212) argues that '[t]abloidization is too complex a phenomenon to judge as a single entity and too fraught with questions of taste and commercialism for simple judgements on its quality. It can be considered as a lowering of the standards of idealized journalism or as a re-orientation of popular national markets within globalized competition for news within wider media markets'.

tag question

A way of turning an utterance into a question by 'tagging' an interrogative fragment at the end. Typically fragments include *isn't it*, *would you*, *all right*, *eh*, *no* and *must I*.

Tag questions were theorized by Lakoff (1975) as being a form of WOMEN'S LANGUAGE, as she claimed they were linked to politeness; the speaker appears to be seeking agreement or confirmation. However, tag questions can sometimes be used to indicate emphasis or irony, so they do not always have polite functions. Holmes (1984) distinguishes between modal tags, which request information or confirmation of information when the speaker is unsure, and affective tags, which are used to indicate concern for the hearer. Affective tags are further split into softeners, which are used to express politeness, and facilitative tags, which invite the hearer to comment on the speaker's assertion. Dubois and Crouch (1975) found that in the context of academic conferences, males used more tag questions than females, while Cameron et al. (1988) also found more male use of tag questions in a corpus of spoken English, and while both sexes used more affective tags than modal tags, this was more pronounced in women. When Cameron et al. (1988) examined a different set of data, where the speakers were identified as being in relatively powerful or less powerful positions, it was found that powerful speakers tended to use the affective tags, and there was no significant difference in overall tag use between the sexes.

technologization of discourse

Fairclough (1992: 215) talks about the invasion of existing orders of discourse by new discourse technologies. Examples of such technologies include advertising, counselling and conversation control skills. Fairclough and Wodak (1997: 260) note that '[t]he increased importance of language in social life has led to a greater level of conscious intervention to control and shape language practices in accordance with economic, political and institutional objectives'.

Fairclough (1996: 73) points out a number of features of discourse technologization: the appearance of 'discourse technologists', such as communication specialists who advise people on how to use language for specific strategic purposes; a move towards standardizing discourse practices, such as the use of 'scripts' in call centres, along with the surveillance techniques that are used to ensure that workers follow the script; and the creation of various discourse techniques that can be transferable across a range of difference contexts.

tense

Tense refers to the linguistic expression of time. Tense has the 'now' or what is happening currently as its point of reference (or deictic centre). Tense then expresses events as happening before or after the 'now'. English recognizes the present, past and future tenses.

Examples
> *I am eating* (present tense).
> *He ate all the vegetables* (past tense).
> *He will eat all my vegetables* (future tense).

Tense goes hand in hand with aspect. Aspect in grammar refers to the expression of whether an event is ongoing or complete. We can distinguish between perfective aspect (expressing completion of an event) or continuous aspect (which indicates that an event is ongoing).

Examples
> *He sings very well* (simple present tense).

> *He was singing a very beautiful song* (past tense, continuous aspect, otherwise referred to as past continuous tense).

> *He is singing a very beautiful song* (present tense, continuous aspect, otherwise present continuous tense).

> *He has sung a very beautiful song* (present tense, perfective aspect, otherwise present perfect tense).

Vet and Vetters (1994:1) argue for a consideration of discourse when carrying out analysis of tense, writing that '. . . a considerable part of the meanings of tense and aspect forms strongly depends on contextual factors and probably on the type of text as well, so that tense and aspect cannot be properly studied if their contribution to text cohesion is not taken into account'.

terms of address

Terms of address are words, usually nominals, used to refer to people. They can express a range of different social phenomena. Many indicate degree of formality: *Mr*, *Mrs*, *Sir* and *Dr* are honorifics and are used in formal contexts to signal respect and distance. Others, like *darling*, *love*, *mate* and *dude*, may be used to signal informal relations. Terms of address thus can be manifestations of different types of POLITENESS and deference depending on the social distance between the addressor and addressee.

text

Definitions of the term *text* are difficult as different researchers have conceptualized texts in a range of ways. A prototypical text would be something which has lots of written words in it, such as a book. However, De Beaugrande and Dressler (1981) define a text as a communicative occurrence that meets seven standards of textuality: cohesion, coherence, intentionality, acceptability, informativity, situationality and intertextuality. Along similar lines, Halliday and Hasan (1976) define a text as being a semantic unit that has a particular social meaning, made up of related sentences whose main characteristic is unity of meaning. A text has cohesion; that is, each sentence in a text is related to the previous ones through cohesive ties. So any stretch of language that functions as a unity is a text. This definition could include posters, shopping lists, emails, poems, film reviews and so on. We could also view a text as anything which involves a recognized language system (not just writing but speech also). This could mean that we consider a conversation or a song as a text.

In discourse analysis, the notion of text tends to get extended much further than 'anything with words'. For example, Bernstein (1990: 17) refers to a text as 'the form of the social relationship made visible, palpable, material', while Talbot (1995: 14) calls a text 'the fabric in which discourses are manifested'. Barker and Galasinksi (2001: 5) position a text as 'any phenomenon that generates meaning through signifying practices. Hence dress, television programmes, advertising images, sporting events, pop stars and so on can all be read as texts'. Some researchers (e.g. Hodge and Kress 1988, Caldas-Coulthard and van Leeuwen 2002) have considered objects such as toys as texts.

Fairclough (1995: 4), however, argues against an understanding of text as *anything* that generates meaning. Instead, he proposes that a text is an inherently linguistic event, and two fundamental processes, cognition and representation of the world, are materialized in texts (1995: 6).

Even if we take the definition of text to mean 'linguistic event', we should still bear in mind that there are additional aspects of texts which may communicate meaning, even if not through language. For example, advertisements combine written words with images, and the meaning of the advert can only be decoded by taking into account the relationship between these different parts. In addition, typographic information such as font size, colour and style may also impact on the meanings we ascribe to texts.

textual orientation

This refers to an approach to discourse analysis which pays special attention to features of a TEXT, especially linguistic features such as vocabulary, grammar, COHESION and COHERENCE. Textually-Oriented Discourse Analysis (TODA) includes the analysis of 'actual instances of discourse' such as texts. Fairclough (1992: 37) argues that TODA is different from 'Foucault's more abstract approach' to discourse analysis. This means that TODA must involve 'linguistic *description* of the language text, *interpretation* of the relationship between the (productive and interpretative) discursive processes and the text, and *explanation* of the relationship between the discursive processes and the social processes' (Fairclough 1995: 97, original emphasis).

theme

The 'topic' of a particular stretch of discourse, as opposed to what is said about the topic (the RHEME). There are several ways of defining themes – for example, we could say that the SUBJECT is also the theme, or we could focus on the position of the theme within a stretch of discourse. A distinction can be made between themes at the level of discourse and at the level of clause:

> The house was full of little flights of steps where he least expected them. There were many dark, stained rooms. 'I would have had it done,' said the owner, a small, pale woman, 'but I'm selling up to go and live with my sister and it didn't seem worth it'. (BNC, A0R)

Here, the theme at the discourse level is 'the house'. The rheme is therefore everything that comes after the first two words as the entire paragraph is about 'the house'. However, we could also point to an additional 'local' theme 'the owner' which is established at the level of the sentence, along with a local rheme 'a small pale woman'. Despite this, the discourse-level theme continues to be the 'The house' as the owner is continuing to talk about the house.

topoi

Topoi (sometimes called *loci*, singular *topos*) are an aspect of ARGUMENTATION, being defined as persuasive strategies or rules which connect an argument to a claim or conclusion. Topoi are thus broad beliefs which help to maintain an argument without actually constituting the argument itself. Reisigl and Wodak (2001) have identified a number of topoi which are often used to justify discriminatory practices towards particular groups. For example, a topos of burden could be stated as 'if a group is burdened by another group, then actions should be taken in order to alleviate this burden'. This topos could be activated by someone who was opposed to immigration. Such a person might say something like, 'they come here to claim benefits and soon there won't be enough for everyone else!' Other topoi include the following: danger/threat (if x is a threat to y, then x must be stopped), authority (x is true because an authority said it is true) and justice (everyone should be treated the same).

transcription

Transcription conventions refer to established rules for converting spoken text to written text for the purposes of analysis. Transcriptions are often used in CONVERSATION ANALYSIS or the analysis of FOCUS GROUPS or RESEARCH INTERVIEWS. Generally, each line of speech in a transcription is numbered. Some transcription schemes can be detailed, for example, covering exact lengths of pauses in milliseconds as well as annotating overlapping speech or extralinguistic information. Some commonly used transcription conventions include the following:

(1.0)	– A number in round brackets indicates a pause of that many seconds.
.	– A full stop indicates a very short pause.
((laugh))	– Double round brackets indicate paralinguistic behaviour.
{leaves room}	– Curly brackets could indicate nonverbal behaviour.
[are you] [no]	– Square brackets can indicate overlapping speech.
so= =well	– Equals signs show latching between turns of two speakers.
yes::::	– Multiple colons can indicate a drawn-out syllable.
WHY	– Capitalization can indicate loud volume.

See Chafe (1982), Atkinson and Heritage (1984) and Dressler and Kreuz (2000).

transitivity

Transitivity is a system of representation in which the CLAUSE (in English) plays a crucial role. A VERB can be transitive (taking a direct object), intransitive (not able to take a direct object) or ERGATIVE (sometimes taking a direct object but sometimes not). In addition, monotransitive verbs take only one direct object whereas ditransitive verbs take two objects.

For example,

1. John ate the cheese.
2. Tony slept.
3. Sue gave John the ticket.

In example 1, the verb *ate* is transitive – it relates to an object (in this case, the cheese). However, in example 2, the verb *slept* is intransitive – no object is referred to. In example 3, the verb *gave* is ditransitive, taking two objects (John and the ticket). Rather than viewing transitivity as a binary distinction, some people see it as more of a continuum, with some verbs having higher transitivity than others.

It is through the transitivity system that we represent our perception and experience of the world around and inside us (Halliday 1994). This experience, according to Halliday, consists of what he calls 'goings on', such as 'happening, doing, sensing, meaning, being and becoming' (ibid.: 106).

Transitivity is important in discourse analysis as clause patterns can represent different ways of viewing the world or constructing reality, for example, by representing some people as actors and others as goals. This may have implications for which individuals or groups are represented as having AGENCY or POWER (Fairclough 1992: 177–185).

triangulation

Triangulation refers to the use of multiple approaches to research. This could involve data – for example, collecting data from different sources, or using different methods of data collection (focus groups, interviews, questionnaires) or it could involve using different methods of analysis (e.g. corpus analysis vs. a close qualitative analysis). The term originates from geometry and land surveying, where an accurate view is obtained from looking at things from two or more positions. Layder (1993: 128) points out several advantages of triangulation: It facilitates validity checks of hypotheses, it anchors findings in more robust interpretations and explanations, and it allows the researcher to respond flexibly to unforeseen problems and aspects of the research.

Discourse-based social research advocates the use of triangulation. For example, Reisigl and Wodak (2001: 35) state,

> One methodological way for critical discourse analysis to minimise the risk of critical biasing and to avoid simply politicising, instead of accurately analysing, is to follow the principle of triangulation [. . . and] endeavour to work interdisciplinarily, multimethodically and on the basis of a variety of empirical data as well as background information.

truth conditions

Truth conditions refer to the semantic content of sentences and utterances. The meanings of certain types of utterances depend on their truth conditions. A statement such as 'the sun rises in the east' can be subjected to investigation and found to be true or false. Truth conditions are different to FELICITY CONDITIONS, which are more concerned with the circumstances that are required for a performative to succeed.

turn-taking

Turn-taking is the set of practices through which conversation is organized and is therefore an important aspect of CONVERSATION ANALYSIS. Patterns of turn-taking were first described following a study of the use of English in telephone conversations and group talk (Sacks et al. 1974), although Cook (1989) notes that turn-taking mechanisms may vary between cultures or between languages. In English-speaking societies, turn-taking usually means that in a conversation one participant speaks at a time. The first speaker, A, speaks and then stops. The next speaker, B, speaks and then stops, so there is a conversational pattern that looks like this:

A-B-A-B-A-B.

According to Sacks et al. (1974), rules that govern turn-taking constitute a *local management system*. In this system, speakers compete over a scarce resource, namely, the control of the *floor*. The *floor* here refers to the right to speak and be listened to. The speakers share the floor by taking turns to utilize it. The minimal units by which turns are shared are called *turn-construction units*, and they are made up of sentences, clauses or phrases. They are identified in part by prosodic features such as intonation.

The end of such a unit marks the point at which speakers may change. This point is known as the *transition relevance place*. The transition relevance place does not mean that speakers must or will change at that point. It simply means that it is possible, at that point, for speakers to change.

There are rules that govern speaker change or how the floor is shared in the course of an interaction. This has to do with speaker selection. When A is the current speaker and B is the next speaker,

1. If A selects B in the current turn, then A must stop speaking and B must speak next. Transition occurs at the first transition relevance place after B's selection.
2. If A does not select B, then any (other) party may self-select, the first speaker gaining rights to the floor then makes a contribution.
3. If A has not selected B, and no other party self selects, A may (but need not) continue speaking. In other words, he or she may claim the right to the next turn constructional unit but does not have to.

The pattern then repeats itself (adapted from Levinson 1983: 298).

These rules mean that generally only one person speaks at a time. Overlaps can occur as competing first starts. Alternatively, they may occur where a transition relevance place has been mis-projected, such as where a tag or address term has been appended (ibid.: 299).

Conversation analysts may be interested in cases where turn-taking appears to break down, as this may indicate something important is happening in the conversation. They may also examine how participants orient to such break-downs and attempt to REPAIR them. In addition, an analysis of turn allocation in conversation can reveal a lot about the relative power of speakers and can therefore be utilized in CRITICAL DISCOURSE ANALYSIS.

unsolicited talk

Unsolicited talk refers to spoken research data that occurs in 'authentic' or 'natural' circumstances, rather than being elicited by the researcher.

utterance

An utterance refers to a unit of speech. Unlike sentences in written language, which are marked with particular features (capitalization at the start and a punctuation mark at the end), utterances can be difficult to delineate at times – some definitions of utterances note that they are marked by silence at their start and end, although in naturally occurring conversations, people can interrupt each other's utterances, so they appear to be cut off prematurely. In addition, pauses can potentially occur within utterances, for example, if someone forgets a word and pauses to remember it. The length of silence that is required to mark the end of one utterance and the start of another can also be contestable.

verb

Words which relate to actions, occurrences or states of being. Different languages can modify verb forms according to tense, aspect, mood and voice. Verbs may also need to agree with the person, gender and number that they refer to. See also AGENCY, ERGATIVITY, MODALITY, PERFORMATIVE, TRANSITIVITY.

vernacular

The term vernacular has several related meanings. (1) A vernacular language is one that is indigenous to a country or locality. (2) Labov (1966) identifies a vernacular as an unself-conscious style of speech – the sort of language we would use in relaxed conversation, without having to make an effort about how we talk. (3) It can refer to a nonstandard variety of language, such as a particular dialect. Such vernaculars are normally spoken, rather than written. (4) A vernacular has also been conceptualized as 'an abstract set of norms' (Lodge 2005: 13).

vocabulary

Vocabulary refers to the set of words available to a particular language and is sometimes known as a *lexicon*. There are different types of vocabulary and each person acquires different levels of different types of vocabulary. For example, a speaking vocabulary is all the words that a person is able to utilize when speaking, while a reading vocabulary is all the words that a person is able to recognize when reading. A similar distinction can also be made between active vocabulary (words that are currently used by a particular speaker) and passive vocabulary (words which are known even if not used). The vocabulary of any language grows all the time because language is productive and new words are coined continuously. However, words also fall out of the vocabulary of a language as people stop using them.

warrants

Warrants are forms of justification. Toulmin et al. (1979: 43) define 'warrants' as 'statements indicating the *general ways of arguing* being applied in each particular case and *implicitly relied on* as ones whose *trustworthiness* is well established'. In ARGUMENTATION theory, a TOPOS is a content-related warrant or conclusion rule that connects an argument to a claim (Reisigl and Wodak 2001: 75). In racist, xenophobic, homophobic or sexist discourse, warrants are used to justify the social EXCLUSION of marginal groups and to create 'out-groups' which must be separated from mainstream society or the 'in-group'.

Swann (2002) uses the term *warrant* in relation to language and gender research to refer to the evidence that is needed to support conclusions about gender when analysing linguistic data. For example, what warrants do we have for being able to say that a piece of language is gendered. Based on analysing different types of research, she lists a number of different types of warrants:

1. Quantitative and general patterns of language use (such as corpus analysis)
2. Indirect reliance on quantitative/general patterns
3. Participants' orientation as evident in the text
4. Speakers/participants' solicited interpretation (e.g. interviews)
5. Analyst's theoretical position (e.g. critical discourse analysis)
6. Analyst's intuition
7. Speakers/participants are male/female

women's language

Issues surrounding the definition or existence of 'women's language' have been the subject of many language studies, especially within feminist linguistics. A chapter by the linguist Otto Jespersen in 1922 conceived of women using language distinctly from men. Jespersen's claims, now seen as sexist, presented a form of women's language use as 'deficient' to men's. Robin Lakoff's 1975 book *Language and Women's Place* put forward a different position, that men use language to dominate women and, resultingly, women's language is polite, hyper-correct and concerned with ensuring that conversations run smoothly. Her work has since been criticized for making

ING

overgeneralizations and extrapolating conclusions based on observing a small sample of her peers. A later position advocated by self-help writer and interactional sociolinguist Deborah Tannen (1990), that men and women use language differently (whether due to socialization or other reasons), avoided accusing men of being bullies and women of being victims, but it fell open to criticisms of an apolitical perspective. However, all of the above research has been grounded on the existence of a distinct 'women's language', which has since been problematized. Since the 1990s, a position which takes into account diversity, considers how particular women and men use language in specific settings, and the complex ways that gender interacts with other IDENTITY categories (Eckert and McConnell-Ginet 1998) has arisen.

word order

This refers to the order in which words in a sentence follow to form a well-formed sentence. For example, the words '*killed man the dog, vicious the*' make no sense until they are ordered according to the rules of English grammar: '*The vicious dog killed the man.*' Rules of transformation can be applied to change the basic word order of sentences in order to foreground certain aspects of the sentence. For example, a headline in a newspaper can appear in two different forms:

Two hundred people die in train crash.
Train crash kills two hundred people.

In the first sentence, the two hundred people are thematized and therefore foregrounded. In the second sentence, it is the train crash that is thematized and foregrounded.

The Key Thinkers

Louis Althusser

An Algerian philosopher, Althusser was influenced by Marx as well as the psychoanalysts Freud and Lacan. He wrote on the concept of ideology, believing that our choices, intentions, values and desires are inculcated by ideological practices. In other words, social practices impose certain roles upon the individual which determine the concept of the self. In his 1971 essay *Ideology and State Apparatuses*, Althusser claimed that ideological practices are constituted by an assortment of institutions he refers to as ideological State Apparatuses such as religious systems, the family, political systems, trade unions and communications (the media). Such structures are both agents of repression and inescapable – everyone is subjected to ideology. Althusser's conceptualization of ideology has been influential to critical discourse analysis.

J. L. Austin

A British philosopher of language who developed the concept of the speech act and its associated theory. Austin's most influential work was his short book *How to Do Things with Words* (1962), based on a series of lectures he gave in 1955, in which he criticises the notion that statements can only be either true or false. He introduces the idea of statements that are not truth-evaluable, including those which are deemed as 'performative' because they are used to perform a certain type of action (speech acts). Such performatives only succeed or are 'felicitous' if certain circumstances are met (e.g. you may try to leave an antique clock to someone in your will, but if you do not own the clock, or the person does not exist, then the performative will be infelicitous). Austin's research was later expanded by John Searle and has been influential in the development of pragmatics as well as helping to inspire Judith Butler's performativity theory of gender.

Allan Bell

A New Zealand sociolinguist who has published in the area of language and the media as well as examining New Zealand English and language style. Bell is most well known for his theory of audience design (1984), which proposes that style-shifting occurs primarily in response to a speaker's audience. Bell identified a classification system for different types of audiences, depending on three criteria: whether the audience is known to be part of a speech context, whether the speaker ratifies or acknowledges the listener's presence and whether the listener is directly addressed. Bell is one of the founding editors of the *Journal of Sociolinguistics*. His publications include *The Language of News Media* (1991) and *Approaches to Media Discourse* (1998) with Peter Garrett. He also co-edited *New Zealand Ways of Speaking* (1990) with Janet Holmes and *Languages of New Zealand* (2006) with Ray Harlow and Donna Starks.

Pierre Bourdieu

A French sociologist and cultural theorist who was influenced by writers such as Marx, Wittgenstein and Weber. His works include *Distinction: A Social Critique of the Judgement of Taste* (1984), *Language and Symbolic Power* (1991) and *The Field of Cultural Production* (1993). Bourdieu wrote about the concept of *capital*, extending the term to cover categories such as social capital, cultural capital and symbolic capital in order to argue that individuals occupy multiple social positions. Such types of capital help the ruling and intellectual classes to maintain power in postindustrial societies. In *Distinction*, he argues that people internalize aesthetic dispositions from an early age and that social class is thus demonstrated and maintained by how people present their social spaces to the world. Rather than emphasizing economic factors in social domination, Bourdieu was instead more interested in how social actors engaged with symbolic capital. He viewed language as a mechanism of power and also coined the term *symbolic violence*, which involves the imposition of symbolic capital in order to influence people. Bourdieu also emphasized the importance of reflexivity in sociological analysis, being critical of the idea of scientific objectivity.

Judith Butler

An American post-structuralist philosopher who has published extensively in the areas of gender, feminism, queer theory, ethics and political philosophy. Her work has often focused on the concept of the embodied self, and she is also known for her theory of gender performativity which views gender identity as constituted by repeated stylizations of bodily acts. However, she underlines that the performance of identity is not a matter of deliberate choice but a result of discourses which determine what categories of gender, sex and sexuality are permissible and that masculinities and femininities are socially constructed. Her publications include *Gender Trouble: Feminism and the Subversion of Identity* (1990), *Bodies That Matter: On the Discursive Limits of Sex* (1993), *Excitable Speech: The Politics of the Performative* (1997), *Undoing Gender* (2004) and *Giving an Account of Oneself* (2005). Her work has been particularly influential to feminist branches of discourse analysis.

Deborah Cameron

An English philologist who has made numerous contributions to a range of linguistic and social topics. In *Verbal Hygiene* (1995), she employs moral panic theory to examine debates around political correctness and declining standards in language, while in *Good to Talk?* (2000) she examines the surge of concern about the importance of talk in a range of social contexts. A large part of her work has focused around issues of gender and sexuality from a feminist perspective, an early example being *Feminism and Linguistic Theory* published in 1992. In *Language and Sexuality* (co-written with Don Kulick in 2003), she queries definitions of queer theory and suggests that desire might be a better paradigm than identity in order to make sense of language in sexual contexts. In *The Myth of Mars and Venus* (2007), she critiques the gender differences view of language which has popularized relationship advice literature. Her *Working with Spoken Discourse* is a guide to analysis of spoken texts, covering approaches like conversation analysis and critical discourse analysis.

Paul Chilton

A discourse analyst and cognitive linguist who has also published in literary studies. His interests include conceptual metaphor theory, cognitive stylistics and the analysis of political discourse. His books include *Orwellian Language and the Media* (1988), *Security Metaphors: Cold War Discourse from Containment to Common European Home* (1996) and *Analysing Political Discourse: Theory and Practice* (2004). Chilton has drawn on Grice's Co-operative Principle, Sperber and Wilson's Relevance Theory and Chomsky's Generative Linguistics in order to formulate principles for a cognitive approach to political discourse. As well as focusing on metaphors, he has developed a theory of discourse analysis which takes into account the concepts of space, vectors and co-ordinates. He argues that anyone who processes discourse will locate arguments and predicates according to the dimensions of space (s), time (t) and modality (m) and has used this to build a three-dimensional model of discourse analysis which he has applied to his own work, for example, an analysis of President Clinton's speeches.

Jennifer Coates

A British linguist who has published extensively in the field of language and gender, mainly looking at spoken language using a range of quantitative and qualitative discourse analysis techniques. In 1986, she wrote *Women, Men and Language*, which went beyond a 'genderlect' view of talk to consider the more nuanced concept of men and women performing gender in everyday interactions. The book considers social networks as well as attempting to explain the causes and consequences of gender differentiated language. This book was followed by two empirical sets of studies, which considered the informal interactions of males and females in friendship groups: *Women Talk* (1996), which investigates how women contribute towards a discourse of solidarity, and *Men Talk* (2003), where she shows how men's talk and particularly men's story-telling relate to norms of hegemonic masculinity. Coates has also edited or co-edited a number of collections of papers, including *Women in Their Speech Communities* (1989), *Language and Gender: A Reader* (1998) and *The Sociolinguistics of Narrative* (2003).

Guy Cook

An applied linguist who has published a number of works on discourse, including *Discourse* (1989), *The Discourse of Advertising* (1992) and *Discourse and Literature* (1994). He has been the editor of the journal *Applied Linguistics* and chair of the British Association for Applied Linguistics. Cook views discourse as hierarchically progressing from substance through to form and then interaction, and he has written about discourse from the perspective of a language teacher, applying theory to classroom activities so that students' discourse skills can be improved. In his book on advertising, Cook deals with the issue of incorporating the analysis of music and images into more traditional forms of discourse analysis which deal with written texts, while in his book on literature he examines how schema theory can be used in the discourse analysis of literary texts.

Malcolm Coulthard

A linguist who is well known in both the fields of discourse analysis and forensic linguistics. Coulthard wrote one of the first introductions to discourse analysis in 1977. In 1980, with David Brazil and Catherine Johns, he co-wrote *Discourse Intonation and Language Teaching*, which focused on intonational semantics. This was followed a year later by *Studies in Discourse Analysis* (with Martin Montgomery). In his 1992 edited collection *Advances in Spoken Discourse Analysis*, he has a chapter on forensic discourse analysis, where he applies concepts like the conversational maxims and analysis of discourse structure to examine legal interviews and confessions. In his later work on forensic linguistics, Coulthard has used frequency-based corpus approaches to determine whether language use is typical in a particular context. For example, in a 2000 paper he demonstrated that Derek Bentley, a young man who had been executed in 1953, almost certainly did not say the words which were supposed to be a transcript of his confession.

Jacques Derrida

A prolific Algerian-born French philosopher who founded the deconstructionist approach, which aimed to show that within any text there are numerous (and often conflicting) meanings or interpretations. This approach, although never formally described as a method of analysis, influenced approaches to discourse analysis, particularly from the early 1990s onwards, helping to provide the basis of critiques of the more traditional ways of carrying out social research which had been based on researcher-defined categorizations. Some authors have conceptualized deconstruction as a form of discourse analysis, although others (such as Ernesto Laclau) disagree. Derrida tended to define deconstruction based on what it is not rather than what it is. He was influenced by Freud, Nietzsche, de Saussure, Heidegger and Husserl, among others. Derrida's most well-known work is *Of Grammatology* (1976), which focused on the implications of understanding language in its written form, rather than as speech, which formed the basis of deconstruction. Another book, *Speech and Phenomena* (1973), is also concerned with deconstruction.

Norman Fairclough

A discourse analyst who developed one of the first approaches to critical discourse analysis, based on extending critical linguistics to take social practices and different types of context more thoroughly into account (see *Language and Power* 1989, *Discourse and Social Change* 1992, *Critical Discourse Analysis* 1995, *Discourse in Late Modernity* (co-authored with Lilie Chouliaraki) 1999, and *Analysing Discourse: Textual Analysis for Social Research* 2003). Fairclough has been influenced by Halliday and Bakhtin at the linguistic level and theorists such as Foucault, Gramsci, Althusser and Bourdieu at the sociological level. He has applied his own three-stage model of critical discourse analysis (CDA) (sometimes called Textually Oriented Discourse Analysis or TODA) in order to address how language is used to create, maintain and challenge power relationships and ideologies. He is particularly interested in concepts which refer to current social changes: globalization, neoliberalism and the knowledge economy. His research has shown how marketing discourses and associated linguistic phenomena such as informalization and conversationalization have crossed over into many other forms of everyday life. In 2000, he authored *New Labour, New Language*, which examined the discourse of Tony Blair's Labour government. More recently, he has worked on aspects of 'transition' in Central and Eastern Europe.

Michel Foucault

A French philosopher, historian, sociologist and activist who studied with Althusser and was influenced by Hegel, Nietzsche and Heidegger. His works include *Madness and Civilisation: A History of Insanity in the Age of Reason* (1967), *The Archaeology of Knowledge* (1972), the three-volume *The History of Sexuality* (1979a, 1986, 1988) and *Discipline and Punish: The Birth of the Prison* (1979b). His writing tended to focus on criticisms of social institutions, particularly the prison system, psychiatry and medicine. He also wrote widely on sexuality and the relationships between power, knowledge and discourse. His theory of discourse (in the *Archaeology*) is an influential work in contemporary discourse analysis, especially critical discourse analysis.

Roger Fowler

A British critical linguist whose main field was stylistics (his early books include *The Languages of Literature* and *Linguistics and the Novel*). In 1979, he co-authored *Language and Control* which contains a chapter (with Gunther Kress) on critical linguistics, which was influential in the development of critical discourse analysis. Fowler and Kress applied Halliday's functional linguistics to the critical examination of texts, in particular paying attention to transitivity, modality, nominalizations, passivizations, relexicalization, over-lexicalization and coherence, order and unity of discourse. In 1991, he published *Language in the News: Discourse and Ideology in the Press*, arguing that newspaper coverage of world events is not unbiased recording of hard facts but is instead socially constructed, making use of stereotypes, incorporating biases and subject to various social and economic factors.

Erving Goffman

A Canadian sociologist whose most famous book *The Presentation of Self in Everyday Life* was published 1956 and was one of the first works to discuss face-to-face interaction from a sociological perspective. He viewed social interaction as a kind of theatrical performance, with a 'front' region, where people maintain face to others, and a 'back' region which is private. Goffman developed a theory of face, based on the idea that individuals try to control the impression they make on other people, engaging in various practices, called 'face work' to avoid embarrassing themselves or each other. He argued that cultural differences aside, societies have basically similar ways of ensuring self-regulation, based on concepts like dignity, pride and honour. His theories are continued in his later books: *Stigma* (1963) and *Interaction Ritual* (1967). In *Frame Analysis* (1974), he developed a theory for how people organize experiences, using a picture frame metaphor where the frame represents the structure which holds together the picture, which is the context of the experience.

Paul Grice

A British-born philosopher of language whose work helped to found the field of pragmatics. He was particularly interested in the relationship between speaker meaning and linguistic meaning and developed the Cooperative Principal (Grice 1975) along with four Conversational Maxims in order to help to explain how non-literal utterances are understood and how speakers adhere to or flout certain maxims at particular points in order to express meaning. He developed a theory of implicature, making distinctions between conversational and conventional implicature as well as making distinctions between four types of content: encoded/non-encoded content and truth-conditional/non-truth-conditional content. His 1989 valedictory book *Studies in the Way of Words* covers a large amount of his work, including a series of influential William James lectures he gave in 1967. Grice's theory of meaning and pragmatic inference has been built on and challenged by Dan Sperber and Deirdre Wilson's (1986) Relevance Theory.

John Gumperz

An American sociolinguist whose early work focused on dialect differences in rural Michigan. He then carried out anthropological work in a North Indian village community, examining issues of language contact. In the 1970s, he became more interested in discourse and conversation analysis, concentrating on bilingualism and communication between cultures. In 1972, he co-edited *Directions in Sociolinguistics* with Dell Hymes, while in 1982 he wrote *Discourse Strategies*. Gumperz is most well known for developing an approach called interactional sociolinguistics which foregrounds how speakers signal and make sense of meaning in social interaction. The approach involves the close analysis of recorded interactions. Gumperz went against the 'information theory' perspective of communication which views context as separate from communicative content by arguing that sociocultural knowledge is embedded within the talk and behaviour of interactions. He postulates that we communicate interpretive frames through 'contextualization cues', such as prosody, lexical choice and visual and gestural phenomena. Such cues help us to interpret the propositional content of utterances.

Stuart Hall

A Jamaican-born sociologist and cultural theorist who is particularly interested in hegemony, race, youth subcultures and media. In 1973, he wrote *Encoding and Decoding in the Television Discourse* where he developed an approach to textual analysis which did not view audiences as passive recipients of texts but instead focused on their ability to negotiate or oppose meanings. Hall's emphasis on reception positions the meaning of a text as somewhere between the producer and the reader. In 1978, he co-wrote *Policing the Crisis: Mugging, the State and Law and Order*, where he employed Cohen's moral panic theory to show how media reports and crime statistics can be used to further moral panics as part of the social production of news. His 1997 book *Representation: Cultural Representations and Signifying Practices* focuses on the construction of identities, particularly those classed as 'the other' in a variety of social contexts, including photography, soap opera, film, museum exhibits and advertising.

Michael Halliday

A British-born linguist who mainly worked in Australia, Halliday founded the field of social semiotics and developed systemic functional grammar (sometimes called systemic functional linguistics or SFL). Halliday's research was influenced by John Firth and is based on people's real-world systems and requirements – for example, he outlines seven functions that language has for developing children. Likewise, with SFL, Halliday foregrounded functional (as opposed to structural) aspects of language. SFL has been influential in a number of areas of linguistics, including computational linguistics. It was also used as the basis of analysis for critical linguistics and was subsequently influential in the descriptive stage of Fairclough's Critical Discourse Analysis as well as other forms of critical discourse analysis (CDA). In 1990, Halliday published a paper which challenged applied linguists to address issues that were relevant to the twenty-first century, particularly the destruction of eco-systems. This paper triggered the emergence of eco-critical discourse analysis.

John Heritage

A British sociologist who was influenced by ethnomethodology and later became a leading figure in the field of conversation analysis. His *Garfinkel and Ethnomethodology* (first published in 1984) gives an analysis of the origins and development of ethnomethodological theory and research from the mid-1940s onwards. He has co-edited several collections of works on conversation analysis, including *Structures of Social Interaction* (1984), *Interaction and Language Use* (1986), *Talk at Work* (1992) and *Conversation Analysis* (2006). His later research has focused on applying conversation analysis techniques in both public and institutional settings, such as televised news and political interviews, medical care, legal trials and calls to emergency services. He has often published work jointly with Paul Drew and Steven Clayman.

Susan Herring

A linguist who specializes in information technology. In 1996, she edited one of the first books on interaction in online environments: *Computer-mediated Communication: Linguistic, Social and Cross-Cultural Perspectives*. This was followed by *The Multilingual Internet: Language, Culture, and Communication Online*, which was co-edited with Brenda Danet in 2007. Herring has examined a wide range of computer-mediated communication (CMC) practices: SMS, Twitter, weblogs, online game environments and bulletin boards. Her work has tended to be based around two main strands. First, she has particularly examined electronic participation from a gender differences/dominance perspective, arguing that in CMC male participants can dominate discourse, for example, through rhetorical intimidation. Second, she has considered multilingualism in CMC contexts, drawing on theories of performance and speech communities, and investigating how multilingual CMC users develop their own conventions for communication in contexts where English is the dominant language.

Janet Holmes

A sociolinguist who specializes in language and gender, language and the workplace and New Zealand English. Her work utilizes a range of qualitative and quantitative approaches, including corpus linguistics, while she has examined aspects of pragmatics, including politeness strategies, sexist language, pragmatic particles and hedges, compliments, directives, apologies, disagreement, humour and small talk. She has particularly focused on sex as a variable in hierarchical workplace settings by examining, for example, how male and female managers negotiate power differently. Her publications include *An Introduction to Sociolinguistics* (1992), *Women, Men and Politeness* (1995) and *Gendered Talk at Work* (2006). With Miriam Meyerhoff, she has co-edited *The Handbook of Language and Gender* (2003).

Dell Hymes

An American anthropologist and sociolinguist who developed a linguistic model (Hymes 1974) which stated that language users not only need to learn the vocabulary and grammar of a particular language but they also have to take into account a number of other components. The model has the acronym SPEAKING (having 16 components under eight main divisions): Setting and Scene, Participants, Ends, Act Sequence, Key, Instrumentalities, Norms, Genre. This model was influential in that it foregrounded social context, which is a central tenet of discourse analysis. Hymes also proposed the term 'communicative competence' (1966) in contrast with Chomsky's notion of 'linguistic competence' (1965). His later work focused on folklore and poetics, particularly in Native American oral narratives. Hymes is a founder of the journal *Language in Society*, and his books include *Language in Culture and Society* (1964), *Foundations in Sociolinguistics* (1974) and *Essays in the History of Linguistic Anthropology* (1983).

Gunther Kress

A linguist and semiotician whose areas of interest include language and ideology, literacy, media language, new media, and the analysis of visual design. In 1979, he co-authored *Language as Ideology* with Robert Hodge, which was influential in the development of critical linguistics. He and Theo van Leeuwen developed a systematic theory of visual design in which, they claim, visual images have a 'grammar' very similar to linguistic grammar in that, for example, a picture can represent an actor, an action and a goal, much like a clause. His work has thus added a dimension to discourse analysis which for a long time was not considered core: visual image analysis. His other publications include *Learning to Write* (1982), *Before Writing: Rethinking the Paths to Literacy* (1997) and *Literacy in The New Media Age* (2003). With van Leeuwen, he has co-authored *Reading Images: The Grammar of Visual Design* (1990) and *Multimodal Discourse: The Modes and Media of Contemporary Communication* (2001).

William Labov

The founder of variationist sociolinguistics, Labov has published extensively on the relationship between social factors that influence language change, such as sex, age, ethnicity, and social class. His methods of eliciting data for study of varieties of English in New York City have been widely cited. He also studied English used by African-American communities, arguing that rather than stigmatize this variety as nonstandard English, it should be given full recognition as a variety of English in its own right with its own grammatical rules. His publications include *The Social Stratification of English in New York City* (1966), *Language in the Inner City* (1972a), *Sociolinguistic Patterns* (1973), *Principles of Sociolinguistics: The Internal Factors. Vol 1* (1994), *Principles of Sociolinguistics: Social Factors. Vol 2* (2000) and *Studies in Sociolinguistics by William Labov* (2001).

Ernesto Laclau

An Argentinian political theorist who co-authored *Hegemony and Socialist Strategy* with Chantal Mouffe in 1985. Laclau's approach is sometimes referred to as post-Marxist as he examines the Marxist concept of hegemony from a discourse-analytical perspective. Laclau has reworked Foucault's conceptualization of discourse analysis in order to produce a more systematic, general and clear form of discourse theory. He defines discourse as a structural totality of differences (but because discourse cannot be fixed in place or maintained by locating something outside discourse to define itself in relation to, it collapses from within). Furthermore, Laclau defines discourse as not a practice but the result of a practice and argues that discourse analysis is in opposition to deconstruction and that the two work in a circular relationship to each other. Most of Laclau's work is theoretical rather than empirical.

Robin Tolmach Lakoff

A pioneering feminist linguist whose areas of specialization include pragmatics and sociolinguistics. She is particularly interested in the relationship between language and gender and is well known for her groundbreaking book *Language and Woman's Place* (1975) in which she argues that men use language to dominate women, citing a number of disempowering speech styles such as hedges, tag questions, hyper-correctness and super polite forms which she claims women use more than males. Her ideas on gender, although often criticized, formed the basis for feminist approaches to discourse analysis. She has also published work on language and power with her books *Talking Power* (1990) and *The Language War* (2001).

Stephen Levinson

A linguist who has helped to develop the field of pragmatics. Strongly influenced by Paul Grice, his most well-known work (co-authored with Penelope Brown) was published in 1987: *Politeness: Some Universals in Language Use* (although most of it had been previously published in 1978 in an edited collection by Esther Goody called *Questions and Politeness*). In the book, the authors develop a set of principles for constructing polite speech, incorporating and developing Goffman's concept of *face* to include positive and negative face as well as face-threatening acts. They detail a taxonomy of different types of positive and negative politeness strategies, applying their theories to a range of different cultures and conversational contexts. In 1983, Levinson wrote a general overview of the field called *Pragmatics*. In his later work, he has focused on conversational implicature, publishing *Presumptive Meanings: The Theory of Generalized Conversational Implicature* in 2000. He has also written books on language acquisition, linguistic relativity, language and space, human sociality, and evolution and culture.

Karl Marx

A German philosopher, political theorist, historian and communist. In his most famous work, *The Communist Manifesto* (1848), he argued that the history of society is the history of class struggles. He was especially interested in the organization of labour and how this related to means of production and relations of production. He argued that societies tend to develop the means of production more quickly than the relations (such as laws to regulate new technologies), which results in social disruption. He argued that in capitalist societies the working class is exploited by bourgeois classes and that relations of production are mediated through commodities, including labour, which results in people becoming alienated from their own nature. However, Marx believed that capitalism would result in a crisis and eventually be replaced by socialism, leading to a classless and communist society. His class-based perspective has been influential in the social sciences and is particularly relevant to critical discourse analysis, which has addressed similar issues of political and social oppression and inequality.

Sara Mills

A feminist linguist whose areas of interest include linguistic politeness, feminist linguistic theory and text analysis, critical discourse analysis and feminist postcolonial theory. Her books include *Discourses of Differences: Women's Travel Writing and Colonialism* (1991), *Discourse* (1997), *Michel Foucault* (2003a), *Gender and Politeness* (2003b), *Gender and Colonial Space* (2005) and *Language and Sexism* (2008). In a 1998 paper, she demonstrates post-feminist text analysis by showing how an advert for a dating agency contains subtle sexist discourses. She has edited a number of collections of papers on language and gender and travel, and has edited the *Journal of Politeness Research* and *Gender and Language*.

Jonathan Potter

A discourse analyst who was one of the main founders (along with Derek Edwards and Margaret Wetherell) of the field of discursive psychology. He co-authored *Discourse and Social Psychology* (1987) with Margaret Wetherell, which presented a critique of traditional experimental ways of conducting research in social psychology (such as attitude questionnaires and categorization), pointing out that such methods can result in flawed or oversimplified analyses. Discursive psychology offered a different approach, partly based on conversation analytical methods but combining these with a perspective that takes social context into account when carrying out detailed qualitative analyses of human talk and writing. His later book *Representing Reality: Discourse, Rhetoric and Social Construction* (1996) gives an overview and critique of social constructionism in the social sciences, while an edited collection that he co-authored with Hedwig te Molder called *Conversation and Cognition* (2005) attempts to apply discourse analytical methods to cognitive research.

Harvey Sacks

An American sociologist who founded the discipline of conversation analysis in the 1960s and 1970s. Sacks was influenced by ethnomethodology and much of his work, including transcripts of his lectures, was published after his premature death in 1975. Sacks initially studied transcripts of conversations from a suicide hotline which he worked at in the 1960s, gradually developing a theory of conversation that was based around structured routines (and was in opposition to established thinking which saw conversation as disorganized and spoken language as degenerate). Sacks developed a number of important concepts in relation to conversation analysis, including turn-taking, speaker selection preference, adjacency pairs, conversational openings and closing, pre-sequences, accounts and repairs. Conversation analysis is widely accepted in applied linguistic research, and elements of it often occur in spoken discourse analysis or discursive psychology.

Deborah Schiffrin

An American linguist who has published on a wide range of discourse-based topics, including language and identity, discourse and history, narratives and oral histories, grammar and interaction. Her 1987 book *Discourse Markers* was a comparative piece of fieldwork analysis which examined frequently used particles and connectives that perform important functions in conversation. In 1994, she wrote *Approaches to Discourse*, which gave a comparative review of six dominant approaches to carrying out discourse analysis (speech act theory, pragmatics, ethnomethodology, interactional sociolinguistics, ethnography of communication, and variation theory). She has also co-edited two large collections of works on discourse analysis: *The Handbook of Discourse Analysis* (2001) and *Discourse and Identity* (2006).

Ron Scollon

An American linguist who has published in the fields of new literacy studies, discourse analysis and intercultural communication. Scollon was influenced by John Gumperz and has helped to develop the field of interactional sociolinguistics by showing how speakers create conversational coherence with a framework laid out in his 1995 book *Intercultural Communication: A Discourse Approach*, which he co-authored with Suzanne Wong Scollon. This was followed in 1998 with *Mediated Discourse as Social Interaction*, which focuses on the ethnographic study of the role of print and television news media in the construction of identity. Scollon also developed a framework for Mediated Discourse Analysis, which foregrounds social actions and their consequences rather than taking discourse and language as the central focus. His 2003 book (also with Suzanne Wong Scollon) *Discourses in Place: Language in the Material World* established the field of geosemiotics, offering an analysis of the ways that people interpret language as it is materially placed in the world.

Michael Stubbs

A linguist who specializes in language teaching, literacy, educational linguistics, discourse analysis and corpus linguistics. He published one of the first books on discourse analysis in 1983 (*Discourse Analysis: the Sociolinguistic Analysis of Natural Language*). In the 1990s, he began to use computer-assisted methods to carry out discourse analysis, first publishing *Text and Corpus Analysis* in 1996, then *Words and Phrases* in 2001. He also co-authored *Text, Discourse and Corpora* in 2007. Stubbs has shown how corpus methods can help to reveal hidden patterns of language use that tend to be used subconsciously and can have ideological functions. He has examined the impact of fixed collocational patterns such as *Jewish intellectual* or *working mother* and has extended theories of collocation by helping to develop the terms *semantic preference* and *discourse prosody*. Stubbs has also applied corpus techniques to further the concept of *cultural keywords* – words which reveal something important about a culture.

John Swales

An American linguist who has published in the areas of genre analysis, applied linguistics and English as a Foreign Language. His book *Genre Analysis* (1990) is of particular interest to discourse analysts. He has also analysed comparative rhetoric, the use of English in academic settings and used corpus linguistics methods in his research. Swales was one of the leaders of the

MICASE (Michigan Corpus of Academic Spoken English) project and has used MICASE in his own research in order to examine discourse management in academic contexts. He has also examined corpora of corporate 'mission statements' to see how such texts are designed to be rhetorically attractive to employees. Swales also has a 100,000 word spoken corpus named after him (The John Swales Conference Corpus). As another strand of his research, Swales developed the concept of the discourse community, which had been used previously by Martin Nystrand. Swales' six characteristics of a discourse community are regularly referenced by researchers who are seeking a clear definition of the term.

Deborah Tannen

An American linguist who has published widely on gender and interpersonal communication in everyday conversation. She has edited collections of papers on coherence in spoken and written discourse (1982) and framing in discourse (1993) as well as publishing books on everyday conversation: *Conversational Style: Analysing Talk among Friends* (1984) and *Talking Voices: Repetition, Dialogue and Imagery in Conversational Discourse* (1989). She is best known for her book: *You Just Don't Understand: Women and Men in Conversation* (1990), where she argues that women and men come from different subcultures and therefore their conversational styles reflect those subcultures. Tannen is critical of earlier approaches to language and gender which viewed women's language as weak or deficient, instead emphasizing the notion of gender 'difference' (a position that other writers have since criticized). Her later books have also tended to focus on gender differences: *Talking from 9 to 5: Women and Men in the Workplace: Language, Sex and Power* (1995) and *You Were Always Mom's Favourite: Sisters in Conversation throughout Their Lives* (2009).

Teun Van Dijk

A leading figure in the field of critical discourse analysis, he is a proponent of an approach to critical discourse analysis (CDA) which takes the relationship between cognition, discourse and society into account. He has theorized on how people produce, comprehend and remember texts and talk and is also interested in the relationship between discourse, ideology and power. Two related strands of his research have involved analysis of the reproduction of racism and prejudice in discourse, and the analysis of news discourse. He has founded a number of journals in discourse analysis, and his books include *Prejudice in Discourse* (1984), *News as Discourse* (1988), *Racism and the Press* (1991), *Elite Discourse and Racism* (1993), *Ideology* (1998) and *Discourse and Context: A Socio-cognitive Approach* (2008).

Theo van Leeuwen

A linguist who has also been involved in film and television production. He was one of the founding editors of the journal *Visual Communication* and has published widely in media discourse, critical discourse analysis and multimodal communication. With Gunther Kress, he developed an approach to the analysis of visual images in *Reading Images: The Grammar of Visual Design* (1990). The two authors later co-wrote *Multimodal Discourse: the Modes and Media of Contemporary Communication* (2001). van Leeuwen has also developed a system of analysis for social actor representation in language use (1996, 1997), which has been influential in the field of critical discourse analysis. His approach often involves examining non-traditional 'texts' such as computer games, toys or photographs.

Margaret Wetherell

A social psychologist who helped to develop the field of discursive psychology. Wetherell has applied the discursive psychology framework to issues related to identity, especially ethnicity, racism and gender. She has examined discursive practices around accounts of illness, gendered division of labour and negotiation of being single. In 1987, she co-authored *Discourse and Social Psychology* with Jonathan Potter. In 2001, she co-edited two collections of papers on discourse analysis called *Discourse Theory and Practice: A Reader* and *Discourse as Data: A Guide to Analysis*. In 2003, she co-authored the edited collection *Analysing Racist Discourse*, while in 2009 she published two edited collections on identity, *Identity in the 21st Century* and *Theorising Identities and Social Action*. She has argued for the omnipresence of gender as salient for conversation analysis. She has also explored connections between psychoanalysis and discourse theory in order to carry out analyses of subjectivity.

Henry Widdowson

A linguist who has published research in or *about* applied linguistics, language teaching, discourse analysis and critical discourse analysis. His short book *Discourse Analysis* (2007) serves as a good introduction to the subject, with chapters covering the range of different meanings of discourse and approaches such as conversation analysis, critical analysis, corpus linguistics, pragmatics, cohesion and coherence and schema theory. With regard to critical discourse analysis, Widdowson's (2004) *Text, Context, Pretext* presents a more cautious approach, admitting that he has 'serious reservations about the way it [critical discourse analysis] does its work' (2004: ix). He is concerned that people involved in CDA are not critical enough of their own practices, that they selectively attend to certain linguistic features, and are subjective in their interpretations, which are conditioned by contextual and pretextual factors.

Ruth Wodak

A leading figure in the field of critical discourse analysis who has published widely in the areas of racism and anti-Semitism, gender studies, political discourse, organizational discourse and the construction of Austrian and European identities. With Martin Reisigl, she developed the discourse-historical approach to critical discourse analysis, which involves using triangulation and emphasizes combining textual analysis with the analysis of historical and political context. Her analytical framework makes use of argumentation theory, systemic functional linguistics and ethnography. Her publications include *Disorders of Discourse* (1996), *The Discursive Construction of National Identity* (1999/2009) (co-authored with Rudolf de Cillia, Martin Reisigl and Karin Liebhart), *Discourse and Discrimination: Rhetorics of Racism and Antisemitism* (2001) (co-authored with Martin Reisigl), *The Politics of Exclusion: Debating Migration in Austria* (2008) (with Michal Krzyzanowski) and *The Discourse of Politics in Action: Politics as Usual.* (2009). She has edited several collections of papers on methodology in critical discourse analysis.

The Key Texts

Austin, J. L. (1962) *How to do Things with Words*. **Oxford: Oxford University Press.**

This relatively short but influential book comprises transcripts of 12 lectures that Austin delivered at Harvard University in 1955. Austin develops a theory of speech acts, arguing that in language there are constatives (statements that can either be true or false) and performatives which are not truth-evaluable but instead can be felicitous ('happy') or infelicitous ('unhappy') and are used as part of 'doing' an action, such as betting, marrying, naming or bequeathing. If the performative is not uttered under the right set of circumstances (e.g. you cannot marry someone if you are not ordained to do so), then the performative is infelicitous. As the lecture series develops, Austin makes a distinction between explicit and implicit performatives and later in the book develops further classifications based on a distinction between locutions, illocutions and perlocutions. Austin's theories were later developed by John Searle (see Searle 1969).

Bell, A. and Garrett, P. (1998) *Approaches to Media Discourse*. Oxford: Malden.

This edited collection (1998) brings together scholars from linguistics, discourse analysis and media studies and discusses different approaches to the study of media texts such as television news interviews, opinion letters in newspapers, and front pages of newspapers. The approaches to discourse analysis used include textual analysis, narrative analysis, reception analysis and visual image analysis (e.g. Gunther Kress and Theo van Leeuwen examine the layout of newspapers and show that the analysis of texts are no longer structured by linguistic means exclusively but also through the spatial arrangement of blocks of text, pictures and other graphic features). Because of the diverse approaches to text and discourse analysis, this book is a valuable resource for discourse analysts.

Benwell, B and Stokoe, E. (2006) *Discourse and Identity*. Edinburgh: Edinburgh University Press.

Considering the relationship between discourse and identity (and defining *identity* broadly as how people display who they are to each other), this accessible book is divided into seven chapters which each considers a different discursive environment in which people do 'identity work'. These include everyday conversations and different types of narratives, computer-mediated or virtual contexts, advertising and institutions. Analyses of naturally occurring data are combined with discussions of key studies by other authors, and the book critically considers a range of approaches, including Conversation Analysis, Critical Discourse Analysis, discursive psychology, politeness theory, positioning theory and narrative analysis. Interestingly, the book also tackles a somewhat neglected aspect of discourse and identity research, spatial or place-relevant aspects of identity.

Brown, G. and Yule, G. (1983) *Discourse Analysis*. Cambridge: Cambridge University Press.

A relatively early book on discourse analysis, focusing on the concept of discourse as 'language in use' rather than viewing discourse as associated with power relations and ideologies. The book takes a wide range of discourse-based research and linguistic terminology into account and is organized around central topics which include the role of context in making meaning (which deals with presupposition, implicature and inferencing), topic and representation of discourse content, thematic structure, information structure, reference (which covers cohesion) and coherence (which includes speech act theory, frames and scripts). As such, the bulk of the book focuses on linguistic analysis in reference to how people communicate, using many real-life examples (rather than analysing abstracted cases), although it does not take into account other aspects of analysis such as intertextuality or processes of production and reception.

Brown, P. and Levinson, S. (1987) *Politeness: Some Universals in Language Usage*. **Cambridge: Cambridge University Press.**

A reissue of an earlier work, this book seeks to outline a theory of politeness which can be applied universally (i.e. across cultures). Brown and Levinson's framework is influenced by aspects of Gricean pragmatics, such as the Cooperative Principle and communication as intentional. However, more central to their model is the concept of face, which can be positive (desire for approval/closeness) or negative (desire to be unimpeded). The bulk of the book is concerned with different sorts of FTAs (face threatening acts) and the different sorts of conversational strategies that are associated with positive and negative politeness. Utterances from various languages (English, Tamil, Japanese, Tzeltal etc.) are given as illustrations of different cultural contexts. Towards the end of the book, the authors consider implications of their model for social and linguistic theory.

Butler, J. (1990) *Gender Trouble*. **London and New York: Routledge.**

An influential feminist and post-structuralist text which critiques the notion of fixed gender identities, instead arguing that gender and sexual categories are produced as a result of powerful discourses that are articulated through language. Thus, gender appears fixed through its repeated performance in everyday life. The title of the book derives from Butler's view that contemporary feminist debates on the meaning of 'gender' lead to a sense of 'trouble'. Butler draws mainly on philosophers including Foucault, Irigaray, Kristeva and Wittig as well as referencing psychoanalytic theories from Freud and Lacan. The book covers a range of topics and concepts, including the subject of the woman in feminism, compulsory heterosexuality, the incest taboo and the maternal body. It ends with a discussion of the link between gender parody and politics.

De Saussure, F. (1966) *Course in General Linguistics.* **C. Bally and A. Sechehaye (eds) Translated by Wade Baskin. New York: McGraw-Hill Book Company.**

A groundbreaking book which outlined Saussure's central ideas of structuralism. It is based on Saussure's lecture notes given at the University of Geneva between 1906 and 1911. The book covers a range of topics that are important to discourse analysis including the division of language into langue/parole, as well as the investigation of the sign as a linguistic unit which is made up of the signifier and the signified – the two having an arbitrary relationship. Saussure also argues that language works through relations of difference, and he describes two types of relations: syntagmatic and pragmatic. The book is divided into six parts: introduction, which covers writing systems and phonetics; general principles which describes sign theory and makes the distinction between static linguistics and evolutionary linguistics; synchronic linguistics which tends to focus on grammatical aspects of language; diachronic linguistics which is more interested in sound change; geographical linguistics which considers dialects and questions of retrospective linguistics which functions as a conclusion to the book.

Fairclough, N. (1989) *Language and Power*. London: Longman.

The opening book in Longman's Language in Social Life series, where Fairclough first lays out the theory and procedures surrounding critical discourse analysis. Fairclough draws on a range of existing literature, including work on postmodernism, systemic linguistics, discourse analysis, sociolinguistics, pragmatics, critical linguistics and social theory, to argue that language is social practice and that a purely descriptive account of language will offer an incomplete picture. He thus postulates a three-stage model of critical discourse analysis comprising description, interpretation and explanation. Illustrations of analysis are given, with examples focusing on how power relations are expressed and maintained in newspaper articles, adverts and conversations. Fairclough also argues that the position of the analyst needs to be taken into account. In later chapters, he focuses on discourses of Thatcherism, advertising, consumerism, bureaucracy and therapy, ending with recommendations for the introduction of Critical Language Study in schools and educational contexts.

Fairclough, N. (1995) Critical Discourse Analysis: The Critical Study of Language. London: Longman.

A collection of key papers written by Fairclough mainly between 1983 and 1993 plus three new papers. The chapters are organized into four themes: (1) language, ideology and power, which reflects on the development of the analytical framework for studying the relationships between language, power and ideology; (2) discourse and sociocultural change, which integrates discourse analysis with social analysis of sociocultural change, presenting critical discourse analysis as a three-dimensional framework; (3) textual analysis in social research – this section is addressed to discourse analysts who are working outside language studies, arguing that textual analysis (which includes both linguistic and intertextual analysis) should be included in this kind of research; and (4) critical language awareness, where Fairclough focuses on educational applications of critical work in discourse analysis, particularly examining concepts of language awareness and language appropriateness in schools.

Fowler, R., Hodge, B., Kress, G. and Trew, T. (eds) (1979)
Language and Control. **London: Routledge.**

This is a collection of ten essays which work towards developing the concept of critical linguistics written by the four authors . The book's three aims are to show how (1) language is used in order to embody specific views of reality, (2) linguistic variation reflects and expresses structured social differences and (3) language use is part of social process. The authors analyse a variety of naturally occurring data, including newspapers, interviews, children's language and birth registration documentation, in order to show how linguistic structures impact on our perceptions of reality, regulate behaviour, categorize people, events and objects, and assert status. In doing so, the authors make use of Halliday's model of systemic functional linguistics. *Language and Control* strongly influenced the development of critical discourse analysis, which supplemented many of the linguistic tools and techniques of analysis described here with additional analyses of context.

Grice, P. (1989) *Studies in the Way of Words*. **Cambridge, MA: Harvard University Press.**

This valedictory book contains much of Grice's work, covering his influential William James lectures delivered in 1967, along with newer material. It is divided into two parts, Logic and Conversation, and Explorations in Semantics and Metaphysics. The book focuses on how people make sense of each other's utterances, particularly in terms of how they interpret meaning and the intention of the speaker as well as covering language philosophy, the philosophy of perception and metaphysics. Grice develops his theory of the Cooperative Principle and describes the four conversational Maxims (quantity, quality, relevance and manner). The book also contains Grice's work on implicature and presupposition.

Halliday, M. and Matthiessen, C. (2004) *An Introduction to Functional Grammar.* **Third Edition. London: Edward Arnold.**

This book gives a detailed account of Halliday's theory of systemic functional grammar, first published in 1985. Halliday's work on the functions of grammar has been utilized by critical linguists and critical discourse analysts who have focused on the choices that grammars offer speakers and writers, and the ways such choices can impact on interpretation of meaning, thus having ideological functions. In systemic functional grammar, language is analysed in three ways – as semantics, phonology and lexico-grammar – and text can be analysed with respect to three meta-functions: ideational, interpersonal and textual. The third edition of the book retains the original organization and coverage from the earlier two editions but adds new material, particularly from corpus data, as well as giving more emphasis to the systematic perspective and grammaticalization.

Hoey, M., Mahlberg, M., Stubbs, M. and Teubert, W. (2007) *Text, Discourse and Corpora.* **London: Continuum.**

A collection of eight chapters (with an introduction by John Sinclair) which examines how corpus linguistic approaches can be utilized in various aspects of discourse or text analysis. Unlike many other forms of discourse analysis, this approach concentrates on how computational analysis of large collections of electronic texts can be utilized in order to reveal patterns of language use that would not normally be available to the human eye. Case studies involve the use of large reference corpora such as the British National Corpus, smaller purpose-built corpora and the use of the web as corpus (via search engine queries). Hoey outlines a theory of lexical priming, Teubert examines words that represent key concepts (such as *globalization, work* and *property*), Stubbs examines multi-word sequences and the implications that the corpus approach has on linguistic models, while Mahlberg examines corpora of newspapers and literary texts (the latter involving the conceptualization of corpus stylistics).

Kress, G. and van Leeuwen, T. (1990) *Reading Images: The Grammar of Visual Design*. **Victoria: Deakin University Press.**

This book covers an approach to the systematic analysis of visual design, with the authors arguing that there are significant correspondences between the grammar of language and that of visual culture. Using a wide range of examples, including children's drawings, textbook illustrations, photojournalism, images taken from advertising and fine art, they show that elements such as use of colour, perspective, framing and composition can communicate meaning or act as rhetorical devices. They also consider three-dimensional images, including sculpture and architecture. An updated version of the book, published in 2006, considers new materials on moving images, colour, websites and web-based images as well as looking at the future of visual communication.

Lakoff, R. (1975) *Language and Women's Place.* **New York: Oxford University Press.**

A pioneering text in the study of gender and language, Lakoff argues that there is a direct relationship between language use and women's powerlessness by focusing on two main areas: language used by women and language used to talk about women. Her main argument in the book is that there is a distinctive women's language which reflects their subordinate status. Among the examples she cites are that women use tag questions, hedges, 'empty' adjectives and a rising intonation which render their language tentative and weak. Her assertion that the language of and about women expresses powerlessness began a long-running debate among gender and feminist scholars so that today her work is widely referenced. A recent expanded edition of the book was edited by Mary Bucholtz (2004) and contains some of the responses to the earlier text and brings a diversity of voices from across disciplines, such as language and linguistics, anthropology, information sciences and others, and situates the earlier work within contemporary feminist and gender studies.

Potter, J. and Wetherell, M. (1987) *Discourse and Social Psychology*. **London: Sage.**

Viewing discourse as all forms of talking and writing, this book applies concepts and techniques of discourse analysis to various topics in or related to social psychology, showing how discourse analysis offers a more sophisticated way of making sense of data. The authors are critical of traditional social psychology approaches, pointing out that they can sometimes reflect researcher bias or be inaccurate. As a contrast, they demonstrate how detailed qualitative analyses of texts (particularly conversation and interview data) reveal how concepts such as attitudes (that have traditionally been seen as easily measurable and stable) often appear contradictory and complex in people's talk. Techniques from Conversation Analysis are contrasted with those involving categorization based on predetermined typologies in order to demonstrate how the latter model is inadequate at explaining how people formulate accounts. Towards the end of the book, the authors present a ten-stage model for carrying out discourse analysis.

Reisigl, M. and Wodak, R. (2001) Discourse and Discrimination: Rhetorics of Racism and Antisemitism. London and New York: Routledge.

An important text in critical discourse analysis which relates discourse to social exclusion, more specifically to racism, antisemitism and ethnicism. The authors describe their discourse-historical framework for critical discourse analysis of texts, which takes into account the political, historical and cultural contexts in which the texts are produced and consumed. The theory is grounded in empirical data in the form of newspaper articles, political speeches and other policy texts in Austria. The authors use argumentation theory to show how different argumentation strategies are used to legitimate racist and other discriminatory discourses and practices. They also draw on and expand van Leeuwen's (1996) framework of representation of social actors in order to show how referential and predicational strategies are used to label and evaluate social actors in order to provide warrants for their social exclusion. The book also discusses how stereotypes are used as the basis for discrimination.

Sacks, H. (1992) *Lectures on Conversation*. Oxford: Blackwell.

This 1,400 page two-volume work comprises lectures given by Harvey Sacks between 1964 and 1972 on conversation and related topics (it is edited by Gail Jefferson). Sacks outlines many aspects of Conversation Analysis, using transcripts of conversations he collected (including those from when he worked at a suicide hotline). Volume 1 focuses on membership categorization devices and the rules of sequences in conversation, giving a full outline of the rules of turn-taking. Volume 2 covers the poetics of ordinary talk, the function of public tragedy and story-telling in conversation. The volume ends with a discussion of one of the most well-known facets of Conversation Analysis: adjacency pairs. Throughout both volumes, Sacks also includes commentary on a range of methodological issues relating to Conversation Analysis.

Schiffrin, D., Tannen, D. and Hamilton, H. E. (eds) (2001) *The Handbook of Discourse Analysis*. Oxford: Blackwell.

This 850-page edited collection contains 41 chapters on a range of subjects relating to the various conceptualizations of discourse analysis and is therefore one of the most wide-ranging and inclusive books available on the topic (although see also Jaworski and Coupland 2006). The chapters are split into six main sections: (1) discourse – meaning, function and context; (2) methods and resources for analysing discourse; (3) sequence and structure; (4) negotiating social relationships; (5) identity and subjectivity and (6) power, ideology and control. Each section ends with a number of discussion points. Many of the papers were previously published elsewhere, so this key text is in itself a collection of key texts, although other papers are from more contemporary specialists, and some are reflexive commentaries which highlight differences between some of the subdivisions in the field.

Stubbs, M. (1983) Discourse Analysis: The Sociolinguistic Analysis of Natural Language. Oxford: Blackwell.

An early book on discourse analysis which understands discourse as being 'language above the sentence or above the clause' as well as occurring in social contexts, especially in interactions between two or more people.

The book is split into five main sections. Section 1 is concerned with defining basic terminology. Section 2 offers three different approaches to carrying out discourse analysis of conversation: analysing transcripts for organization patterns, taking an ethnographic approach which focuses on underlying meanings of utterances and focusing on discourse particles such as *well* and *please*. Section 3 focuses on the concept of conversational exchanges and their structures, while Section 4 is concerned with cohesion, coherence and propositions. Finally, Section 5 considers methodological aspects, reflecting on the fact that there are no established ways of doing discourse analysis and addressing issues of sampling, data size, bias and triangulation.

Sunderland, J. (2004) *Gendered Discourses*. London: Palgrave.

Sunderland develops a system for identifying and naming discourses through analysing their 'traces' in language use. She distinguishes between descriptive discourses (such as classroom discourse) and interpretive discourses, which represent a particular view or ideology (such as racist discourse). Specific examples of gendered discourses such as 'women beware women' or 'poor boys' are illustrated. The book focuses on relationships between different types or orders of discourses, noting that discourses are arranged in hierarchies and that they can also be supportive, contradictory and conflicting. In the middle part of the book, Sunderland draws on examples from texts in parenting magazines, children's literature and classroom interactions, while the book ends with a section on linguistic intervention, which focuses on the concept of damaging discourses.

Van Dijk, T. (ed.) (1997) *Discourse as Social Interaction*.
London, Thousand Oaks and New Delhi: Sage.

An edited collection of chapters on different forms of discourse analysis but heavily featuring perspectives that focus on context, power and ideology. The collection establishes a theoretical link between discourse and social life as the contributors focus on the functions of text and talk, showing that discourse is not only about form and meaning but also about social (inter)action. The approaches to discourse analysis represented in this volume include Critical Discourse Analysis, Conversation Analysis and socio-cognitive analysis and cover areas such a racism and ethnicism, gender, corporate power, institutional settings, politics and culture. The book is suitable for discourse analysts at different levels of sophistication but is also useful for those whose interests include communication studies, cultural studies, law and anthropology.

Widdowson, H. (2004) Text, Context, Pretext: Critical Issues in Discourse Analysis. Oxford: Blackwell.

In this book, Widdowson critically reflects on critical discourse analysis itself, arguing that while the motivations behind CDA practitioners are laudable, the way that they approach analysis is problematic in that they tend to rely on subjective interpretations in their analyses, for example, by engaging in selective attention to certain textual features. He claims that 'critical discourse analysis' is a misnomer, since its findings usually consist of interpretations which are conditioned by contextual and pretextual factors. Widdowson also devotes a chapter to the critique of corpus approaches, arguing that corpus linguists cannot infer contextual factors from co-textual ones and therefore cannot use textual data as evidence for discourse. In his conclusion, Widdowson proposes that CDA requires more academic rigour, suggesting a number of directions, such as establishing default interpretations of texts based on psycholinguistic research or by carrying out detailed investigations of production and consumption via ethnographic enquiry.

Wodak, R. and Meyer, M. (eds.) (2001). *Methods of Critical Discourse Analysis*. London, Thousand Oaks and New Delhi: Sage.

This book serves as an introductory text to Critical Discourse Analysis, bringing together contributions from six prolific scholars of discourse analysis. In the first chapter, Wodak gives an account of the history of CDA along with important concepts and developments in the field. Then, Meyer discusses how CDA uses different approaches, both theoretical and methodological, in doing discourse analysis. He points out, however, that in this diversity, there are a number of key characteristics that the different approaches share: They are interested in the 'social processes of power, hierarchy building, exclusion and subordination' (Meyer 2001: 30), and they aim to uncover the discursive aspects of social inequalities (ibid.). The final chapters cover five influential approaches to CDA research, illustrating theoretical and methodological issues as well as giving examples of analysis: Jäger's discourse and dispositive analysis, Wodak's discourse-historical approach, Van Dijk's 'socio-cognitive' approach, Fairclough's CDA and Scollon's Mediated Discourse Analysis.

References

Aijmer, K. (1996), *Conversational Routines in English. Convention and Creativity*. London: Longman.

Albertazzi, D. and McDonnell, D. (2008), *Twenty-First Century Populism: The Spectre of Western European Democracy*. New York and London: Palgrave Macmillan.

Althussur, L. (1971), *Lenin and Philosophy and Other Essays*. London: New Left Books.

Altman, R. (2008), *A Theory of Narrative*. New York: Columbia University Press.

Anderson, B. (1983), *Imagined Communities*. London and New York: Verso.

Andersen, G. (1998), 'The pragmatic marker *like* from a relevance-theoretic perspective.' In A. H. Jucker and Y. Zov (eds), *Discourse Markers: Descriptions and Theory*. Amsterdam/Philadelphia: John Benjamins, pp. 147–170.

Anderson, A. R., Belnap, N. D. and Dunn, J. M. (1992), *Entailment: The Logic of Relevance and Necessity. Vol. 2.* Princeton, NJ: Princeton University Press.

Armistead, N. (1974), *Reconstructing Social Psychology*. Harmondsworth: Penguin.

Atkinson, J. and Drew, P. (1979), *Order in Court. The Organization of Verbal Interaction in Judicial Settings*. London: MacMillan.

Atkinson, M. and Heritage, J. (eds) (1984), *Structures of Social Action*: *Studies in Conversation Analysis*. Cambridge: Cambridge University Press.

Auer, P. (1984), *Bilingual Conversation*. Amsterdam: John Benjamins.

Austin, J. L. (1962), *How To Do Things With Words: The William James Lectures Delivered at Harvard University in 1955*. Oxford: Clarendon.

Bakhtin, M. M. (1986), *Speech Genres and Other Late Essays*. Edited by C. Emersen and M. Holquist. Translated by V. McGee. Austin, TX: University of Texas Press.

Baker, P. (2002), *Polari – The Lost Language of Gay Men*. London: Routledge.

Baker, P. (2005), *Public Discourses of Gay Men*. London: Routledge.

Baker, P. (2006), *Using Corpora in Discourse Analysis*. London: Continuum.

Baker, P. (2008), *Sexed Texts*. London: Equinox.

Baker, P. (2010), 'Will Ms ever be as frequent as Mr? A corpus-based comparison of gendered terms across four diachronic corpora of British English.' *Gender and Language*, 4.

Barker, C. and Galasinski, D. (2001), *Cultural Studies and Discourse Analysis. A Dialogue on Language and Identity*. London: Sage.

Baron-Cohen, S. (2004), *The Essential Difference: Men, Women and the Extreme Male Brain*. London: Penguin.

Baxter, J. (2002), 'Competing discourses in the classroom: A post-structuralist discourse analysis of girls' and boys' speech in public contexts.' *Discourse and Society*, 13, 827–842.

Baxter, J. (2003), *Positioning Gender in Discourse: A Feminist Methodology*. Basingstoke: Palgrave Macmillan.

Baxter, J. (2008), 'Feminist post-structuralist discourse analysis: A new theoretical and methodological approach?' In K. Harrington, L. Litosseliti, H. Sauntson and J. Sunderland (eds), *Gender and Language Research Methodologies*. Basingstoke: Palgrave MacMillan, pp. 243–255.

Beetham, D. (1991), *The Legitimation of Power*. London: Macmillan Education Ltd.

Beier, L. (1995), 'Anti-language or jargon? Canting in the English underworld in the sixteenth and seventeenth centuries.' In P. Burke and R. Porter (eds), *Languages and Jargons*, Cambridge: Polity Press, pp. 64–101.

Bell, A. (1984), 'Language style as audience design.' *Language in Society*, 13(2), 145–204.

Bell, A. (1991), *The Language of News Media*. Oxford: Blackwell.

Bell, A. and Garrett, P. (1998), *Approaches to Media Discourse*. Oxford: Blackwell.

Bell, A., Harlow, R. and Starks, D. (eds) (2006), *Languages of New Zealand*. Wellington: Victoria University Press.

Bell, A. and Holmes, J. (eds) (1990), *New Zealand Ways of Speaking*. Wellington: Victoria University Press.

Benveniste, E. (1954), 'Civilisation: Contributions à l'histoire du mot.' In E. Benveniste (ed.), *Problèmes de linguistique générale*. Paris: Gallimard (1966), pp. 336–345.

Bernard, H. R. and Ryan, G. W. (2010), *Analyzing Qualitative Data: Systematic Approaches.* Los Angeles, CA: Sage.

Bernstein, B. (1990), *The Structuring of Pedagogic Discourse: Class, Codes and Control. Vol. 4.* London: Routledge.

Bhatia, V. K. (2004), *Worlds of Written Discourse: A Genre-Based View.* London: Continuum.

Biber, D., Conrad, S. and Reppen, R. (1998), *Corpus Linguistics: Investigating Language Structure and Use.* Cambridge: Cambridge University Press.

Biber, D., Johansson, S., Leech, G., Conrad, S. and Finegan, E. (1999), *Longman Grammar of Spoken and Written English.* London: Longman.

Biber, D., Conrad, S. and Cortes, V. (2004), 'If you look at . . .: Lexical bundles in University teaching and textbooks.' *Applied Linguistics*, 25(3), 371–405.

Billig, M. (1987), *Arguing and Thinking: A Rhetorical Approach to Social Psychology.* Cambridge: Cambridge University Press.

Blaikie, N. (2003), *Analyzing Quantitative Data: From Description to Explanation.* London: Sage.

Bloome, D. and Green, J. (2002), 'Directions in the sociolinguistic study of reading.' In P. D. Pearson, R. Barr, M. L. Kamil and P. Mosenthal (eds), *Handbook of Reading Research vol 1.* Mahwah, NJ: Lawrence Erlbaum, pp 395–421.

Bloomfield, L. (1926), 'A set of postulates for the science of language.' *Language*, 2, 153–154.

Boas, F. (1887), 'Museums of ethnology and their classification.' *Science*, 9, 589.

Boas, F. (1889), 'On alternating sounds.' *American Anthropologist, 2,* 47–53.

Bordo, S. (1993), *Unbearable Weight: Feminism, Western Culture, and the Body.* Berkeley, CA: University of California Press.

Bourdieu, P. (1984), *Distinction: A Social Critique of the Judgement of Taste.* London: Routledge and Kegan Paul.

Bourdieu, P. (1986), 'The forms of capital.' In J. Richardson (ed.), *Handbook of Theory and Research for the Sociology of Education.* New York: Greenwood, pp. 241–258.

Bourdieu, P. (1991), *Language and Symbolic Power.* Cambridge: Harvard University Press.

Bourdieu, P. (1993), *The Field of Cultural Production.* New York: Columbia University Press.

Bowell, T. and Kemp, G. (2002), *Critical Thinking. A Concise Guide. Second Edition*. London: Routledge.

Brazil, D., Coulthard, M. and Johns, C. (1980), *Discourse Intonation and Language Teaching*. London: Longman.

Brewer, J. (2000), *Ethnography*. Buckingham: Open University Press.

Brown, G. and Yule, G. (1983), *Discourse Analysis*. Cambridge: Cambridge University Press.

Brown, P. (1973), *Radical Psychology*. London: Tavistock.

Brown, P. and Levinson, S. (1987), *Politeness: Some Universals in Language Usage*. Cambridge: Cambridge University Press.

Burr, V. (1995), *An Introduction to Social Constructionism*. London: Routledge.

Butler, J. (1990), *Gender Trouble: Feminism and the Subversion of Identity*. New York: Routledge.

Butler, J. (1991), 'Imitation and gender insubordination.' In D. Fuss (ed.), *Inside/Out. Lesbian Theories, Gay Theories*. New York: Routledge, pp. 13–31.

Butler, J. (1993), *Bodies That Matter: On the Discursive Limits of Sex*. New York: Routledge.

Butler, J. (1997), *Excitable Speech: A Politics of the Performative*. New York: Routledge.

Butler, J. (2004), *Undoing Gender*. London: Routledge.

Butler, J. (2005), *Giving an Account of Oneself*. New York: Fordham University Press.

Button, G., Drew, P. and Heritage, J. (eds) (1986), *Interaction and Language Use, Special Double Issue of Human Studies, 9*. Republished in 1991 by Lanham: University Press of America.

Caldas-Coulthard, C. R. and van Leeuwen, T. (2002), 'Stunning, shimmering, iridescent: Toys as the representation of gendered social actors.' In L. Litosseliti and J. Sunderland (eds), *Gender Identity and Discourse Analysis*. Amsterdam: John Benjamins, pp. 91–108.

Cameron, D. (1992), *Feminism and Linguistic Theory*. London: Palgrave.

Cameron, D. (1994), 'Words, words, words: The power of language.' In S. Dunant (ed.), *The War of the Words: The Political Correctness Debate*. London: Virago, pp. 15–34.

Cameron, D. (1995), *Verbal Hygiene*. London: Routledge.

Cameron, D. (2001), *Working with Spoken Discourse*. London: Sage.

Cameron, D. (2002), *Good to Talk? Living and Working in a Communication Culture*. London: Sage.

Cameron, D. (2007), *The Myth of Mars and Venus*. Oxford: Oxford University Press.

Cameron, D. and Kulick, D. (2003), *Language and Sexuality*. Cambridge: Cambridge University Press.

Cameron, D., McAlinden, F. and O'Leary, K. (1988), 'Lakoff in context: The social and linguistic function of tag questions.' In J. Coates and D. Cameron (eds), *Women in Their Speech Communities*. Harlow, GA: Longman, pp. 74–93.

Canary, D. J. and Hause, K. S. (1993), 'Is there any reason to research sex differences in communication?' *Communication Quarterly*, 41, 129–44.

Canovan, M. (1981), *Populism*. New York and London: Harcourt Brace Jovanovich.

Carter, R. and Nash, W. (1990), *Seeing Through Language: A Guide to Styles of English Writing*. Oxford: Blackwell.

Cazden, C. B. (2001), *Classroom Discourse: The Language of Teaching. Second Edition*. Portsmouth, NH: Heinemann.

Chafe, W. (1982), 'Integration and involvement in speaking, writing, and oral literature.' In D. Tannen (ed.), *Spoken and Written Language*. Norwood, MA: Ablex, pp. 35–54.

Chapman, S. and Routledge, C. (2009), *Key Ideas in Linguistics and the Philosophy of Language*. Edinburgh: Edinburgh University Press.

Choi, P. Y. L. (2000), *Femininity and the Physically Active Woman*. London: Routledge.

Chomsky, N. (1965), *Aspects of the Theory of Syntax*. Cambridge, MA: MIT Press.

Coates, J. (1986), *Women, Men and Language*. London: Longman.

Coates, J. (1996), *Women Talk: Conversation between Women Friends*. Oxford: Blackwell.

Coates, J. (ed.) (1998), *Language and Gender: A Reader*. Oxford: Blackwell.

Coates, J. (2003), *Men Talk. Stories in the Making of Masculinities*. Oxford: Blackwell.

Coates, J. and Cameron, D. (eds) (1989), *Women in Their Speech Communities*. London: Longman.

Cohen, S. (1973), *Folk Devils and Moral Panics*. St Albans: Paladin.

Conboy, M. (2006), *Tabloid Britain: Constructing a Community through Language*. London: Routledge.

Connell, R. W. (1987), *Gender and Power*. Stanford, CA: Stanford University Press.

Connell, R. W. (1995), *Masculinities*. Oxford: Polity Press.

Cook, G. (1989), *Discourse*. Oxford: Oxford University Press.

Cook, G. (1992), *The Discourse of Advertising*. London: Routledge.

Cook, G. (1994), *Discourse and Literature: The Interplay of Form and Mind*. Oxford: Oxford University Press.

Cossard, P. K. (2006), 'Electronic Medievalia: Global warming for humanities computing? Strategic changes in the economic forecast.' *A Journal of Early Medieval Northwestern Europe 9*. Online journal http://www.mun. ca/mst/heroicage/issues/9/em.html.

Coulthard, M. (1977), *An Introduction to Discourse Analysis*. London: Longman.

Coulthard, M. (ed.) (1992), *Advances in Spoken Discourse Analysis*. London: Routledge.

Coulthard, M. (2000), 'Whose text is it? On the linguistic investigation of authorship.' In S. Sarangi and M. Coulthard (eds), *Discourse and Social Life*. London: Longman, pp, 270–287.

Coulthard, M. and Montgomery, M. (1981), *Studies in Discourse Analysis*. London: Routledge and Kegan Paul.

Davies, B. and Harré, R. (1990), 'Positioning: The discursive production of selves.' *Journal for the Theory of Social Behaviour,* 20(1), 43–63.

De Beaugrande, R. and Dressler, W. U. (1981), *Introduction to Text Linguistics*. London: Longman.

De Fina, A., Schiffrin, D. and Bamberg, M. (eds) (2006), *Discourse and Identity*. Cambridge: Cambridge University Press.

Derrida, J. (1973), *Speech and Phenomena, and Other Essays on Husserl's Theory of Signs*. Translated by D. B. Allison. Evanston, IL: Northwestern University Press.

Derrida, J. (1976), *Of Grammatology*. Baltimore, MD: John Hopkins Press. Translation of *De la Grammatologie*. Translated by G. S. Spivak (1967). Paris: Editions de Minuit.

Derrida, J. (1978), *Writing and Difference*. London: Routledge.

De Saussure, F. (1966), *Course in General Linguistics*. Edited by C. Bally and A. Sechehaye. Translated by Wade Baskin. New York: McGraw-Hill Book Company.

Dindia, K. and Allen, M. (1992), 'Sex differences in self-disclosure: a meta-analysis.' *Psychological Bulletin*, 112(1), 106–24.

Dressler, R. A. and Kreuz, R. J. (2000), 'Transcribing oral discourse: A survey and model system.' *Discourse Processes*, 29, 25–36.

Drew, P. and Heritage, J. (eds) (1992), *Talk at Work: Interaction in Institutional Settings*. Cambridge: Cambridge University Press.

Drew, P. and Heritage, J. (eds) (2006), *Conversation Analysis* (4 Volumes), London: Sage.

Dubois, B. and Crouch, I. (1975), 'The question of tag questions in women's speech: They really don't use more of them.' *Language in Society*, 4, 289–294.

Dunant, S. (ed.) (1994), *The War of the Words: The Political Correctness Debate*. London: Virago.

Duncan, S. (1973), 'Towards a grammar for dyadic conversation.' *Semiotica*, 9, 29–46.

Dyer, R. (ed.) (1977), *Gays and Film*. London: British Film Institute.

Eagleton, T. (1991), *Ideology: An Introduction*. London: Verso.

Eckert, P. and McConnell-Ginet, S. (1998), 'Communities of Practice: Where language and gender and power all live.' In J. Coates (ed.), *Language and Gender: A Reader*. Oxford: Blackwell, pp. 484–494.

Edley, N. (2001), 'Analysing masculinity: Interpretative repertoires, ideological dilemmas and subject positions.' In M. Wetherell, M. Taylor and S. J. Yates (eds), *Discourse as Data: A Guide for Analysis*. London: Sage, pp. 189–228.

Edwards, D. (2005), 'Discursive psychology.' In K. L. Fitch and R. E. Sanders (eds), *Handbook of Language and Social Interaction*. Mahwah, NJ: Lawrence Erlbaum, pp. 257–273.

Edwards, D. and Potter, J. (1992), *Discursive Psychology*. London: Sage.

Ehrenreich, B. (1992), 'The challenge for the left.' In P. Berman (ed.), *Debating PC: The Controversy over Political Correctness of College Campuses*. New York: Laurel, pp. 333–338.

Epstein, S. (1998), 'Gay politics, ethnic identity: The limits of social constructionism.' In P. M. Nardi and B. E. Schneider (eds), *Social Perspectives in Lesbian and Gay Studies*. London: Routledge, pp. 134–159. Reprinted from *Socialist Review 93/94* (May–August 1987), pp. 9–54.

Fairclough, N. (1989), *Language and Power*. London: Longman.

Fairclough, N. (1992), *Discourse and Social Change*. Oxford: Wiley-Blackwell.

Fairclough, N. (1993), 'Critical discourse analysis and the marketization of public discourse: The universities.' *Discourse and Society*, 4(2), 133–168.

Fairclough, N. (1994), 'Conversationalization of public discourse and the authority of the consumer.' In K. Russell, N. Whiteley and N. Abercombie (eds), *The Authority of the Consumer*, London: Routledge, pp. 253–268.

Fairclough, N. (1995), *Critical Discourse Analysis*. London: Longman.

Fairclough, N. (1996), 'Technologisation of discourse.' In C. R. Caldas-Coulthard and M. Coulthard (eds), *Texts and Practices: Readings in Critical Discourse Analysis*. London: Routledge, pp. 71–83.

Fairclough, N. (2000a), *New Labour, New Language?* London: Longman.

Fairclough, N. (2000b), 'Language and neo-liberalism.' *Discourse and Society*, 11(2), 147–148.

Fairclough, N. (2001), 'Critical discourse analysis as a method in social scientific research.' In R. Wodak and M. Meyer (eds), *Methods of Critical Discourse Analysis*. London, Thousand Oaks and Delhi: Sage, pp. 121–138.

Fairclough, N. (2003), *Analysing Discourse: Textual Analysis for Social Research*. London: Routledge.

Fairclough, N. (2009), 'A dialectical-relational approach to critical discourse analysis in social research.' In R. Wodak and M. Meyer (eds), *Methods for Critical Discourse Analysis*. London: Sage, pp. 162–200.

Fairclough, N. and Wodak, R. (1997), 'Critical discourse analysis.' In T. Van Dijk (ed.), *Discourse as Social Interaction*. London: Sage, pp. 258–284.

Fetterman, D. M. (1998), *Ethnography: Step by Step. Second Edition.* Thousand Oaks, CA: Sage.

Foucault, M. (1967), *Madness and Civilisation: A History of Insanity in the Age of Reason.* London: Tavistock Publications.

Foucault, M. (1971), 'Orders of discourse.' *Social Science Information*, 10(2), 7–30.

Foucault, M. (1972), *The Archaeology of Knowledge*. London: Tavistock. Translated by A. M. Sherdidan Smith.

Foucault, M. (1979a), *The History of Sexuality: The Will to Knowledge. Vol. 1.* London: Allen Lane.

Foucault, M. (1979b), *Discipline and Punish*. Harmondsworth: Penguin.

Foucault, M. (1984), 'The order of discourse.' In M. Shapiro (ed.), *Language and Politics*. New York: New York University Press, pp. 108–138.

Foucault, M. (1986), *The History of Sexuality: The Use of Pleasure. Vol. 2.* London: Viking.

Foucault, M. (1988), *The History of Sexuality: The Care of the Self. Vol. 3.* London: Allen Lane.

Fowler, R. (1971), *The Languages of Literature.* London: Routledge and Kegan Paul.

Fowler, R. (1977), *Linguistics and the Novel.* London: Methuen.

Fowler, R. (1991), *Language in the News: Discourse and Ideology in the Press.* London: Routledge.

Fowler, R., Hodge, G., Kress, G. and Trew, T. (eds) (1979), *Language and Control.* London: Routledge and Kegan Paul.

Garfinkel, H. (2002), *Ethnomethodology's Program.* New York: Rowman and Littlefield.

Gilbert, G. N. and Mulkay, M. (1984), *Opening Pandora's Box: A Sociological Analysis of Scientists' Discourse.* Cambridge: Cambridge University Press.

Glaser, B. G. (1965), 'The constant comparative method of qualitative analysis.' *Social Problems*, 12(4), 436–445.

Gleason, P. (1983), 'Identifying identity: A semantic history.' *Journal of American History*, 69(4), 910–931.

Goffman, E. (1956), *The Presentation of Self in Everyday Life.* Edinburgh: University of Edinburgh Social Sciences Research Centre.

Goffman, E. (1963), *Stigma: Notes on the Management of Spoiled Identity.* Englewood Cliffs, NJ: Prentice-Hall.

Goffman, E. (1967), *Interaction Ritual: Essays on Face-to-face Behavior.* New York: Garden City.

Goffman, E. (1974), *Frame Analysis: An Essay on the Organization of Experience.* Cambridge: Harvard University Press.

Goffman, E. (1981), *Forms of Talk.* Oxford, Blackwell.

Goodman, S. (1996), 'Market forces speak English.' In S. Goodman and D. Graddol (eds), *Redesigning English: New Texts, New Identities.* London: Routledge, pp. 141–180.

Goode, E. and Ben-Yehuda, N. (1994), *Moral Panics: The Social Construction of Deviance.* Oxford: Blackwell.

Goody, E. (ed.) (1978), *Questions and Politeness: Strategies in Social Interaction. Cambridge Papers in Social Anthropology, 8.* Cambridge: Cambridge University Press.

Gramsci, A. (1971), *Selections from Prison Notebooks*. Translated by Q. Hoare and G. Nowell-Smith. London: Lawrence and Wishart.

Gramsci, A. (1985), *Selections from the Cultural Writings 1921–1926*. Edited by D. Forgacs and G. Nowell Smith. Translated by W. Boelhower. London: Lawrence and Wishart.

Grice, P. (1975), 'Logic and conversation.' In P. Cole and J. Morgan (eds), *Syntax and Semantics 3: Speech Acts*. New York: Academic Press, pp. 41–58.

Grice, P. (1989), *Studies in the Way of Words*. Harvard: Harvard University Press.

Gumperz, J. (1968), 'The speech community.' In D. Sills (ed.), *International Encyclopedia of the Social Sciences*. New York: Macmillan, pp. 381–386.

Gumperz, J. (1982), *Discourse Strategies*. Cambridge: Cambridge University Press.

Gumperz, J. and Hymes, D. (eds) (1972), *Directions in Sociolinguistics: The Ethnography of Communication*. New York: Holt, Rinehart and Winston.

Habermas, J. (1979), *Communication and the Evolution of Society*. Boston: Beacon Press.

Habermas, J. (1984), *The Theory of Communicative Action: Reason and the Rationalization of Society. Vol. 1*. Translated by T. McCarthy. London: Heinemann.

Habermas, J. (1985), *Legitimation Crisis*. Boston: Beacon Press.

Hall, D. E. (2003), *Queer Theories*. London: Palgrave.

Hall, S. (1973), *Encoding and Decoding in the Television Discourse*. Birmingham University, Centre for Cultural Studies.

Hall, S. (1997), *Representation: Cultural Representations and Signifying Practices*. London: Sage in Association with the Open University.

Hall, S., Critcher, C., Jefferson, T., Clarke, J. and Roberts, B. (1978), *Policing the Crisis*. London: Macmillan.

Halliday, F. (1999), 'Islamophobia reconsidered.' *Ethnic and Racial Studies*, 22(5), 892–902.

Halliday, M. A. K. (1961), 'Categories of the theory of grammar.' *Word*, 17, 241–292.

Halliday, M. A. K. (1978), *Language as a Social Semiotic: The Social Interpretation of Language and Meaning*. London: Edward Arnold Ltd.

Halliday, M. A. K. (1990), 'New ways of meaning: The challenge to applied linguistics.' *Journal of Applied Linguistics*, 6, 7–36.

Halliday, M. A. K. (1994), *An Introduction to Functional Grammar. Second edition*. London: Edward Arnold.

Halliday, M. A. K. and Hasan, R. (1976), *Cohesion in English*. London: Longman.

Halliday, M. A. K. and Hasan, R. (1985), *Language, Context and Text: Aspects of Language in a Socio-Semiotic Perspective*. Australia: Deakin University Press.

Halliday, M. and Matthiessen, C. (2004), *An Introduction to Functional Grammar. Third Edition*. London: Edward Arnold.

Hamblin, C. L. (1970), *Fallacies*. London: Metheun.

Hardt-Mautner, G. (1995), *Only Connect: Critical Discourse Analysis and Corpus Linguistics, UCREL Technical Paper 6*. Lancaster: University of Lancaster. Available at http://www.comp.lancs.ac.uk/ucrel/tech_papers.html.

Harré, R. and Secord, P. F. (1972), *The Explanation of Social Behaviour*. Oxford: Blackwell.

Harré, R., Brockmeier, J. and Mühlhäusler, P. (1999), *Greenspeak: A Study of Environmental Discourse*. London: Sage.

Harrington, K. (2008), 'Perpetuating difference? Corpus linguistics and the gendering of reported dialogue.' In K. Harrington, L. Litosseliti, H. Sauntson and J. Sunderland (eds), *Gender and Language Research Methodologies*. Basingstoke: Palgrave MacMillan, pp. 85–102.

Hart, C. and Luke, D. (eds) (2007), *Cognitive Linguistics in Critical Discourse Analysis: Theory and Application*. Newcastle: Cambridge Scholars.

Harvey, D. (2005), *A Brief History of Neoliberalism*. Oxford: Oxford University Press.

Hayward, S. (2000), *Cinema Studies: The Key Concepts*. London: Routledge.

Hekman, S. (2004), *Private Selves, Public Identities: Reconsidering Identity Politics*. University Park: Pennsylvania State University Press.

Heritage, J. (1991), *Garfinkel and Ethnomethodology*, Cambridge: Polity.

Hewings, M. (2005), *Grammar and Context*. London: Routledge.

Hodge, R. and Kress, G. (1988), *Social Semiotics*. Cambridge: Polity Press.

Hoey, M. (1986), 'The discourse colony: A preliminary study of a neglected discourse type.' In R. M. Coulthard (ed.), *Talking about Text, Discourse Analysis Monographs 13*, English Language Research. Birmingham: University of Birmingham, pp. 1–26.

Hogg, M. A. and Abrams, D. (eds) (1999), *Social Identity and Social Cognition*. Malden, MA: Blackwell.

214 References

Hoggart, R. (1957), *The Uses of Literacy*. London: Chatto and Windus.

Hollway, W. (1995), 'Feminist discourses and women's heterosexual desire.' In S. Wilkinson and C. Kitzinger (eds), *Feminism and Discourse: Psychological Perspectives*. London: Sage, pp. 86–105.

Holmes, J. (1984), 'Hedging your bets and sitting on the fence.' *Te Reo*, 27, 47–62.

Holmes, J. (1992), *An Introduction to Sociolinguistics*, London: Longman.

Holmes, J. (1995), *Women, Men and Politeness*. London: Longman.

Holmes, J. (2006), *Gendered Talk at Work*. Oxford: Blackwell.

Holmes, J. and Meyerhoff, M. (eds) (2003), *The Handbook of Language and Gender*. Oxford: Blackwell.

Huang, Y. (2007), *Pragmatics*. Oxford: Oxford University Press.

Hunston, S. (2002), *Corpora in Applied Linguistics*. Cambridge: Cambridge University Press.

Hutcheon, L. (1989), *The Politics of Postmodernism*. New York: Routledge.

Hyde, J. (2005), 'The gender similarities hypothesis.' *American Psychologist*, 60(6), 581–592.

Hymes, D. (ed.) (1964), *Language in Culture and Society: A Reader in Linguistics and Anthropology*. New York: Harper and Row.

Hymes, D. (1966), 'Two types of linguistic relativity.' In W. Bright (ed.), *Sociolinguistics*. The Hague: Mouton, pp. 114–158.

Hymes, D. (1972), 'Models of the interaction of language and social life.' In J. Gumperz and D. Hymes (eds), *Directions in Sociolinguistics: The Ethnography of Communication*. Oxford: Blackwell, pp. 35–71.

Hymes, D. (1974), *Foundations in Sociolinguistics: An Ethnographic Approach*. London: Tavistock Publications.

Hymes, D. (1983), *Essays in the History of Linguistic Anthropology*. Amsterdam: John Benjamins.

Israel, M. and Hay, I. (2006), *Research Ethics for Social Scientists*. London: Sage.

Jäger, S. (2001), 'Discourse and knowledge: Theoretical and methodological aspects of a critical discourse analysis and dispositive analysis.' In R. Wodak and M. Meyer (eds), *Methods of Critical Discourse Analysis*. London: Sage, pp. 32–62.

Jaworski, A. and Coupland, N. (eds) (2006), *The Discourse Reader. Second Edition*. London: Routledge.

Jespersen, O. (1922), *Language, Its Nature, Development and Origin*. London: Allen and Unwin.

Jørgensen, M. and Phillips, L. (2002), *Discourse Analysis as Theory and Method*. London: Sage.

Jucker, A. H. and Smith, S. W. (1998), 'And people just you know like "wow". Discourse markers as negotiating strategies.' In A. H. Jucker and Y. Zov (eds), *Discourse Markers: Descriptions and Theory*. Amsterdam/Philadelphia: John Benjamins, pp. 171–201.

Kitetu, C. and Sunderland, J. (2000), 'Gendered discourses in the classroom: The importance of cultural diversity.' In A. Yamashiro (ed.), *Temple University of Japan Working Papers 17*. Tokyo: Temple University, pp. 26–40.

Kitzinger, J. (1995), 'Qualitative research: introducing focus groups.' *British Medical Journal*, 311, 299–302.

Klein, N. (2007), *The Shock Doctrine: The Rise of Disaster Capitalism*. New York: Metropolitan Books/Henry Holt.

Krane, V. (2001), ' "We can be athletic and feminine," but do we want to? Challenges to femininity and heterosexuality in women's sport.' *Quest*, 53, 115–33.

Kreidler, C. W. (1989), *The Pronunciation of English: A course book in phonology*. Oxford: Blackwell.

Kress, G. (1982), *Learning to Write*. London: Routledge.

Kress, G. (1997), *Before Writing: Rethinking the Paths to Literacy*. London: Routledge.

Kress, G. (2003), *Literacy in the New Media Age*. London: Routledge.

Kress, G. and Hodge, R. (1979), *Language as Ideology*. London: Routledge.

Kress, G. and van Leeuwen, T. (1990), *Reading Images: the Grammar of Visual Design*. Victoria: Deakin University Press.

Kress, G. and van Leeuween, T. (2001), *Multimodal Discourse: the Modes and Media of Contemporary Communication*. London: Arnold.

Krippendorff, K. (2004), *Content Analysis: An Introduction to its Methodology. Second edition*. Thousand Oaks, CA: Sage.

Kronman, A. T. (1983), *Max Weber*. London: Edward Arnold.

Krzyzanowski, M. and Wodak, R. (2008), *The Politics of Exclusion: Debating Migration in Austria*. New Brunswick, NJ: Transaction.

Kunda, Z. (1999), *Social Cognition: Making Sense of People*. Cambridge, MA: MIT Press.

216   **References**

Kvale, S. (1996), *Interviews: An Introduction to Qualitative Research Interviewing*. Thousand Oaks, CA: Sage.

Labov, W. (1966), *The Social Stratification of English in New York City*. Columbia University PhD Thesis.

Labov, W. (1972a), *Language in the Inner City*. Philadelphia, PA: University of Pennsylvania Press.

Labov, W. (1972b), 'The logic of nonstandard English.' In P. Giglioli (ed.), *Language and Social Context*. Harmondsworth: Penguin, pp. 179–215.

Labov, W. (1973), *Sociolinguistic Patterns*. Philadelphia, PA: University of Pennsylvania Press.

Labov, W. (1994), *Principles of Sociolinguistics: Internal Factors. Vol. 1*. Oxford: Basil Blackwell.

Labov, W. (2000), *Principles of Sociolinguistics: Social Factors. Vol. 2*. Oxford: Basil Blackwell.

Labov, W. (2001), *Studies in Sociolinguistics by William Labov*. Beijing: Beijing Language and Culture University Press.

Laclau, E. and Mouffe, C. (1985), *Hegemony and Socialist Strategy: Towards a radical democratic politics*. London: Verso.

Lakoff, G. (2004), *Don't Think of an Elephant! Know your Values and Frame the Debate: The Essential Guide for Progressives*. White River Junction, VT: Chelsea Green.

Lakoff, R. (1975), *Language and Woman's Place*. New York: Harper and Row.

Lakoff, R. (1990), *Talking Power: The Politics of Language*. New York: Basic Books.

Lakoff, R. (2001), *The Language War*. Berkeley and Los Angeles, CA: University of California Press.

Landry, D. and MacLean, G. (eds) (1996), *The Spivak Reader*. New York and London: Routledge.

Lave, J. and Wenger, E. (1991), *Situated Learning: Legitimate Peripheral Participation*. Cambridge: Cambridge University Press.

Layder, D. (1993), *New Strategies in Social Research*. Cambridge: Polity Press.

Lazar, M. (ed.) (2005), *Feminist Critical Discourse Analysis: Gender, Power and Ideology in Discourse*. Basingstoke: Palgrave.

Leech, G. (1966), *English in Advertising*. London: Longman.

Leech, G. (1983), *Principles of Pragmatics*. London: Longman.

Leech, G. (2002), 'Recent grammatical change in English: Data, description, theory.' In K. Aijmer and B. Altenberg (eds), *Proceedings of the 2002 ICAME Conference*, Gothenburg, pp. 61–81.

Leech, G. and Short, M. (2007), *Style in Fiction: A Linguistic Introduction to English Fictional Prose. Second Edition.* Harlow, GA: Pearson.

Levinson, S. (1983), *Pragmatics.* Cambridge: Cambridge University Press.

Levinson, S. (2000), *Presumptive Meanings: The Theory of Generalized Conversational Implicature.* Cambridge, MA: MIT Press.

Levy, A. (2005), *Female Chauvinist Pigs: Women and the Rise of Raunch Culture.* London: Pocket Books.

Likert, R. (1932), 'A technique for the measurement of attitudes.' *Archives of Psychology*, 140, 1–55.

Lindlof, T. R. and Taylor, B. C. (2002), *Qualitative Communication Research Methods. Second Edition.* Thousand Oaks, CA: Sage.

Linell, P. (1998), *Approaching Dialogue.* Amsterdam: John Benjamins.

Litosseliti, L. (2003), *Using Focus Groups in Research.* London: Continuum.

Lodge, R. A. (2005), *A Sociolinguistic History of Parisian French.* Cambridge: Cambridge University Press.

Louw, B. (1993), 'Irony in the text or insincerity in the writer? – The diagnostic potential of semantic prosodies.' In M. Baker, G. Francis and E. Tognini-Bonelli (eds), *Text and Technology: In Honour of John Sinclair.* Amsterdam and Philadelphia: John Benjamins, pp. 157–176.

Lyons, J. (1977), *Semantics.* Cambridge: Cambridge University Press.

Lyotard, J. F. (1979 [1984]), *The Postmodern Condition: A Report on Knowledge.* Manchester: Manchester University Press.

Malinowski, B. (1923), 'The problem of meaning in primitive languages.' In C. Ogden and I. Richards (eds), *The Meaning of Meaning.* London: Routledge, pp. 146–152.

Marshall, C. and Rossman, G. B. (1999), *Designing Qualitative Research.* Thousand Oaks, CA: Sage.

Martin, J., R. and Rose, D. (2003), *Working with Discourse: Meaning Beyond the Clause.* London and New York: Continuum.

Martin, J. (2004), 'Positive discourse analysis: Power, solidarity and change.' *Revista*, 49, 179–200.

Marx, K. and Engels, F. (1848 [1998]), *The Communist Manifesto.* New York: Penguin.

Marx, K. (1977), *Capital.* London: Dent.

Mason, J. (2002), *Qualitative Researching.* London: Sage.

McEnery, T. (2006), *Swearing in English.* London: Routledge.

McEnery, T. and Wilson, A. (1996), *Corpus Linguistics. An Introduction.* Edinburgh: Edinburgh University Press.

McKee, A. (2003), *Textual Analysis*. London: Sage.

McRobbie, A. (2009), *The Aftermath of Feminism: Gender, Culture and Social Change*. London: Sage.

Memmi, A. (1992), *Rassimus*. Hamburg: Europäische Verlagsanstalt.

Merton, R. K. and Kendall, P. (1946), 'The focused interview.' *American Journal of Sociology*, 51(6), 541–557.

Mey, C. (2001), *Pragmatics: An Introduction*. London: Blackwell.

Meyer, M. (2001), 'Between theory, method and politics: Positioning of the approaches to CDA.' In R. Wodak and M. Meyer (eds), *Methods of Critical Discourse Analysis*. London: Sage, pp. 14–31.

Meyerhoff, M. (2006), *Introducing Sociolinguistics*. London: Routledge.

Mills, S. (1991), *Discourses of Difference: Women's Travel Writing and Colonialism*. London: Routledge.

Mills, S. (1997), *Discourse*. London: Routledge.

Mills, S. (1998), 'Post-feminist text analysis.' *Language and Literature*, 7(3), 235–253.

Mills, S. (2003a), *Michel Foucault*. London: Routledge.

Mills, S. (2003b), *Gender and Politeness*. Cambridge: Cambridge University Press.

Mills, S. (2005), *Gender and Colonial Space*. Manchester: Manchester University Press.

Mills, S. (2008), *Language and Sexism*. London: Routledge.

Minsky, M. (1975), 'A framework for representing knowledge.' In P. H. Winston (ed.), *The Psychology of Computer Vision*. New York: McGraw-Hill, pp. 211–277.

Moi, T. (ed.) (1990), *The Kristeva Reader*. Basil Blackwell, Oxford.

Money, J. (1955), 'Hermaphroditism, gender and precocity in hyperadreno-corticism: Psychologic findings.' *Bulletin of the Johns Hopkins Hospital*, 96, 253–264.

Mumby, D. K. and Clair, R. P. (1997), 'Organizational discourse.' In T. Van Dijk (ed.), *Discourse Studies: Discourse as Social Interaction. Vol. 2*. London, Thousand Oaks and New Delhi: Sage, pp. 181–205.

Namaste, V. K. (2000), *Invisible Lives. The Erasure of Transsexual and Transgendered People*. Chicago, IL: University of Chicago Press.

Norris, S. and Jones, R. H. (eds) (2005), *Discourse in Action: Introducing Mediated Discourse Analysis*. London: Routledge.

Nussbaum, M. (1995), 'Objectification.' *Philosophy and Public Affairs*, 24(4), 279–283.

Nystrand, M. (1982), *What Writers Know: The Language, Process, and Structure of Written Discourse.* New York: Academic Press.

O'Halloran, K. (2003), *Critical Discourse Analysis and Language Cognition.* Edinburgh: Edinburgh University Press.

Ochs, E. (1992), 'Indexing gender.' In B. D. Miller (ed.), *Sex and Gender Hierarchies.* Cambridge: Cambridge University Press, pp. 335–358.

Partington, A. (2003), *The Linguistics of Political Argument.* London: Routledge.

Partington, A. (2004), 'Corpora and discourse, a most congruous beast.' In A. Partington, J. Morley and L. Haarman (eds), *Corpora and Discourse.* Bern: Peter Lang, pp. 11–20.

Pauley, B. F. (2002), *From Prejudice to Persecution: A History of Austrian Anti-Semitism.* Chapel Hill, NC: University of North Carolina Press.

Phillips, L. and Jorgensen M. W. (2004), *Discourse Analysis as Theory and Method.* London, Thousand Oaks, New Delhi: Sage.

Pinker, S. (1994), *The Language Instinct: How the Mind Creates Language.* London: Penguin.

Potter, J. (1996), *Representing Reality: Discourse, Rhetoric and Social Construction.* London: Sage.

Potter, J. and Wetherell, M. (1987), *Discourse and Social Psychology. Beyond Attitudes and Behaviour.* London: Sage.

Potter, J. and Wetherell, M. (1995), 'Discourse analysis.' In J. Smith, R. Harré and L. van Langenhove (eds), *Rethinking Methods in Psychology.* London: Sage, pp. 80–92.

Rayson, P., Leech, G. and Hodges, M. (1997), 'Social differentiation in the use of English vocabulary: Some analyses of the conversational component of the British National Corpus.' *International Journal of Corpus Linguistics*, 2, 133–150.

Reisigl, M. and Wodak, R. (2001), *Discourse and Discrimination: Rhetorics of Racism and Antisemitism.* London: Routledge.

Rich, A. C. (1980), 'Compulsory heterosexuality and lesbian existence.' *Signs*, 5(4), 631–660.

Richardson, J. (2004), *(Mis)representing Islam: The Racism and Rhetoric of British Broadsheet Newspapers.* London: Routledge.

Riggins, S. H. (ed.) (1997), *The Language and Politics of Exclusion: Others in Discourse*. Thousand Oaks, CA: Sage.

Routley, R. and Meyer, R. K. (1973), 'Semantics of entailment.' In H. Leblanc (ed.), *Truth, Syntax, and Modality*. Amsterdam: North-Holland, pp. 194–243.

Rühlemann, C. (2007), *Conversation in Context. A Corpus-Driven Approach*. London: Continuum.

Runnymede Trust (1997), *Islamophobia: A Challenge for Us All*. Document downloaded from http://www.runnymedetrust.org/uploads/publications/pdfs/islamophobia.pdf.

Sacks, H., Schegloff, E. A. and Jefferson, G. (1974), 'A simplest systematics for the organization of turn-taking for conversation.' *Language*, 50, 696–735.

Said, E. (1979), *Orientalism*. New York: Vintage.

Schank, R. C. and Abelson, R. P. (1977), *Scripts, Plans, Goals and Understanding*. Hillsdale, NJ: L. Erlbaum.

Schegloff, E. A. and Sacks, H. (1973), 'Opening up closings.' *Semiotica*, 8, 289–327.

Schmid, H-J. and Fauth, J. (2003), 'Women's and men's style: Fact or fiction? New grammatical evidence.' Paper presented at the *Corpus Linguistics Conference*, Lancaster, March 2003.

Schiffrin, D. (1987), *Discourse Markers*. Cambridge: Cambridge University Press.

Schiffrin, D. (1994), *Approaches to Discourse*. Oxford: Blackwell.

Schiffrin, D., Tannen, D. and Hamilton, H. (eds) (2001), *The Handbook of Discourse Analysis*. Oxford: Blackwell.

Scollon, R. (1998), *Mediated Discourse as Social Interaction*. London: Longman.

Scollon, R. (2001), 'Action and text: Towards an integrated understanding of the place of text in social (inter)action, mediated discourse analysis and the problem of social action.' In R. Wodak and M. Meyer (eds), *Methods of Critical Discourse Analysis*. London: Sage, pp. 139–183.

Scollon, R. and Scollon, S. W. (1995), *Intercultural Communication: A Discourse Approach*. Oxford: Blackwell.

Scollon, R. and Scollon, S. W. (2003), *Discourses in Place: Language in the Material World*. London: Routledge.

Scott, M. and Lyman, S. (1968), 'Accounts.' *American Sociological Review*, 31, 46–62.

Searle, J. R. (1969), *Speech Acts: An Essay in the Philosophy of Language*. Cambridge: Cambridge University Press.

Searle, J. R. (1975), 'A taxonomy of illocutionary acts.' In K. Günderson (ed.), *Language, Mind, and Knowledge*. Minneapolis, MN, pp. 334–369.

Secher, H. P. (1962), *Basic Concepts in Sociology*. New York: Citadel Press.

Short, M. (1996), *Exploring the Language of Poems, Plays and Prose*, London: Longman.

Simpson, P. (1993), *Language, Ideology and Point of View*. London: Routledge.

Sperber, D. and Wilson, D. (1986), *Relevance: Communication and Cognition*. Cambridge, MA: Harvard University Press.

Stibbe, A. (2006), 'Deep ecology and language: The curtailed journey of the Atlantic salmon.' *Society and Animals*, 14(1), 61–77.

Stoller, R. (1968), *Sex and Gender: On the Development of Masculinity and Femininity*. New York: Science House.

Stubbs, M. (1983), *Discourse Analysis: The Sociolinguistic Analysis of Natural Language*. Chicago, IL: University of Chicago Press.

Stubbs, M. (1996), *Text and Corpus Analysis*, London: Blackwell.

Stubbs, M. (2001), *Words and Phrases*. London: Blackwell.

Sumner, W. G. (1906), *Folkways*. New York: Ginn.

Sunderland, J. (2004), *Gendered Discourses*. Basingstoke: Palgrave.

Swales, J. M. (1990), *Genre Analysis: English in Academic and Research Settings*. Cambridge: Cambridge University Press.

Swann, J. (2002), 'Yes, but is it gender?' In L. Litosseliti and J. Sunderland (eds), *Gender Identity and Discourse Analysis*. Amsterdam: John Benjamin, pp. 43–67.

Talbot, M. (1995), *Fictions at Work – Language and Social Practice in Fiction*. London: Longman.

Talbot, M. (1998), *Language and Gender: An Introduction*. Cambridge: Blackwell, Polity Press.

Tannen, D. (ed.) (1982), *Coherence in Spoken and Written Discourse*. Norwood, MA: Ablex.

Tannen, D. (1984), *Conversational Style: Analysing Talk among Friends*. Norwood, MA: Ablex.

Tannen, D. (1989), *Talking Voices: Repetition, Dialogue and Imagery in Conversational Discourse*. Cambridge: Cambridge University Press.

Tannen, D. (1990), *You Just Don't Understand: Women and Men in Conversation*. London: Virago.

Tannen, D. (ed.) (1993), *Framing in Discourse*. New York: Oxford University Press.

Tannen, D. (1995), *Talking from 9 to 5: Women and Men in the Workplace: Language, Sex and Power*. London: Virago.

Tannen, D. (2009), *You Were Always Mom's Favourite: Sisters in Conversation throughout their Lives*. London: Random House.

Tasker, F. (2004), 'Lesbian parenting: Experiencing pride and prejudice.' *Psychology of Women Section Review*, 6, 22–28.

Tasker, F. (2005), 'Lesbian mothers, gay fathers and their children: A review.' *Journal of Developmental and Behavioral Pediatrics*, 26, 224–240.

Te Molder, H. and Potter, J. (eds) (2005), *Conversation and Cognition*. Cambridge: Cambridge University Press.

Thiesmeyer, L. (ed.) (2003), *Discourse and Silencing: Representation and the Language of Displacement*. Amsterdam: John Benjamins.

Thomas, J. (1995), *Meaning in Interaction*. Harlow, London and New York: Longman.

Thompson, K. (1998), *Moral Panics*. London: Routledge.

Thornborrow, J. and Coates, J. (2003), *The Sociolinguistics of Narrative*. Amsterdam: John Benjamins.

Tognini-Bonelli, E. (2001), *Corpus Linguistics at Work* (Studies in Corpus Linguistics: 6). Amsterdam/Atlanta, GA: John Benjamins.

Toulmin, E., Rieke, R. and Janik, A. (1979), *An Introduction to Reasoning*. New York: Macmillan.

Troemel-Plotz, S. (1991), 'Review essay: Selling the apolitical.' *Discourse and Society*, 2(4), 489–502.

Van Den Berg, H., Wetherell, M. and Houtkoop, H. (eds) (2003), *Analysing Racist Discourse*. Cambridge: Cambridge University Press.

Van Dijk, T. (1984), *Prejudice in Discourse: An Analysis of Ethnic Prejudice in Cognition and Conversation*. Amsterdam: Benjamins.

Van Dijk, T. (1988), *News as Discourse*. Hillsdale, NJ: L. Erlbaum.

Van Dijk, T. (1991), *Racism and the Press*. London: Routledge.

Van Dijk, T. (1993), *Elite Discourse and Racism*. Newbury Park, CA: Sage.

Van Dijk, T. (1996), 'Discourse, power and access.' In C. Caldas-Coulthard and M. Coulthard (eds), *Texts and Practices: Readings in Critical Discourse Analysis*. London: Routledge, pp. 84–100.

Van Dijk, T. (ed.) (1997), *Discourse As Structure and Process*. London: Sage.

Van Dijk, T. (1998), *Ideology: A Multidisciplinary Approach*. London: Sage.

Van Dijk, T. (2001), 'Multidisciplinarity CDA: A plea for diversity.' In R. Wodak and M. Meyer (eds), *Methods of Critical Discourse Analysis*. London: Sage, pp. 95–120.

Van Dijk, T. (2008), *Discourse and Context: A Socio-cognitive Approach*. Cambridge: Cambridge University Press.

Van Leeuwen, T. (1996), 'The representation of social actors.' In C. Caldas-Coulthard and M. Coulthard (eds), *Texts and Practices: Readings in Critical Discourse Analysis*. London: Routledge, pp. 32–70.

Van Leeuwen, T. (1997), 'Representing social action.' *Discourse and Society*, 6(1), 81–106.

Van Leeuwen, T. (2007), 'Legitimation in discourse and communications.' *Discourse and Communication*, 1(1), 91–112.

Verspoor, M. and Sauter, K. (2000), *English Sentence Analysis*. Amsterdam: John Benjamins.

Vet, C. and Vetters, C. (eds) (1994), *Tense and Aspect in Discourse*. Berlin: Mouton de Gruyter.

Von Sturmer, J. (1981), 'Talking with Aborigines.' *Australian Institute of Aboriginal Studies Newsletter*, 15, 13–30.

Walsh, S. (2006), *Investigating Classroom Discourse*. London: Routledge.

Walvis, T. H. (2003), 'Avoiding advertising research disaster: Advertising and the uncertainty principle.' *Journal of Brand Management*, 10(6), 403–409.

Walton, D. (1990), 'What is reasoning? What is an argument?' *Journal of Philosophy*, 87, 399–419.

Wardhaugh, R. (2005), *An Introduction to Sociolinguistics*. London: Blackwell.

Warner, M. (ed.) (1993), *Fear of a Queer Planet*. Minneapolis, MN: University of Minnesota Press.

Watson, J. and Hill, A. (2000), *Dictionary of Media and Communication Studies*. London: Arnold.

Weber, M. (1925), *Wirtschaft und Gesellschaft*. Tübingen: JCB Mohr.

Weber, M. (1947) *The Theory of Social and Economic Organisation*. New York: The Free Press.

Weber, R. P. (1990), *Basic Content Analysis. Second Edition*. Newbury Park, CA: Sage.

Wernick, A. (1991), *Promotional Culture: Advertising, Ideology and Symbolic Expression*. London: Sage

Wetherell, M. (1998), 'Positioning and interpretative repertoires: Conversation analysis and post-structuralism in dialogue.' *Discourse and Society*, 9, 387–412.

Wetherell, M., Taylor, S. and Yates, S. (eds) (2001a), *Discourse as Data: A Guide to Analysis*. London: Sage.

Wetherell, M., Taylor, S. and Yates, S. (eds) (2001b), *Discourse Theory and Practice: A Reader*. London: Sage.

Wetherell, M. (ed.) (2009a), *Identity in the 21st Century: New Trends in Changing Times*. Basingstoke: Palgrave.

Wetherell, M. (ed.) (2009b), *Theorizing Identities and Social Action*. Basingstoke: Palgrave.

Widdowson, H. G. (2004), *Text, Context, Pretext: Critical Issues in Discourse Analysis*. Oxford: Blackwell.

Widdowson, H. G. (2007), *Discourse Analysis*. Oxford: Oxford University Press.

Wierzbicka, A. (1999), *Emotions across Languages and Cultures: Diversity and Universals*. Cambridge: Cambridge University Press.

Wilkins, B. M. and Andersen, P. A. (1991), 'Gender differences and similarities in management communication: a meta-analysis.' *Management Communication Quarterly*, 5, 6–35.

Williams, R. (1976), *Keywords*. London: Fontana.

Wittig, M. (1992), *The Straight Mind and Other Essays*. Boston: Beacon Press.

Wodak, R. (1996), *Disorders of Discourse*. London: Longman.

Wodak, R. (2001), 'The discourse-historical approach.' In R. Wodak and M. Meyer (eds), *Methods of Critical Discourse Analysis*. London: Sage, pp. 63–94.

Wodak, R. (2009), *The Discourse of Politics in Action: Politics as Usual*. Basingstoke: Palgrave Macmillan.

Wodak, R. and Chilton, P. (eds) (2005), *A New Agenda in (Critical) Discourse Analysis*. Amsterdam: John Benjamins.

Wodak, R., de Cillia, R., Reisigl, M. and Liebhart, K. (2009), *The Discursive Construction of National Identity. Second edition.* Edinburgh: Edinburgh University Press.

Wolcott, H. F. (1999), *Ethnography: A Way of Seeing.* Walnut Creek, CA: AltaMira.

Woodward, K. (1997), *Identity and Difference.* London: Sage.

Wouters, C. (1977), 'Informalisation and the civilising process.' In P. R. Gleichmann, J. Goudsblom and H. Korte (eds), *Human Figurations: Essays for Norbert Elias.* Amsterdam: Amsterdams Sociologisch Tidjschrift, pp. 437–455.

Yule, G. (1996), *Pragmatics.* Oxford: Oxford University Press.

Index

Lightning Source UK Ltd.
Milton Keynes UK
UKOW06f0124170516

274395UK00014B/227/P